Philosophy, and Public Affairs

ROYAL INSTITUTE OF PHILOSOPHY SUPPLEMENT: 45

EDITED BY

John Haldane

CAMBRIDGE
UNIVERSITY PRESS

PUBLISHED BY THE PRESS SYNDICATE OF THE UNIVERSITY OF CAMBRIDGE
The Pitt Building, Trumpington Street, Cambridge, CB2 1RP,
United Kingdom

CAMBRIDGE UNIVERSITY PRESS
The Edinburgh Building, Cambridge CB2 2RU, United Kingdom
40 West 20th Street, New York, NY 10011–4211, USA
10 Stamford Road, Oakleigh, Melbourne 3166, Australia

Printed in the United Kingdom at the University Press, Cambridge
Typeset by Michael Heath Ltd, Reigate, Surrey

*A catalogue record for this book is available
from the British Library*

ISBN 0 521 66784 4 paperback
ISSN 1358-2461

To Greta and Struther Arnott

Contents

Contents

Notes on Contributors

David Alton is a Member of the Upper House in the UK Parliament having previously served as an MP for eighteen years. He was formerly Deputy Leader of Liverpool City Council and founder of the Jubilee Campaign. Currently Director of the Foundation for Citizenship at Liverpool John Moores University, he is the author of six books, including *Citizen Virtues* (Harper Collins, 1999).

Bryan Appleyard is a journalist and cultural commentator who writes regularly for, among other publications, *The Sunday Times*. He is the author of a number of books including *Understanding the Present* (Picador, 1992) and *Brave New Worlds: Genetics and the Human Experience* (Harper Collins, 1999), which was highly commended in the BMA Medical Book Competition.

Samuel Brittan is a writer on political economy He has a regular column on *The Financial Times* and contributes to other journals. His most recent books are Capitalism with a Human Face (Fontana/Harper Collins, 1996) and *Essays, Moral, Political and Economic* (Edinburgh University Press for David Hume Institute, 1998).

Gordon Graham is Regius Professor of Moral Philosophy at the University of Aberdeen where he also directs the Centre for Philosophy, Technology and Society. He is a frequent contributor to academic journals as well as radio and the press. His most recent books are *The Internet: a Philosophical Inquiry* (Routledge, 1999), and *Evil and Christian Ethics* (Cambridge University Press, 2000).

John Haldane is Professor of Philosophy and Director of the Centre for Philosophy and Public Affairs in the University of St Andrews. He co-authored *Atheism and Theism* in the Great Debates in Philosophy series (Blackwell, 1997) and a collection of his papers entitled *Faithful Reason* will be published by Routledge. Besides being widely published academically he contributes to the press and broadcasting

Russell Keat is Professor of Political Theory and Head of the School of Social and Political Studies at the University of Edinburgh. He co-edited *Enterprise Culture* (Routledge, 1992) with Nicholas Abercrombie, and *The Authority of the Consumer* (Routledge, 1994) with Nigel Whitely and Nicholas Abercrombie. A collection of his essays, *Cultural Goods and the Limits of the Market* is shortly to be published by Macmillan.

David Marquand was MP for Ashfield from 1966-1977 and is now Principal of Mansfield College, Oxford and Honorary Professor of Politics at the University of Sheffield. His books include *Ramsay*

Notes on Contributors

MacDonald (second edition, Cohen Books, 1997), *The New Reckoning: Capitalism, States and Citizens* (Polity Press, 1997), and the recently republished *The Progressive Dilemma* (second edition, Phoenix Press, 1999).

Anthony O'Hear is Professor of Philosophy in the University of Bradford and Director of the Royal Institute of Philosophy. His most recent books are *Beyond Evolution* (Oxford University Press, 1997) and *After Progress* (Bloomsbury, 1999). From 1989 to 1997 he was a government advisor on education and teacher training.

Melanie Phillips is a *Sunday Times* columnist who writes about social policy and political culture. She is also the author of *The Sex-Change Society: Feminised Britain and the Neutered Male*, published by the Social Market Foundation, 1999; and *All Must Have Prizes*, published by Little Brown, 1996.

Alan Ryan is Warden of New College, where he teaches philosophy and politics. His most recent books are *Liberal Education and Liberal Anxieties* (Profile Books, 1999), *John Dewey and the High Tide of America Liberalism* (Norton & Co., 1995) and *Bertrand Russell: A Political Life* (Oxford University Press, 1993). He has written extensively on J.S. Mill, property rights, and liberal politics generally, for both an academic and a more general audience.

John Skorupski is Professor of Moral Philosophy in the University of St Andrews. He is the author of *John Stuart Mill* in the Arguments of the Philosophers series (Routledge, 1989) and of *English-Language Philosophy 1750-1945* in the OPUS History of Western Philosophy (Oxford, 1993). He edited the *Cambridge Companion to Mill* (1988) and a collection of his essays is published under the title *Ethical Explorations* (Oxford, 2000).

George Walden is a journalist and writer. A former Russian and Chinese specialist in the Foreign Office, he became a Conservative MP but resigned his seat at the last election and is no longer a member of a political party. His latest book is *Lucky George: Memoirs of an Anti-Politician* (Penguin, 1999). Other books include *Ethics and Foreign Policy* (Weidenfeld, 1989), *We Should Know Better: Solving the Education Crisis* (Fourth Estate, 1996). He is currently completing a book on Anarchism.

Introduction

JOHN HALDANE

> Whoever promotes the common good of the community simultaneously promotes their own good; first, because individual well-being cannot exist without the well being of the family, the city or the realm ... and second because being part of the family or of the city it is right to consider personal well-being in the light of what is prudent with regard to the common good.
>
> Thomas Aquinas, *Summa Theologiae*, IIa, IIae, q. 47, a. 10

It is sometimes said that philosophy begins with curiosity; but it would be as true to say that it starts in confusion (where any particular enquiry ends up depends on the gifts of those involved). Typically one finds oneself faced with a conflict between experience and reflection, or within thought itself. Certain things seem obviously morally impermissible say, but it appears impossible to conceive how anything could be, in and of itself, always and everywhere absolutely wrong. Justice seems to require redistributing wealth for the sake of welfare, yet compulsory taxation can also appear a paradigm of injustice: state-organised theft. Society represents itself as a voluntary association of free individuals, yet our sense of ourselves as voluntary agents is something formed by society not something antecedent that we bring to it.

So it continues. Natural rights may be as Bentham suggested 'nonsense on stilts', yet the liberal, political sensibility that he did much to form, finds 'rights' talk not just convenient but compelling. Conservatives frequently argue that tradition is the embodiment of social wisdom, yet often denounce entrenched collective practices as inimical to sound policy making. Those preoccupied with social justice often urge the need to adapt social norms to the interests of immigrant minorities while pursuing general policies that are in direct opposition to the most deeply held beliefs and values of these minorities.

Such notions and conflicts are the concerns of moral, social and political philosophy. It is tempting to say 'such are their starting points'; but the truth of the matter is that conflicts and confusions of these sorts are as much the effects as they are the causes of philosophy.

There is a recurrent idea that first thoughts are best, because somehow closer to the facts. One version of this notion is the belief that young children have an insight into basic truths which time and education only serve to obscure. This belief is sometimes related to the conjecture that there are innate ideas – once cast in the form of an inner mental text, and now in terms of naturally evolved, because adaptive, dispositions.With or without the innateness hypothesis the notion of pre-reflective insight is deeply problematic. Thoughts are expressed in language, in particular natural languages, and these are taught and learned in a social context. Whatever innate endowment there may be, the particular style and substance of thought about the world is a product of the world itself and, to emphasise the point, the child's world is mostly a social one.

In learning language, children learn not just how but what to think. Ironically this fact shows itself in the very questions posed in the effort to elicit innocent truths from the mouths of the young. Of late there has been an interest in encouraging philosophy among children. Teachers wishing to practice this are encouraged to generate group discussion by getting the children to express their views in response to basic quasi-philosophical questions. Thus the mind–body issue might be posed by asking, 'Can you think if you don't have a brain?'; or that of justice introduced by enquiring, 'Is it fair not to give back what you have borrowed or to return it damaged?'. It should be clear enough, however, that questions such as these are heavily laden with presuppositions and assumptions, and serve more to provide than to elicit information. Asking about whether thinking is dependent on having a brain suggests a linkage between them; also young children are generally first introduced to the idea of brains via such phrases as 'use your brain' and 'don't be brainless', that is ones that suggest that something in the head is the organ of thought. Likewise with questions about 'truthfulness', 'honesty', 'justice', 'charity', and so on. Children learn these terms in ways and in contexts that communicate established ways of thinking about them; asking questions is after all a mode of education.

The implication of this is that felt conflicts between thought and experience and within thought itself are as likely as not to express historic conflicts within philosophical thinking itself. The clash between the idea that consciousness is an essentially private reality to which only the self has access, and which is at most only contingently dependent on embodiment, and the thought that one is just another material object in a material world and is best accounted for by the physical senses, is not a conflict between pre-reflective intuition and sophisticated theory but a clash between quasi-philosophical theories the initial absorption of which comes early in the learning of language: 'close your eyes and imagine watching yourself being born' ... 'what do you mean you ... "can't imagine it"?' ... 'we'll have to have your brains looked at'.

It would be too much to say, as Wittgenstein seems sometimes to have supposed, that philosophy consists entirely in tracking down and eliminating from ordinary language confusions sown by earlier philosophy. For one thing a regress threatens: some thinking must have been pre-philosophical if philosophy ever had a beginning, as presumably it did, however vague an origin that might be. For another the process of clarification working upon our confused thinking, often brings us to the point of recognising that our confusions arise from the effort to combine ideas and ideals that enjoy independent coherence and appeal, but which stand in an opposition that could only be resolved by finding good reasons to reject one set and embrace another. Clarification is an essential part of philosophy but so too is refutation and proof. It is not enough to identify sources of conflict, or to embark upon a process of reconciliation, sometimes we need to engage in the battle of ideas with a willingness to kill off error – open up to the possibility that this may involve turning against our own previously held ideas.

Philosophers *per se* tend to be attracted to the most general form of questioning. A judge may be concerned with what punishment to impose; a philosopher will be likely to ask whether punishment itself is or, better, *can* ever be just. A general may be troubled by the conduct of a military campaign; a philosopher will ask whether war can ever be justified. A finance minister may wonder about the social impact of a fiscal measure; a philosopher is likely to ask whether the state is essentially an economic device. But philosophers are not the only ones to be attracted to framework issues. Theorists in other fields such as politics and economics, and social and cultural commentators also aspire to a broader and more topographical view; one of wide range that also discerns the prominent and often recurring features of the field. Also philosophers have of late become aware of the interest and value in engaging in more detailed, topic-specific enquiries.

This range of interests and approaches has developed significantly in the last three decades in recognition of a number of pressures and precedents. The Second World War effected tremendous changes in economic and political arrangements, in moral and religious consciousness and in common human experience. The decade immediately following was given over to efforts at resettlement, but by the 1960s it was clear that the old frameworks had been badly damaged and might not be reconstructable or again enjoy general allegiance. Where free politics was an option it moved to the left,

John Haldane

while at the personal level a greater individualism tested moral conventions. The American (US) experience was perhaps the most traumatic; desegregation, race riots and the civil rights movement, the Korean and Vietnam Wars, Watergate, the abortion issue and so on, forced social theorists to try to give some general description and explanation of what was happening, and caused philosophers to wonder whether purely abstract speculation about mind, language and reality left undischarged intellectual and moral responsibilities. After all, the great figures of the subject, such as Plato, Aristotle, Augustine, Aquinas, Spinoza, Hume, Kant, and Hegel, had all engaged moral and social questions and certainly not regarded this as extra-curricular activity.

The most significant moment of development can be dated; it occurred in 1971 with the publication of John Rawls, *A Theory of Justice*. For the first time in the English-speaking world since Mill, a first-class philosopher had made moral and political issues a main focus of his work. The effect in America, Britain and beyond was and remains considerable. Philosophy began to be deployed in guiding the conduct of life. It soon became common to speak of 'applied philosophy', though some would dearly wish to see that fact undone. The expression suggests a two-stage process: first the philosophy is worked out; second it is applied. Besides demeaning the efforts of those who try to engage practical questions this conception overlooks the possibility that philosophy might arise from, and stay with, practical issues, finding it methodologically more appropriate to use concepts peculiar to the issues in question rather than to replace them with highly general abstract ideas, such as those of the right to liberty, or of the principle of non-maleficence.

Whatever its name, self-conception or methods, the 'practical turn' in philosophy has now produced important work of lasting value. That was already clear to those familiar with the situation in the US, and it was becoming evident in Britain when in 1983 the decision was taken at the University of St Andrews to establish the Centre for Philosophy and Public Affairs. Launched the following year with a major conference on *Ethics and International Relations*, supported by the US/UK Fulbright Commission, it set out from the start to encourage philosophers to engage in questions of practical import by inviting them to give public lectures and seminars in St Andrews and beyond, and by appointing them to visiting fellowships. At the same time it sought to persuade those in public life and in social institutions to take an interest in the philosophical dimensions of their professional work.

Over the years the leading moral, social and political philosophers of the English-speaking world have lectured under the auspices of the Centre: Anthony Quinton, John Rawls, Ronald Dworkin, Alasdair MacIntyre, Neil MacCormick, Anthony Kenny, Bernard Williams, Mary Warnock, G. M. (Jerry) Cohen, Onora O'Neill, Charles Taylor, Roger Scruton, Richard Rorty, Martha Nussbaum and Derek Parfit. Mindful of the aim of having those outside professional philosophy reflect on the values and principles relevant to public policy and practice, prominent politicians, journalists and religious leaders have also contributed to lecture series.

Until 1997, however, there had not been an opportunity to bring members of the two constituencies together. It was with pleasure, therefore, that the Centre learned of the Royal Institute of Philosophy's decision to support, as one of its annual conferences, a meeting in St Andrews on the theme of *Philosophy and Public Affairs*. Thanks very greatly to the encouragement and help of the Royal Institute of Philosophy's Director, Professor Anthony O'Hear, the conference proved a success. The papers given or developed out of it now appear here as a publication of the Royal Institute of Philosophy. The range of topics covered and styles of approach is quite wide but there is a common underlying concern with the way in which contemporary Western society and its political culture has been shaped, and its policies and practices directed, by broadly philosophical ideas. Whether philosophers or not every contributor shares the belief that philosophy needs to be brought to bear upon the conduct of public affairs.

I am grateful to the Royal Institute for its support, to the contributors and to the staff at Cambridge University Press for their good work and patience, and to Professor Struther Arnott, Principal of the University of St Andrews and Mrs Greta Arnott for their supportive participation in this and other Centre events. The combination of academic philosophy and social commentary achieved looking out to sand, sea and distant mountains, and now represented in print, was a fruitful one. I hope it may serve as an encouragement to others.

In Defence of Individualism

SAMUEL BRITTAN

1 Liberals versus communitarians

There are many writers and critics who regard what they call 'individualist-liberalism' as the root of many of the evils of the modern world; and the emphasis of their attack is on the individualist half of the term. Those who take this line nowadays often call themselves 'communitarians'. I would prefer to call them collectivists, as that brings out their dangerous tendency to regard the group as more important than the individuals of whom it is composed. But in what follows I shall concede on labels and most often refer to them as communitarians.

There are a number of slogans characteristic of communitarian rhetoric. The most frequent of them is that, 'Man is a political (or sometimes social) animal.' The individualist-liberal is then accused of an 'atomistic' view of society. Another slogan is that more emphasis should be put on duties instead of rights. Here there would be no difference between Tony Blair and Margaret Thatcher. In a lower key there is a preference for teamwork as opposed to individual responsibility (apparent even in the new arrangements for monetary policy).

But the emphasis of the attack is on modern market capitalism, The historian of political thought, C. B. MacPherson, called this 'possessive individualism',[1] an expression which has caught on with many who have not read a single word of his work. The more lowbrow version is a contempt for the 'pursuit of the bottom line' which is said to characterise our age. Ordinary citizens are accused of 'consumerism' or of being obsessed by the psychology of 'me, me, me'.

In Britain the debate is confused because almost everyone on the left and centre now adopts a communitarian rhetoric. Having accepted much of the economic counter-revolution of the last decade and a half, the main issue on which Blairites dig in their heels is opposition to supposed Thatcherite individualism. This is based on a false chain of reasoning which identifies individualism with self-interest and self-interest with selfishness. The last is a howler, as testified by anyone who has laboured for a charity, for a

[1] C. B. Macpherson, *The Political Theory of Possessive Individualism* (Oxford: Oxford University Press, 1962).

good cause or any of the arts or religion or merely to improve the lot of his or her own family and intimates.

Many on the left will wonder why I am putting together right-wing authoritarians with benevolent communitarians. The American debate sheds some light here. A whole movement has arisen there to attack the liberal individualist foundations of Western politics and culture. US communitarians dislike almost equally ultra-free market libertarians and the more left-wing liberals, such as the philosopher John Rawls, who support the welfare state and other forms of economic intervention. Communitarians condemn them both for regarding the individual person and his or her choices as the measure of all things in politics, and their failure to find a higher purpose for government.

The softer version of US communitarians can be found in writings of commentators such as Amitai Etzioni, who is pictured with vice-president Al Gore on the dust cover of his book.[2] Its harder version can be found in the Republican Religious Right with its support of compulsory religious practices (of which school prayer is but a symbol), belief in savage punishment for retributive reasons and paranoid nationalist fears that foreigners are taking away American jobs.

The two kinds of anti-individualists come together in their advocacy of a year or two of compulsory national service to knock some patriotism and civic virtue into the American young. They have been answered by an individualist liberal (David Boaz) who replies, 'No group of people has the right to force another group to give up a year or two of their lives – and possibly life itself without their consent. The basic liberal principle of the dignity of the individual is violated when individuals are treated as national resources.'[3] Another tell-tale symptom is propaganda for so-called Asian values and admiration for the Singapore leader Lee Kuan Yew who justifies his brutal punishments by saying, 'To us in Asia, an individual is an ant.'

Are British Conservatives more tolerant? Almost every increase in personal liberty and toleration, from the legalisation of homosexuality among consenting adults to the abolition of theatre censorship and more sensible divorce laws, has been brought about in the face of opposition from the majority of Conservative MPs and activists. In nearly every country the political Right (with a few honourable individual exceptions) is adamantly opposed to any re-examination of the drug laws which have done so much to make

[2] A. Etzioni, *The Spirit of Community* (New York: Crown Publishers, 1993).

[3] D. Boaz, *Libertarianism* (London: Free Press, 1993).

money-laundering one of the world's biggest businesses. Their text is still that of Lord Hailsham thirty years ago when he hoped that the addicts of hashish and marijuana would be pursued 'with the utmost severity the law allows'. He hoped they would 'find themselves in the Old Bailey, and however distinguished their positions in the Top 10, they will be treated as criminals deserve to be treated'. Unfortunately too many Blairites rush to show their political 'moderation' by coming down like a ton of bricks on anyone on the Labour or Liberal side who opposes such Hailshamite blusterings.

2 The academic debate

The communitarian-liberal debate has been going on in the USA for a decade or more; and two Oxford philosophers, S. Mulhall and A. Swift, have recently written a textbook guide to it.[4] This takes as its starting point John Rawls's *Theory of Justice*, which has acquired a canonical status and which I shall not attempt to summarise here. Many individualist-liberals have criticised Rawls for making too many concessions to collective goals. But the communitarian attack is just the opposite. It is on the priority which Rawls says he attaches to personal freedom.

The debate takes place on several levels. What seems to motivate Alasdair McIntyre is an intense hostility to theories in philosophical ethics, such as emotivism, subjectivism and relativism.[5] Such philosophers insist that some ways of life are preferable to others and are incensed by Jeremy Bentham's observation that Push-pin (an early nineteenth century board game) was better than poetry if that was what people preferred. Today the argument would be in terms of Radio One versus Radio Three. But these philosophers are not necessarily committed to the specific proposals urged by more policy-oriented communitarians who are looking for some third way between socialism and market capitalism.

Incidentally, I should like to protest against the pompous habit of many contemporary liberal philosophers on my own side of the debate of talking about the 'pursuit of the good'. This is often a confusion between ethical choices, such as how much to spend on charity and good works, and decisions on how to spend one's time in ways which claim no greater merit than that of satisfying the person following them. In a free society someone who devotes his or her life to gambling is not pursuing a personal vision of the good.

[4] S. Mulhall and A. Swift, *Liberals and Communitarians*, 2nd edn (Oxford: Blackwell, 1997).

[5] A. McIntyre, *After Virtue*, 2nd edn (London: Duckworth, 1985).

9

He is simply doing what he most enjoys. The same applies to a citizen with a passion for painting. There is no need to put such activities on the level of Mother Theresa. The older nineteenth century liberals were surely correct to talk in terms of freedom and liberty rather than the relentless pursuit of 'the good'.

3 Metaphysical anti-individualism

In my experience, communitarians like to start from some metaphysical proposition. They say for instance that an individual is constituted by his or her social relationships. He or she is a grandfather, a doctor, a member of certain clubs, an active Scottish Nationalist and so on. Without these relationships he is said to be 'nothing'. Even a hermit is identified by his decision to abandon the community from which he springs. (One often reads that the individual was an invention of the Renaissance and was unknown to the ancient and medieval world. I am not sure that this can be reconciled with the funeral oration of Pericles, as expounded by Thucydides.)

We soon get into an impasse. Groups are made up of individuals; but individuals form groups. A debate on which fact is 'primary' is the kind of dispute which never gets settled. As Stephen Holmes has pointed out, 'The social nature of Man is too trite to count as an insight and is worthless as an argument for or against any existing institutional arrangements. If all individuals are socially constituted then the social self cannot serve as a critical standard to praise some societies and revile others.'[6]

4 A biological perspective

Communitarians are inclined to say that the issue depends on the 'nature of Man'. To my mind this a biological matter rather than one for armchair speculation. And you do not escape the biological nature of the problem by talking in seemingly more philosophical terms of the 'nature of the person' instead.

It is a cliche to say 'Man is a social animal'. The statement can be given empirical content by noting that for the greater part of his existence on this planet he has belonged to clans of hunter-gatherers of not more than a couple of hundred people. It is therefore not surprising that people feel alienated, both in mass society and if left

[6] S. Holmes, *The Anatomy of Anti-Liberalism* (Cambridge, MA: Harvard University Press, 1993).

entirely to their own devices in nuclear families. This could be held to support the communitarian preference for relying on, whenever possible, local groups rather than the isolated individual or the nation state. Communitarians are, however, seldom specific about how this transfer can be undertaken.

Let us, moreover, not romanticise the small group. It can be very oppressive and stultifying; and even in primitive times there were those who left their groups to start other clans. Many of today's most vibrant communities are not people who are geographically close to each other. The most important communities for users of the Internet in the Orkneys may not consist of village neighbours but other users with whom they form a professional link which can blossom into friendship and mutual support.

The worst side of group psychology is the hostility almost always generated to those outside the group. This long pre-dates modern nationalism. Byzantine emperors were able to generate artificial hostility between groups of citizens by dividing them by an arbitrary line into blues and greens. From here it is but a short distance to the bitter struggles in places like Bosnia where people who had previously lived at ease with each other for generations, and indeed intermarried, went in for the barbarities of ethnic cleansing.

Many of the achievements of civilisation are due to what Graham Wallas, the Fabian sociologist, called 'The Great Society'. This was the linking together through the market process of millions who have no chance of being personally acquainted. One interpretation of globalisation is that the whole world is becoming a Great Society. The problem ever since the Industrial Revolution, if not earlier, has been how to combine the benefits of the Great Society with the human ties generated by the smaller group.

5 Defensible individualism

In current political polemics individualism is a pejorative term used by opponents of the concept. Few political writers call themselves individualists. They are more likely to say they are classical liberals, market liberals, old-fashioned liberals or something of the kind. But there clearly is an individualist component to their beliefs which is worth defending.

The kind of individualism for which I will fight in the last ditch is ethical individualism. In its minimal form it is the belief that actions should be judged by their effects on individual human beings.

How would I justify this judgment? It is individuals who feel, exult, despair and rejoice. And statements about group welfare are a shorthand way of referring to such individual effects. This seems to me a plain statement of fact, despite the numerous 'thinkers' who deny – or more usually – bypass it. Whatever might be said about sharing feelings with a close member of one's family, the rejoicing of a nation or a football club or a school is metaphorical.

The danger of collectivism is that of attributing a superior value to collective entities over and above the individuals who compose it. This disastrous error was made respectable by the teachings of Hegel and reached its apotheosis in the state worship of the Nazi and communist regimes. But it is lurking behind ever the apparently more soft-hearted varieties of communitarianism.

Statements about large abstractions such as the interests of a country and the health of the economy must be translatable into statements about individual human beings. This translation cannot logically prevent the collectivist judgments I find so repellent; but such translations can nevertheless lead us to pose useful questions such as, 'How much suffering is justified by the gratification of my feelings of national pride as a Serb or a Croat?' Analysis along such lines would be likely to make people more self-conscious. It might even lead to a weakening of unreflective willingness to die for one's country or the working class and to a waning of nationalism and ideological enthusiasm in general.

Going beyond this reductionism, we do not find a single individualist creed. Benthamite utilitarianism does involve a commitment to individual welfare but not to personal freedom. (The inhabitants of Aldous Huxley's *Brave New World* were made to take their soma pills.) Post-Bentham individualists from John Stuart Mill onwards, argued for the largest possible measure of individual freedom consistent with avoiding harm to others. They did so formally on the grounds that individuals were less bad judges of their own interests than governments, 'experts' or others who claimed to judge. But it is pretty clear from reading classical liberals that they valued freedom for its own sake.

'What is so wonderful about individual choice?' One can only reply that it lies in the absence of coercion or man-made obstacles to the exercise of people's powers and capacities. This judgment cannot in the final analysis be rigorously demonstrated against those with incompatibly different values. One can only try to remove misunderstandings and to display by anecdote, rhetoric and imaginative literature the virtues of the kind of society in which people have maximum opportunity to satisfy their preferences against societies where others make their judgments for them.

A particular misunderstanding is to pit the individual against the family. Anthropology and biology suggest that human beings are creatures that tend to live in one kind of family or another. The individualist is however more content to let the family evolve and hesitates to put a political imprimatur on the nuclear family in the state it reached among the middle classes of the late nineteenth century. Nevertheless the liberal-individualist passion for choice is always tempered by the proviso that it must not harm others; and if the break up of traditional families is having the adverse effects on individual welfare which Melanie Phillips claims, then governments need to take them into account in legislation. But however important the family, one is still allowed to write on other matters. And it is surely clear that it is not families but collective entities from the state down to local collections of busybodies, from which the individualists want to protect us.

6 Self-realisation

Individualists usually desire to go beyond liberating human beings from collectivist pressures and want to celebrate the achievements of particular people whether in the arts or sciences or sports or in the more mundane art of everyday living. This kind of positive individualism has its antithesis in the idealisation of the team. Indeed it is the British focus on team spirit which heavily qualifies the romantic Continental notion that they are a nation of individualists.

Recently I had occasion to congratulate an economist friend on some well-deserved professional promotion. He thanked me very generously, saying how glad he was that the work of his team had been recognised. But this is not what I meant at all. I was expressing pleasure that he personally had been promoted and that the choice had not been made on political grounds.

To go further into the more positive and indeed romantic aspects of individualism would take a separate paper. This would have to recognise the danger of this form of individualism becoming converted into worship of great men such as Napoleon or Frederick the Great for whom the lives and welfare of millions are sacrificed. Even in everyday life 'rugged individualism' sometimes means a craggy disregard for other people's interests, which is not a quality I wish to celebrate.

7 Political economy

A point requiring some emphasis is that an ethical individualist does not have to be an economic individualist. Generations of socialists have indeed argued that the collective control of economic activity would not only enable more individual citizens to satisfy more of their wants, but enable them to flourish in a broader way.

The argument against collectivist economic systems is that they utterly fail to fulfil their promise. Of course it is a bonus to the individualist that allowing some rein to individual instincts for self-betterment will produce better results than centrally imposed direction. Nevertheless the test of Adam Smith's view of the superiority of Natural Liberty must be that of experiments thrown up by events and not just by its psychological attractiveness or otherwise.

Just as a philosophical individualist does not have to be an economic individualist, the same distinction works the other way round. An economic individualist does not have to share a wider individualist philosophy. He or she may simply accept that a market-based economic system brings better results without having a deeper belief in individual choice or in people 'doing their own thing'. Exponents of free markets often oppose freedom in every other sphere, especially in sexual behaviour and the behaviour of the young. This combination of economic individualism with authoritarian wider beliefs is all too common among many Conservatives even in the so-called Thatcherite wing of that party.

8 Economic individualism

Despite these disclaimers, the type of individualism which is most under a cloud is economic individualism. It is associated with slogans like 'It's every man for himself and let the devil take the hindmost'; or with Charles Dickens' Mr Gradgrind (his name, not the actual character in *Hard Times*); or with thick-skinned city types who celebrate the rat-race in which they boast they are engaged. Even if the collapse of collectivist economic systems leaves people with no alternative, this fact is regarded as a necessary evil rather than anything to celebrate. The greatest obstacle faced by economic individualism is the belief that it is based on or encourages materialism or acquisitiveness.

In fact self-interest in a market economy merely means that people follow their own chosen goals. These may be individual consumption, but they may equally be the acquiring of means to promote charitable, cultural or religious causes. Or they may try to maximise leisure to pursue some hobby or interest; or some mixture of all these. The altruistic businessman should indeed strive harder than his rivals to make profits and differentiate himself by what he does with his gain.

These necessary elaborations only take us a certain way. Defenders of market capitalism have rarely faced up to the shock with which many well brought up people react when they learn that their job in is not to feed or clothe or even entertain their fellow citizens directly, but to promote the profits of its owners; that is irrespective of how worthy or unworthy are the purposes to which the profits are devoted.

The most controversial aspect of economic individualism was expressed two centuries ago, by Adam Smith. No sentence in political thought has attracted more opprobrium than the passsage in *The Wealth of Nations* saying 'It is not from the benevolence of the butcher, brewer or baker that we expect our dinner, but from the regard to their own interest. We address ourselves, not to their humanity but to their self love, and never talk to them of our own necessities but of their advantages'.

The moralist is not appeased to learn that Smith also wrote *The Theory of Moral Sentiments* which emphasised benevolence. Nor is he or she appeased to learn that in *The Wealth of Nations* itself, a few sentences before the notorious ones just quoted, Smith stressed how much Man was a social animal and 'has almost constant occasion for the help of his brethren'. While a human being's 'whole life is scarce sufficient to gain the friendship of a few persons, in civilised society he stands at all times in need of the cooperation and assistance of great multitudes'. It is for this reason that he 'has to enlist their self-love in his favour' and cannot rely on their benevolence alone.

This 'self love' will be effective only if certain background conditions are fulfilled. There has to be a legal system and a political order that enforces contracts, protects property rights, and provides for limited liability or the equivalent. In other words there is no private property without good government. Until the disillusioning experience of post-communist countries, such background considerations were regarded by many modern economists as too obvious or insufficiently mathematical to be worth discussing. Their neglect has made it all too easy for former Communist bosses to flip over to being Mafia style capitalists instead.

But it is not the incompleteness of 'Invisible Hand' statements that worries moralists, but its apparent reliance on the greed motive for the successful workings of an advanced civilisation. (A generation before Adam Smith a similar shock was supplied by Bernard Mandeville's *Fable of the Bees* in which he suggested that the vice of the few was essential for the prosperity of the many).

The two most common reactions are either to reject Smith's doctrine as outrageous or to accept it in a cynical spirit and say that

Smith understood that the world was a jungle and that the animal with the sharpest teeth would inevitably win (which was not what he thought at all).

9 A rule utilitarian approach

There is however a third reaction which involves a little formal philosophy, although nothing more advanced than can be found in John Stuart Mill.[7] This is to explain both the strength and limitations of the Invisible Hand doctrine in terms of a system of utilitarian morality. By utilitarianism I simply mean the view that actions are to be judged by their consequences for the welfare of other people. I do not have to argue whether utilitarianism can provide a complete system or whether it should be constrained by other ideas, such as those of Rawls which I mentioned earlier. It is sufficient to say that public activities, whether in politics or business, are normally judged by utilitarian criteria; and it is difficult to see how this could be otherwise in a complex society.

Mill faced up to the problem of how to fit conventional moral rules such as 'Don't tell lies' or 'Keep promises' into utilitarian morality. He argued that we do not have the knowledge to assess directly on each separate occasion the effects of our actions on other human beings. What he called the 'prima facie' rules of common sense morality arose from the common experience of mankind. The welfare of others will usually be better promoted by observing these rules rather than by trying to work out from first principles the effects of our behaviour on others on each separate occasion.

The Invisible Hand doctrine is in my view one of the more surprising prima facie rules to have been suggested. Surprising because of its apparently cynical flavour. For it does suggest that we will often do others more good if we behave as if we are following our self-interest than by pursuing more obviously altruistic purposes. (I suggested this interpretation of the Invisible Hand in terms of rule utilitarianism several years ago. It has not attracted any attention.)[8]

Prima facie rules of acceptable behaviour are by definition subject to exception and qualification. There are always difficult cases which require reflection on basics in personal life. There will always be exceptional cases in which accepted rules should be overridden.

---

[7] J. S. Mill, *Utilitarianism*, Modern edition, (London: J. M. Dent, 1948).

[8] S. Brittan, Wincott Memorial Lecture, 1985. Reprinted as Ch. 2 of *Capitalism with a Human Face* (London: Edward Elgar, 1995), (London: Fontana, 1996), pbk. edition.

So the maxims of Adam Smith do not enable businessmen to escape moral reflection – and were not intended to. The absence of laws or conventions prohibiting the dumping of poisonous lead would not excuse indiscriminate dumping. Nor do they excuse the sale of landmines to unscrupulous users.

In general the closer to hand are the effects of business conduct the easier it is to know when to make exceptions to the Invisible Hand Doctrine. A takeover tycoon who shows an old retainer the door is a scoundrel and should need not be excused by any market economist. The self-interest maxim comes in when we deal with remoter consequences. A business executive does not have the knowledge to estimate the remoter consequences of supposedly patriotic deviations from commercial self interest, such as buying British when the overseas product gives better value. Nor is such knowledge available to MPs, officials or even academic economists.

A manufacturer who keeps open uneconomic enterprises to 'provide jobs' is not necessarily promoting even the longer-run interests of the workforce itself. This is apart from the fact that if he persists he is likely to be taken over or abruptly closed down by successors who will make the changes in a far more brutal way.

10 Information requirements

An economic system has at least five functions. They are to: co-ordinate the activity of millions of individuals, households, and firms; obtain information about people's desires, tastes and preferences; decide which productive techniques to use; promote new ideas, tastes and activities which people would not have thought of without entrepreneurial initiative and create incentives for people to act on such information. Only the fifth, incentive, function of markets could be abandoned in a community of saints. The others would still be required for the saints to know how best to serve their fellows. They might still be well advised to behave as if they were concerned with their own wordly well being in order to create the market signals by which they could best serve others.

We know that the search for profit does not apply to large sections of activity. Institutions concerned with health and education are usually non profit-making even when their services are sold for cash. A distinguished musician or surgeon will often have a strong sense of occasion and not just play or operate for the money. A doctor or teacher should have some responsibility to his patient or pupil over and above the search for fees. Here market rates of pay have their effects at the margin. They bring in the less dedicated who might have chosen a different field of endeavour and they affect even the dedicated in their choice at the margin between work and leisure, or choice of profession. A hospital management need not be interested in profit maximisation, but at least it should be interested in minimising costs. So condemnation of the 'internal market' without examination is merely childish.

It is however time to query the pious belief that professional values are invariably superior to commercial ones. Professional bodies have their own inherent deficiencies. If left to themselves they often try to keep out new people and ideas and enforce restrictive practices.

Many academics are opera lovers. Have they forgotten the professional guild of the Meistersingers of Nuremburg, which tried to keep out new influences and new types of song and verse from their guild? It was no free market fanatic, but Paul Samuelson the Democrat Nobel Prize winning economist who long ago said that he preferred good clean money to bad dirty power.[9]

11 Business culture

But let us descend to a lower level of abstraction. Part of the communitarian critique arises from an absurd idea of how a profit-seeking concern seeks to promote shareholder value. When I write an article for the *Financial Times*, the editor does not ask whether the article will increase the value of the Pearson equity. But he does know that if the paper does not eventually make a return on its assets comparable to that of alternative investments there is going to be trouble. As indeed there should be.

It is worth looking at the origin of the most criticised business attitudes, such as an exaggerated emphasis on the 'bottom line'. They arise not from profit seeking or individualism as such, but from the separation of ownership from control. Modern economists have recognised something called the 'principal agent' problem. How do we make sure that appointed managers do in fact act as trustees for the ultimate owners and do not squander the resources for their own aggrandisement or alternatively to lead a quiet life? The problem affects state property as well as private corporations. It still arises for enterprises owned by their own workers or by local communities.

It was because of frequent abuses of managerial power that the takeover culture developed. On the continent, and especially in Germany, this same function is performed for large enterprises by

[9] Paul Samuelson, *Problems of the American Economy* (London, Athlone Press, 1962).

banks via the business establishment. It is far from obvious that a closed network is a better method of control than open bids for stock ownership. Admiration for German corporate culture is mostly found in English-speaking countries.

Many of the tensions would be eased if there were a move to smaller units where the managers were also the proprietors. Ownership and control are combined in the German Mittelstand or in the flourishing medium-sized Italian companies who are responsible for most of the real economic miracles on the continent.

A manager who is merely a trustee for shareholders has to make his decisions in two halves. First he has to earn as much as he can for the stockholders. Then he has to apportion the resulting earnings in a way that he believes the owners will approve. No wonder most top executives take the easy way out by some ploughing back, some dividend distribution and some token contribution, such as 1 per cent of profits to good causes. How much easier it is for an owner of a ceramics factory in the Italian Veneto to make all his decisions in one go; and if he has a good year to send an immediate cheque to a local musical society or to help the renovation of a Palladian palace. It is his affair and there is no conflict between profit seeking and civic values.

The issue was brought home to me when I once met at a conference a small American manufacturer whose main motive in life was to run a furniture factory profitable enough to give work to the disabled who were paid something like normal wages. If he had been a mere manager, the shareholders could reasonably have demanded that he maximised his return on assets. They, as the owners, could then decide what they wanted to do with the resulting profits, which might include providing work for the disabled at subsidised rates. But when the owner and the manager are the same person all these stages can be collapsed into one. It remains true that such an entrepreneur still does his best for the disabled or any other good cause by buying in the cheapest market and selling in the dearest.

The trend away from corporate dinosaurs towards smaller service companies who make separate contracts with individual purchasers could eventually lead to a much more dispersed pattern of economic decisions and a more personal form of individualism. But let us not pretend that everyone is going to like it. Salaried employees who are suddenly told to fend for themselves as consultants or suppliers of specialist services often find the process a shock – no matter how many books they have read or written decrying bureaucratic corporate management.

Samuel Brittan

12 The true 'bottom line'

It is not difficult to summarise the economic argument. A stake-holder or communitarian would like to see social and ethical objectives pursued directly by corporations in addition to, or instead of, the search for profit. Market liberals prefer to provide for these objectives in the background conditions and rules which constrain the search for profit. In many particular cases two reasonable members of both schools might agree. But the market liberal will always worry that the stakeholder arrogates to business leaders the role of shaping society for which they are ill suited; and that they would serve us as well as themselves better if they stuck to specific and limited objectives and did not take on the role of Moses and the minor prophets as well.

The debate will not be decided by evidence or formal reasoning alone. To communitarians selfishness is the most hideous of sins, and sometimes the only one. An individualist-liberal does not celebrate selfishness; but he believes that there can be worse sins, such as the sacrifice of individual human beings for the sake of some abstract doctrine or religious or other belief. If I may quote Holmes again: 'Communitarian anti-liberals suggest that once people overcome their self-interest, they necessarily act in an admirable and public spirited way ... but these leave out of account the prominent place of selfless cruelty in human affairs. It is much easier to be cruel in the course of acting in the cause of others than while acting for one's own thing. Those who have homosexuals shot in the name of the Islamic revolution cannot be accused of anti-social individualism or base self interest.'[10]

My own conviction is that people in the grip of greed often do much less harm than people in the grip of self-righteousness, especially when that righteousness is harnessed to the supposed needs of a collectivity or given some theological or metaphysical justification.

Appendix on methodological individualism

One kind of individualism which creates much heat is methodological individualism. This is the desire to ground social science in the behaviour and/or motivations of individual human beings. Neo-classical economic theory is based on this approach – although you would not guess so from the short-term forecaster in front of a screen which forms the public image of an economist. Most sociologists are hostile to methodological individualism; and indeed many

[10] Ibid.

economists write books denouncing the individualist foundations of their own subject.

Methodological individualism is itself a branch of reductionism, which seeks to ground explanation in the most basic units. But why stop at individual human beings? Why not try to reduce motivation to biology, biology to chemistry and chemistry in its turn to sub-atomic physics.

Freud, for instance, started off hoping that his analysis could be reduced in the end to bio-chemistry; and the inability to make this translation at any point has counted against the scientific status of psychoanalysis. Nevertheless the test of success in the social sciences is prediction or explanation. It is better to have a more successful explanation of business cycles, which starts with mere statistical regularities, than one which is well grounded in hypotheses about individual behaviour, but which tells us very little we did not know already.

Purely methodological individualism ought to be neutral in relation to morals and politics. It is a matter of finding from experience the approach that yields the most fruitful hypotheses in a particular context.

Nevertheless there is one reason why a social scientist might want to start from the individual human being rather than the group to which he or she belongs or the quarks of which he or she is composed. This is that the social scientist has an advantage over the physical scientist or the zoologist in being able to take into account motivations and intentions. And these exist at the level of the individual. It is odd to have to labour this point to Christian philosophers who place so much emphasis on the free will and responsibility.

Market Boundaries and Human Goods

RUSSELL KEAT

1 Problems of market boundaries

It is now widely accepted that the market is superior to the state as
a means of organising economic activity. But there remain a number of significant problems about the proper scope of the market
domain, about the range of activities which are appropriately governed by market mechanisms and their associated forms of commercial organisation. Whilst many would agree that the market is an
admirable device, provided it is 'kept in its place', there is much less
agreement about the precise location of that place, about where and
on what grounds the boundaries of the market should be established.

In Britain – though a similar story could be told elsewhere – two
broad developments over the past 20 years or so have given rise to
considerable debate about these issues. First, a politically-driven
programme of reform has led to the introduction of market or
quasi-market principles and forms of organisation into a wide range
of institutions and social practices which had previously operated
on quite different bases. I have in mind here not only the privatisation of publicly owned industries, but also the reconstruction of a
wide range of other institutions which, whilst remaining within the
public sector, have increasingly been required or encouraged to
operate in commercially-modelled ways. Amongst these have been
local government, educational and health-care institutions, and also
those which may be termed 'cultural' in character, namely broadcasting, the various arts, academic research and so on.

Second, and without such obvious political intervention, there
has been a strong tendency for the market to expand its range of
application and, as it were, to intensify the pressures it exerts on the
conduct of both commercial and non-commercial activities. So, for
example, whilst previously amateur sports have become 'professional', already professional clubs have become quoted companies
on the Stock Exchange, joined by de-mutualised building societies;
charitable organisations now compete with each other and with
other retail outlets on the high street; university presses are increasingly indistinguishable from their commercial counterparts, who

themselves make increasingly sales-driven judgments about their potential authors' work; and so on.

These two developments have been greeted neither with universal acclaim nor universal hostility; rather, they have generated considerable disagreement and debate. My aim in this paper, however, is not to join this debate by arguing directly about the substantive merits or defects of these particular changes, but to address the more general and philosophical question of what *kinds* of consideration should be regarded as relevant in such arguments. What are to count as proper grounds for establishing or removing boundaries around the market? On what bases might the expansion of the market be legitimately either challenged or endorsed?

More specifically, I shall attempt to defend the view that one legitimate ground for establishing or maintaining market boundaries is a concern for the effects of the market on the nature and value of the various 'human goods' available to individuals in a society such as ours. This concern is to be distinguished from another, quite different (though at least equally important) one, namely with the justice or injustice of the unequal access to these goods between different individuals or social groups, when such access is limited by their respective abilities to pay. So, for example, the introduction of museum and art gallery admission charges may be challenged on the grounds that this will deprive the poor of access to these goods; by contrast, it may also or instead be claimed that, if such institutions are run along purely commercial lines, their proper aims and purposes will be compromised, with negative consequences for the nature and value of the goods they will then have to offer, however just or unjust the potential beneficiaries' differential access to these may be.

In a similar vein, academics who oppose the marketisation of universities may argue that competitive pressures and the attribution of consumer-status to students will undermine the provision of intellectually challenging degrees; television producers, that the de-regulation of broadcasting will lead to a decline in the quality of programmes; subsidised theatre and dance companies, that the commercially modelled criteria for funding imposed by the Arts Council will inhibit artistic innovation; and so on. In these and many other cases, it seems that what is at issue is the supposedly negative effects of the market on the character of the various goods generated by non-market institutions.

However, whilst objections of this kind to the expansion of the market domain are frequently voiced, they are often met with outright, 'in principle' rejection – especially when accompanied, as they usually are, by proposals that the powers and resources of the state should be employed to limit or regulate the operation of the market, and/or to provide support for non-market institutions. Instead, that is, of engaging critically with the specific claims being made about the value of certain goods, and the likelihood or otherwise of their being adequately provided through the market, it is argued that *any* such grounds for limiting the domain of the market, and for deploying the powers and resources of the state, are in principle unacceptable – they are 'ruled out of court', without reference to the possible merits or defects of the specific case at issue.

2 Liberal neutrality and the market

This objection to goods-based arguments for market boundaries may take a number of closely related forms. For example, especially in cases concerning cultural goods, it may be objected that any attempt either to regulate the commercial production of culture, or to subsidise its non-commercial provision, is inherently elitist, since it implies that judgments of cultural value can and should be made only by those with the requisite expertise and authority, whose views will be given insufficient weight if these decisions are instead made by less knowledgeable 'sovereign consumers' in the market.[1] Or, somewhat more generally, it may be argued that to impose such limitations on the market, where people are able to make their own judgments about what will best contribute to their well-being, and then to express these through their willingness to pay, is unjustifiably paternalistic, implying as it would that certain others know better than oneself about what is good for one, and have the right not only to make such judgments but to enforce them.

But there is another version of this objection to which I shall give most attention here. It is based on a central tenet of certain influential contemporary liberal theorists, the principle of (state) 'neutrality'. According to this principle, it is never justifiable for the state (whether democratically controlled or otherwise) to act in ways that are either designed, or reasonably expectable, to favour certain 'conceptions of the good' over others. Instead, it is claimed, the state should remain 'neutral' as between the various conceptions of the good which individuals may espouse and seek to realise, and must refrain from using its powers and resources

---

[1] I have discussed this objection more fully in 'Scepticism, authority and the market', in R. Keat, N. Whiteley and N. Abercrombie (eds), *The Authority of the Consumer* (London: Routledge, 1994), 23–42.

either to place obstacles in the path of some, or to ease the path of others.[2]

By contrast, it is claimed, the state may and indeed should act so as to prevent the pursuit of any such conception of the good by some individual(s) being conducted in such a way as to impede the rights of other individuals to do likewise. Further, for neutralist liberals who are also welfare liberals, it is also proper for the state to ensure a just distribution of the material resources required by individuals for the effective pursuit of their respective conceptions of the good. But this must be done in a way that is not dependent on making judgments about the substantive merits or defects of these conceptions. Such judgments are to be made, if at all, only by the individuals concerned, and not by the state, or by those who control its actions. To think otherwise – to reject these neutralist limitations on the state – is to espouse some form of 'perfectionism', according to which it is legitimate for actions by the state to be based upon such judgments, and to be aimed at the realisation of some (favourably judged) conceptions of the good rather than others.

Now it may well seem that the principle of neutrality would indeed rule out of court the kinds of goods-based arguments for market boundaries which were noted earlier. For these appear to depend, not only on perfectionist judgments being made about the value of certain kinds of goods which are said to be damaged or threatened by an unduly expansive market, but on the view that it is legitimate for the powers and resources of the state to be used to prevent or rectify these undesirable effects.

Furthermore, it may also seem that the market itself is fully consistent with the requirements of neutrality. For this, surely, is a social domain in which the only judgments made about the respective merits of different goods are those made by their (actual or potential) purchasers, who do so in ways that reflect their overall conceptions of the good, of the kinds of life they wish to live and regard as worthwhile, enjoyable, fulfilling and so on. The market is a procedure for making decisions about the allocation of economic resources to the production of goods in which the only criteria by which the value of these goods are judged are those endorsed and applied by consumers themselves – not by the state, nor by any

---

[2] For an influential statement of this neutralist position, see R. Dworkin, 'Liberalism', in *A Matter of Principle* (Oxford University Press, 1985), 181–204; also J. Rawls, *A Theory of Justice* (Oxford University Press), 1971). For critical discussion of liberal neutrality, see J. Raz, *The Morality of Freedom* (Oxford University Press), 1986, Part II.

other supposedly authoritative body. In a market economy it is the preferences of consumers, and the judgments about their own well-being on which these are based, that count; there is no role for the state in this process through which individuals freely pursue their own conceptions of the good, without having to justify their decisions to anyone but themselves.

So the principle of neutrality, combined with the claim that the market is a system which operates fully in accordance with this principle, appears to provide strong grounds for objecting 'in principle' to the deployment of goods-based arguments for market boundaries. I shall argue, however, that this is not in fact so. My argument will proceed in three main stages. First, I shall make a series of somewhat schematic claims about the nature of human goods and their dependency upon various kinds of social institutions, of which the market is but one. Next, I shall argue that the market may operate or develop in ways that are inimical to the effective functioning of other, non-market institutions, and that when this occurs one cannot appeal to the principle of neutrality to rule out intervention by the state. Finally, I shall suggest that a preferable way of approaching these issues is to conceive of the market, not as a domain of individual liberty counterposed to the state, but rather as a collectively instituted device for the realisation of shared conceptions of the good.

3 Human goods and their social conditions

(1) Human goods – i.e. the 'things' which contribute either directly or indirectly to human well-being – are richly diverse and heterogeneous in character. Along with the products generated by the market, they include *inter alia* such disparate items as friendship, love and conviviality; the exercise of the imagination; the acquisition of knowledge and understanding; the development and application of complex skills and capacities; the aesthetic appreciation of nature, and engagement in activities which are seen as productive of other goods.

Thus although economic 'goods' are properly so called, there is no reason to restrict the class of human goods to these alone. Nor is there any reason to believe that the relative value of different kinds of human goods can be expressed or measured in monetary terms. So when, for example, people are asked 'how much they would be willing to pay' to retain some valued feature of their natural environment, and refuse to answer, or when people refuse to say 'how much they would accept as compensation' for the loss of their spouse, they should not be regarded as stupid or irrational, but as correctly recognising the unpriceable value of certain kinds of human goods and hence their irreplaceability by certain others. In this respect, at least, different kinds of human goods may be said to be incommensurable.[3]

(2) At least many, if not all, such human goods are 'social' in the following sense: their existence and character is either dependent upon, or is constituted by, specific (and similarly various and distinct) kinds of social practices, which themselves involve characteristic forms of social relationships, ethical norms, appropriate attitudes and motivations, and so on. Further, many such social practices either require, or are significantly enhanced by, the existence of certain institutional arrangements of a more or less formally organised nature, at least some of which are either directly or indirectly supported by the powers and resources of the state.[4]

So, for example, the human good(s) of intellectual enquiry (including here both those accruing to participants, and those accruing to others as outcomes) depend upon various established forms of social practice, with their accompanying rules of argumentation and evidence, the exercise of certain intellectual virtues and attitudes, the presence of requisite forms of recognition and trust between participants, and so on.[5] These practices of enquiry are typically conducted in specific institutional contexts, such as universities and research centres, which may be wholly or partly funded by, without being correspondingly subordinated to, the state.

(3) There is no reason to expect that any one institutional form will be equally appropriate as a means of organising every or most kinds of social practice, and hence of supporting the generation of their respective kinds of human goods. Rather, one might reasonably expect a considerable diversity in such practice-supportive institutions, reflecting the diversity of the goods which they make possible. Hence, in particular, there is no reason to believe that the market, which is one such institutional form, provides an appropriate basis for the generation of all human goods, despite its undoubted effectiveness in producing some. One should not expect, for example, the human goods made available through familial relationships

[3] On the environmental example, see J. O'Neill, 'King Darius and the environmental economist', in T. Hayward and J. O'Neill (eds) *Justice, Property and the Environment* (Aldershot: Ashgate, 1997), 114–130; on incommensurability, see J. Raz, op. cit., note 2, ch. 13.

[4] Here I partly follow M. Walzer, *Spheres of Justice* (Oxford: Martin Robertson, 1983), ch. 1, and J. Raz, op. cit., note 2, ch. 12, but with a more institutional emphasis.

[5] See J. Ravetz, *Scientific Knowledge and its Social Problems* (Oxford University Press, 1971).

and practices to be equally well generated through the market; nor should one expect the converse to obtain.

(4) There is no guarantee that the different institutions and practices through which these diverse human goods are made available will always operate in mutually harmonious ways; and even if they do so at one time, they may fail to do so at another. That is, it is always possible that one or more such institutions may operate or develop in ways that are inimical to the continued flourishing of others, and hence damage, limit or undermine their ability to generate their specific kinds of human goods.

This is not to say that such mutually antagonistic relationships between the institutional bases of different goods are inevitable. Indeed, one might reasonably claim that it is a characteristic feature of modern societies that they display a relatively coherent and stable form of institutional differentiation which, correspondingly, makes it possible for the members of those societies to engage in a wide range of different kinds of social practices and relationships and to derive from them the enjoyment of a similarly wide range of goods. They may act as consumers, parents, friends and citizens, and benefit from the various goods associated with each of these roles; there need be no 'contradictions' here, any more than there need be between the correspondingly different institutions which make these activities possible for them.

None the less, even without the politically-driven reconstruction of non-market institutions to bring them closer to a market model which was noted earlier, social institutions may operate or develop in ways that are antithetical to the effective functioning of others. This possibility is especially evident in the case of the market, given its inherently dynamic and expansive nature and the considerable power of what are rightly termed market 'forces'. Just as the unbounded market is potentially and often actually destructive of the *natural* conditions for some human goods – the degradation of the environment depriving humans of certain irreplaceable sources of well-being – so too it can be, and often is, of the *social* conditions for other such goods. There are many ways in which this may occur, amongst them the following:

Sometimes the constant need to create 'new commodities' may be met by introducing commodified forms of goods which had previously existed in a non-commodified form, altering their distinctive character or forcing them out of existence: for example, the displacement of blood-doning by its commercial counterpart, or of amateur sports or artistic activities by 'professional' ones. Sometimes the competition for audiences between commercial and non-commercial broadcasters will force the latter to adjust their programming priorities so that, for example, they no longer give serious attention to the democratic requirement for informed political debate and analysis. And sometimes more subtle processes of 'meaning projection' may occur, so that, without literally becoming commodified, social practices previously conducted on a quite different basis become redefined in market-related terms: for example, when friendship or marriage come to be seen and practised as contractual exchanges, with a consequent loss of reciprocity and commitment.[6]

4 Protecting endangered goods

Suppose now that the members of a democratic society are faced with a situation in which, 'left to its own devices', the market could reasonably be expected to operate in such a way that the continued availability of certain non-market human goods is threatened – that they are likely to become 'endangered species'. I suggest that there are no good grounds for ruling out, as a matter of principle, their deciding to utilise the powers of the state to limit the operation of the market, and/or to employ its resources to provide support for these threatened goods. In particular, I shall argue, such decisions are not prohibited by a liberal principle of neutrality.

To clarify what is at issue here, let us also suppose that, in the situation just noted, no member of the society concerned would in fact wish to see these endangered goods go out of existence: they would all prefer them to be protected, and would be willing to 'sacrifice' their potential enjoyment of market goods in order to achieve this. The problem they face is that, as members of a society with a market economy, they find that the aggregative effect of their individually rational actions as economic agents is something which none of them either intended or desired, namely the loss of other goods which, given the choice, they would prefer to remain available to them. Given that this is so, it is hard to see what would be objectionable about their acting collectively so as to prevent these undesired consequences.[7]

Of course, in doing so they will be placing limitations on the

---

[6] On friendship, marriage and the market see E. Anderson, 'The ethical limitations of the market', *Economics and Philosophy*, 6, (1990), 179–205; on blood-doning see J. O'Neill, 'Egoism, altruism and the market', *Philosophical Forum*, 23, (1992).

[7] On the significance of 'collectively irrational consequences of individually rational actions', see B. Barry, 'The continuing relevance of socialism', in *Liberty and Justice* (Oxford University Press, 1991).

actions they would otherwise have performed as consumers and producers in a market economy: some of the things they had previously been free to do will no longer be so. But if they fail to restrict themselves in this way, they will find that some of the things which they would prefer to be able to achieve, some of the more highly valued sources of their own well-being, will no longer be available to them. So why should they be obliged to subject themselves to such a damaging, self-denying ordinance? More specifically, is this what the principle of neutrality obliges them to do? I suggest not, for the following reasons. (The situation is more complex in the absence of unanimity; but I can see no justification for the freedom of a minority to pursue the goods they prefer having priority over that of the majority to do likewise.)

To think that it does would require one to believe that allowing the market to eliminate such endangered goods would be consistent with that principle, whilst using the powers and resources of the state to prevent this would not be. This would imply that the former course of action would *not* involve the state's favouring certain conceptions of the good over others (i.e. those made available through the market over those which were not), whereas the latter course of action *would* (i.e. it would involve the state's favouring non-market goods over market ones). But there is no reason to regard these two cases as differing with respect to the implied neutrality of the state.

Now it might be objected that there is a relevant difference here, namely that if we decide to 'leave things to the market' to determine, we are deciding to 'keep the state out' of such determinations, i.e. not to rely on its powers, whereas if we decide to use those powers, we are clearly not. But this, I believe, is mistaken. For although the market is indeed an alternative to the state as a means of organising the production of 'economic' goods, it is itself a social institution which depends for its existence and mode of operation on the powers of the state – not least in defining and enforcing an appropriate system of legally enforceable property rights. Indeed, it is worth noting here that the market is itself best seen as a 'public good' – one that requires collective action to institute and sustain, and which is not itself the natural outcome of individually rational action.[8]

Now, given that the market is, *inter alia*, a device through which certain kinds of human goods are produced, there is a significant sense in which the decision to institute and/or sustain the market

---

[8] For an argument to this effect, see D. Mueller, *Public Choice II* (Cambridge University Press, 1989), Part I.

represents a decision to utilise the powers of the state to make these kinds of goods available. As such, this is not necessarily incompatible with the requirement of neutrality, since it does not of itself imply a decision to favour these kinds of goods (and the more general conceptions of the good whose realisation they make possible) over others. But then neither is, by the same line of reasoning, a decision to use the powers and resources of the state to support the provision of other kinds of goods: there are no grounds for regarding the two as inherently different with respect to neutrality.

If, however, in the situation I have been considering, the decision is made to allow the market to operate in ways that are destructive of these endangered non-market goods, it is hard to see how this could be regarded as satisfying, or as required by, the principle of state neutrality. It would surely be more plausible to see it as representing a decision to favour market over non-market goods, i.e. as a thoroughly non-neutral one. Indeed, any 'principled' decision always to allow market goods to triumph in this way – as distinct from merely accepting, in effect, that 'might is good' – would seem to be the equivalent of assigning lexical priority to market goods, i.e. of always preferring them when they conflict with others.

What grounds, if any, there could be for such a decision I shall not consider here, but it seems unlikely that they could fail to involve just those kinds of 'perfectionist' judgments about the relative value of different conceptions of the good which the neutralist liberal is so eager to avoid. Thus, far from liberal neutrality requiring us to leave things to the market, leaving things to the market may require us to abandon neutrality; indeed, we may even come to doubt whether neutrality is a principle that can consistently be applied.

5 Markets, democracy and the common good

I have been arguing that one cannot appeal to a liberal principle of neutrality to rule out decisions to use the powers and resources of the state in order to protect human goods endangered by the foreseeable effects of an unbounded market. For the market itself may operate in ways that are, as it were, non-neutral with respect to potential conflicts between market and non-market goods, and as an institution which itself relies upon the state, it is hard to see why neutrality on the latter's part should require such conflicts always to be resolved in the market's favour.

In the course of this argument, I have also claimed that the market should be regarded as just one – albeit a highly significant one –

of many social institutions through which a variety of different kinds of goods is made available to the members of a society such as ours. In doing so I have implicitly suggested an alternative to the way in which liberal political theorists – whether contemporary neutralists or their historical predecessors – typically conceive of the market: as a realm of freedom in which individuals are at liberty to pursue their own conceptions of the good, and which stands in marked contrast to the state, seen as the prime source of coercion, and hence of limitations upon individual liberty.

This alternative view of the market, which has an equally long and distinguished ancestry in the work of the classical political economists, sees it primarily as a socially instituted device with a remarkable ability to generate – more efficiently and abundantly than any other known system – certain kinds of human goods, and hence to contribute to the well-being of those who purchase and utilise them. It is this which constitutes the market's chief merit; for the liberal, by contrast, any such reference to the goods produced by the market is strictly irrelevant, since what matters is its supposed embodiment of individual liberty.[9]

Now let us suppose that, in a democratic society, it is for this 'classical' reason, and not the liberal one, that the market is accepted. We might reasonably take this to indicate that there is some agreement amongst its citizens that the kinds of goods made available through the market are indeed of considerable value to them, and the decision to support the institution of the market with the powers of the state would thus be based upon a 'shared conception of the good', of the well-being it is thought possible to achieve through the purchase and use of consumer products. Indeed, we could also see this decision as expressing a shared concern with 'the common good', the good of every member of that society – and this would then quite naturally be accompanied by a recognition of the need to adjust or supplement market-determined distributions of consumer goods when this was necessary to meet some agreed criteria of justice.

But there would be no reason to expect that this would be their only shared conception of the good, or that they believed it was only through the activities made possible by consumption that their well-being could be realised. Rather, these citizens might also agree on the potential value to their lives of many other kinds of human goods, which cannot be generated through the market. So, just as

---

[9] I have elaborated this contrast between liberal and classical justifications for the market in 'Delivering the goods: socialism, liberalism and the market', *New Waverley Papers*, No. 96–9 (Department of Politics, University of Edinburgh, 1996).

they are willing to act collectively to secure the provision of market-generated goods, they will also wish to act collectively to ensure that these other goods are likewise made available, and will thus be willing also to deploy, where this is appropriate, the resources of the state to achieve this.

On this account, then, the rationales for establishing and maintaining both market and non-market institutions are essentially the same, in that both rely on agreed judgments about the value of various kinds of goods as means for living what are regarded as humanly worthwhile lives. Since this is so, such citizens will see no 'objection in principle' to deciding, for example, to place limits on the operation of the market when it threatens to damage these other goods, at least in those cases where the relative value placed upon these would make this seem to them an unacceptable sacrifice. Given that, for them, the market is an institution whose chief merit is an 'instrumental' one – its ability to deliver certain kinds of goods – they will have no objection in principle to limiting or replacing it whenever it fails; and when conflicts between market and non-market goods arise, they will attempt to resolve these through agreed judgments about their relative significance. Nor will they regard either the market itself, or what are essentially market-replicating procedures such as cost-benefit analysis, as capable of making such judgments, since they recognise the incommensurability, in monetary terms, of the various goods at stake.[10]

Thus, in broad terms, the kinds of reasons they have for adopting the market are the same as those they appeal to in deciding to place limits upon it: in both cases, judgments about human goods are seen as entirely appropriate. From this perspective, then, arguments for such limitations which rely on claims about human goods are not seen as departing radically from the basic rationale for the market itself. By contrast, this is precisely how they must appear from a liberal perspective, given that its rationale for the market makes no reference to its value in generating human goods.

But the alternative, non-liberal account of the market I have been presenting here is not necessarily at odds with the characteristic concerns of liberal political thought. In particular, it must be emphasised that what is collectively agreed and secured by institutional means is only the availability of various kinds of goods, and the possibilities they represent for individuals: there is no requirement that every individual must 'partake' of all these goods, no coercive pressure by the state so to do, no paternalistic judgment made and enforced by others. This is true not only of the goods

[10] For an application of this argument to environmental decisions, see M. Sagoff, *The Economy of the Earth* (Cambridge University Press, 1988).

made available through the market, where it is clear that individuals may select their own particular 'packages', in ways that will partly express their differing overall conceptions of the good, but also of the differing kinds of goods made available through non-market institutions and the social practices they sustain. What is being secured, here, is essentially a common stock or repertoire of goods, from which individuals may freely choose.

Thus the account I have offered is not incompatible with the liberal requirement that individuals should be free to pursue their own conceptions of the good. But it differs from the way this requirement is normally presented, in that it rejects the highly abstract, idealist and asocial manner in which such conceptions of the good are themselves typically conceived: as if they were either the spontaneous creations of individual minds, or floating freely in some conceptual ether, waiting to be chosen and then acted upon. Instead, I have suggested, conceptions of the good are rooted in, and made possible by, specific forms of social practice and (in many cases) their institutional conditions.

This is not to adopt a crude sociologism, according to which all 'individual preferences' are 'socially determined'; rather, it is to insist that specific social conditions must obtain if certain conceptions of the good are to be possible objects of individual choice. So just as the sociality of human goods leaves room for autonomy, the collective decisions made to secure the common stock of these goods leave individuals free to pursue their own conceptions of the good. The state uses its coercive powers to ensure their conditions of possibility, not to force individuals to actualise them.

Now it might be objected that I am trying to have my cake and eat it here, in claiming both that there are shared conceptions of the good in such a society, and that its members remain free to decide upon those which they wish to pursue. For if the latter is true, and the individuals concerned choose differently from one another, what significance can be given to their being said to share certain conceptions of the good, and to agree as citizens on taking collective action to provide what is required to realise these? Would it not be better, and much less misleading, to say instead that all that is really 'agreed' upon is the right of individuals to pursue their own conceptions of the good, and/or the value of their being free to do so? There is no shared conception of the good, here; the citizens of a properly *liberal* democracy simply 'agree to differ' about human goods, but respect one another's right freely to choose what to regard as such, for themselves.

But I do not think this objection is convincing. For it relies upon conflating the choices we make as individuals as to which goods we wish to pursue, and our judgments about what *are* human goods, and hence possible contributions to human well-being. For example, I may not choose to live the life of a musician or a nature-lover, but this does not mean that I do not recognise them as good lives to live. Nor is this 'recognition' merely a matter of my registering the fact that others happen to see them as such; it involves my accepting that they are good lives, not simply that others wish to live them. My coming to accept this may involve considerable efforts of imagination and reflection, and I reserve the right, as it were, to arrive at a negative judgment. But I do not regard the fact of my own preference for a different life, which I judge to be a good one, as implying either that no others are good, or that what others regard as good is a matter merely of their preferences.

I have put these points in the first-person singular, but I see no reason why they should not also be put in the first-person plural, and thus suggest the possibility of a democratic politics of the common good which recognises diversity without lapsing into subjectivism or a spurious form of tolerance. And given both the need for collective action to secure the institutional conditions for such diverse human goods, and the potential for these institutions to operate in mutually antithetical ways, it is hard to see how supposedly illiberal perfectionist judgments about the respective value of these different goods either can or should be avoided.

A Tale of Three Karls:
Marx, Popper, Polanyi and Post-Socialist Europe

DAVID MARQUAND

The human race, to which so many of my readers belong, has been playing at children's games from the beginning... [O]ne of the games to which it most attached is called... 'Cheat the Prophet'. [The prophets] took something or other that was certainly going on in their time, and then said it would go on more and more until something extraordinary happened. ... The players listen very carefully and respectfully to all that the clever men have to say about what is to happen in the next generation. The players then wait until all the clever men are dead, and bury them nicely. They then go and do something else.

(G. K. Chesterton, *The Napoleon of Notting Hill*)[1]

In part it is due to a genuine misunderstanding of the philosophical implications of the natural sciences, the great prestige of which has been misappropriated by many a fool and imposter since their earliest triumphs. But principally it seems to me to spring from a desire to resign our responsibility, to cease from judging provided we be not judged ourselves and, above all, are not compelled to judge ourselves – from a desire to flee for refuge to some vast, amoral, impersonal, monolithic whole – nature, or history, or class, or race, or the irresistible evolution of the social structure ... which it is senseless to evaluate or criticise, and which we resist to our certain doom. This is a mirage which has often appeared in the history of mankind, always at moments of confusion and inner weakness. It is one of the great alibis, pleaded by those who cannot and do not wish to face the facts of human responsibility... This they do in the service of an imaginary science, and, like the astrologers and magicians whom they have succeeded ... make use of hypnotic formulae with little regard for experience, or rational argument, or tests of proven reliability.
(Isaiah Berlin on 'social determinism')[2]

[1] Quoted, in Jonathan Gershuny, *After Industrial Society: The Emerging Self-service Economy* (Basingstoke: Macmillan Press, 1978) p. 1.
[2] Isaiah Berlin, *Historical Inevitability* (Oxford: Oxford University Press, 1954) pp. 77–8.

David Marquand

In the summer of 1997, a meeting of Socialist leaders took place in Malmo. The star turn was the newly installed head of the first Labour Government in Britain for nearly twenty years, Tony Blair. The world, Blair told his colleagues, had undergone 'a veritable revolution of change'. Technology, trade and travel were transforming our lives. The young people of Europe would be working in communications and design rather than in mass production. Jobs for life had gone. Women worked. South East Asia could compete with Europe, often on equal terms. Money was traded across international boundaries in vast amounts, for twenty-four hours a day. 'New, new, new', Blair exclaimed excitedly, 'everything is new'.[3]

On one level, these sentiments were hardly remarkable. If they had been uttered by anyone other than the luminous Young Lochinvar of the British centre-left, in the immediate aftermath of one of the most spectacular election victories in his country's history, they might have passed without notice. Not long ago, I was privileged to hear both a highly placed member of the present Italian Government and an even more highly placed former member of the Spanish Socialist Government say virtually the same things, in almost identical language. On another level, however, Blair's Malmo speech was more significant than it might appear. It was a distillation of the conventional wisdom of the *fin-de-siècle*: the epitome of a curious, a-historical (not to say anti-historical) conception of modernity and modernisation which has become one of the hallmarks of the age – most obviously in the English-speaking world, but to some extent in continental Europe as well. I believe it to be a profoundly misleading conception; and I also believe it to be profoundly dangerous. In the rest of this essay I shall try to show why.

The new worlders

According to this conventional wisdom, we live in a new world, in which old theories have no purchase. Globalisation is dissolving national frontiers, dethroning nation-states, stultifying national economic policies and, in some versions, destroying the ties that hold national communities together. Jobs for life have disappeared; social classes have merged; the labour force has been feminised; the family has been transformed; old elites have been toppled; and old traditions have lost legitimacy. In economies, cultures and polities, a new individualism is carrying all before it, perhaps robbing the very

[3] Quoted, in Stephen Driver and Luke Martell, *New Labour, Politics After Thatcherism*, (Cambridge: Polity Press, 1998), p. 41.

notion of a collective social project of its former resonance, perhaps merely making such projects unfeasible in practice.

Among the prophets of this wisdom – I shall call them the 'new worlders' – there are differences of emphasis and focus. Anthony Giddens, the John the Baptist of New Labour's Third Way, thinks we are in the throes of a global process of 'reflexive modernisation', which is carrying us beyond left and right. Robert Reich, Clinton's first Secretary for Labour, dwells on the effective disappearance of the national corporation as an institution, and on the emergence of a new class of what he calls 'symbolic analysts'. Philip Gould, the most famous of the polling gurus who helped to shape Tony Blair's electoral strategy, predicts a 'permanent revolution' of intensifying competition and technological advance, and celebrates the emergence of a vast new middle class which will give New Labour continuing hegemony into the next century.[4]

By the same token, different prophets appraise the alleged new world through different ideological spectacles. Broadly speaking, the Hayekian New Right see it as unproblematic. To paraphrase John Reed's famous remark about the Bolshevik Revolution, they have seen the future; it is self-evidently neo-liberal; and it works. Exit has triumphed, once and for all, over Voice and the collectivist temptations of Voice. On the left and centre-left, attitudes are more complicated. There, Voice is still prized. Citizens are not equated with consumers. Public power is still thought to have a role. Social justice (albeit sometimes re-packaged as social cohesion) is still cherished. The question is how to pursue these values in the face of ineluctable, but inimical trends: how to 'adapt' – a favourite word, that – traditional left and centre-left doctrines to changes which have made it impossible to apply them in practice.

In one crucial respect, however, the differences between the new-worlders matter less than the similarities. The new world may have cruel and destructive features, they concede; the gales of change that emanate from it may do violence to cherished values and customs. But, for good or ill, its advent is inexorable and unstoppable. Above all, it is homogeneous. From it, there is no hiding place: in it, no room for local ways of life with which its imperatives are in conflict. To think otherwise is to succumb to sentimentality or nostalgia. It is even more foolish to seek to protect local ways of life from

[4] Anthony Giddens, *Beyond Left and Right, The Future of Radical Politics* (Cambridge: Polity Press, 1994); Robert Reich, *The Work of Nations, Preparing Ourselves for 21st Century Capitalism* (New York: Vintage, 1992) and Philip Gould, *The Unfinished Revolution, How the Modernisers Saved the Labour Party* (London: Little Brown and Company, 1998).

its incursions. The global market-place and global culture which are of its essence are or soon will be sovereign. Resistance is futile and will do more harm than good. The 'revolution of change', of which Tony Blair spoke, is a kind of treadmill from which we cannot dismount.

If this essay has a single message it is that the right response to all this is, 'up to a point, Lord Copper'. Of course, we live in a new world: each new generation lives in a world new to it. John Donne famously complained that 'the new philosophy calls all in doubt'. De Tocqueville called for a 'new science' to explain the bewildering novelties of the nineteenth century. Plato, Hobbes and Burke, the great philosophers of conservatism, wrote in reaction to the flux and insecurity of revolutionary change. By the same token, it is true that the political economies of the 1990s differ radically from those of the Keynesian 'golden age', as Eric Hobsbawm calls it, in which I grew up;[5] that some (though not all) of the political approaches of that era now lead nowhere; that in many ways the world is a smaller place than it was then; and that recent changes have made it more difficult to realise the values of solidarity and common citizenship.

Cheating the prophet

But it is one thing to say that changes have taken place, another to add that those same changes are bound to continue, far into the future. Mankind has played 'Cheat the Prophet' more than once in the last couple of centuries. The proposition that an autonomous, ineluctable and irresistible force called globalisation is bound to carry all before it echoes, in twentieth-century language, one of the central themes both of the economic liberalism and of the classical Marxism of the nineteenth century. They too insisted that the global market place was governed by iron laws, which mere governments could not defy, and that its imperatives would break down what Marx and Engels called the 'Chinese walls' that separated national economies and cultures from each other. Nothing of the sort happened. Politics turned out to be more potent than economics; specific, 'thick' cultural traditions rather than the 'thin' universalities of Marxist and laissez-faire theory. Friedrich List, the apostle of German economic nationalism, was a better prophet than Adam Smith. The Germans, the Japanese, even, in those days, the Americans did not want their societies to be re-made in the image of Engels's Manchester or Dickens's Coketown. Still less did they

[5] Eric Hobsbawm, *Age of Extremes, The Short Twentieth Century* (London: Michael Joseph, 1994), Part II.

want their economic destinies to be controlled by a hegemonic Britain, acting as the agent for supposedly impersonal economic laws. They refused to take the Smithian, laissez-faire route to modernity and took the Listian, economic-nationalist route instead. The result was a mosaic of different modernities, not the single, monolithic modernity envisaged by the one-worlders of that day.

That is only the beginning of the story. As Albert Hirschman shows in his elegant study, *The Rhetoric of Reaction*, a favourite trope of progressive rhetoric, ever since the French Revolution, has been the claim that irrevocable laws of motion are carrying mankind, willy-nilly, in the direction which progressives in any case wish to take.[6] Marx was perhaps the greatest master of this trope in the history of social thought, but he was by no means alone in employing it. The interwar pioneers of the post-war mixed economy did so too. According to them, history inevitably progressed from the disorganised to the organised, from the dispersed to the concentrated, from the individual to the collective. So the maverick Conservative, Harold Macmillan, saw existing forms of economic organisation as 'a temporary phase in the onward march of developing social history', which would sooner or later terminate in a planned economy. And so the Labour economist, Evan Durbin, dismissed the liberal economics of Von Mises, Hayek and Robbins with what he evidently assumed was the unanswerable objection that 'social systems have rarely developed backwards'.[7]

But those who lived by determinism died by determinism. In our day, it has been the turn of the New Right to pray in aid of irrevocable laws of motion – this time, of course, pointing in the opposite direction. The inexorable tides of economic and social change, it appeared, had changed direction. They no longer ran from the small to the big or the disorganised to the organised. Like a de-coagulant dissolving a blood clot, ineluctable technological changes were disempowering the state and dissolving the great power blocks that impeded the free flow of market forces. 'The unplanners', as the British Conservative, David Howell, put it during the high noon of the New Right, had 'defeated the planners completely' – not so much because they had better arguments, but because the centralism on which they depended had become (another favourite word) 'outdated'.[8]

[6] Albert O. Hirschman, *The Rhetoric of Reaction: Perversity. Futility, Jeopardy* (Cambridge, Mass: Harvard University Press, 1991), pp. 154–9.

[7] David Reisman (ed.), *Theories of the Mixed Economy* (London: William Pickering, 1994), Vol. IV; Harold Macmillan, *The Middle Way*, p. 109 and Vol. V, Evan Durbin, *The Politics of Democratic Socialism*, p. 361.

[8] David Howell, *Blind Victory: A Study in Income, Wealth and Power* (London: Hamish Hamilton, 1986), p. 4.

David Marquand

The death of socialism

Of course, none of this proves that the new-worlders are wrong. But it does prove that irrevocable laws of motion have a nasty habit of turning traitor. And it does at least suggest that it would be unwise to assume that they will never turn traitor again. That is only one reason for taking the conventional wisdom with a pinch of salt. Another is that it actually obscures the true nature of the strange politico-economic conjuncture which it purports to illuminate. Four features of this conjuncture stand out. The first is that socialism, at least as the term was used and understood for most of its history, has ceased to be a political or intellectual force. (This may seem an odd thing to say at a time when professedly socialist parties are doing better than they have done for years, but I shall try to show that the oddity is only apparent.) For the best part of a century, the socialist vision of a world re-made inspired passionate loyalties, mobilised extraordinary energies and survived innumerable betrayals and disappointments. Now it is little more than a memory. The epic struggle between capitalism and socialism is over; and capitalism has won. Nominally socialist parties still exist. For reasons I shall come to in a moment, some of them are prospering. But their relationship to socialism as traditionally understood is reminiscent of that of the Renaissance Popes to the Sermon on the Mount.

For classical socialism had at least five dimensions. It was an ethic, an economic theory, a science (or purported science) of society, the vehicle of a social interest and a secular religion. Socialists were for 'co-operation', for 'commonwealth, for 'solidarity'; they thought, with William Morris, that fellowship was heaven and lack of fellowship, hell. They were against capitalism because they thought these values could not be realised in a society based on private ownership. At the same time, they took it for granted that social ownership would be more efficient than private, and a planned economy than the free market. Whether gradualists or revolutionaries, they also took it for granted that they had discovered the laws of social change; and that their prescriptions for the future were uniquely compelling because they had done so. Also whether gradualists or revolutionaries, they saw their creed as the instrument, inspiration and mentor of the labour movement and allotted a unique redemptive role to the working class. Last, but by no means least, they had a heaven and a hell; saints and sinners; martyrs and persecutors; heretics and heresy-hunters; saved and damned. Above all, they had an eschatology – a science of last things. One day, the expropriators would be expropriated, the humble would be exalted

42

and a new society, free of exploitation and injustice, would arise from the ruins of the old.

Of these five dimensions only the first survives. The ethic of solidarity and fellowship has at least as much to say to the Europe of our time as it had to the Europe of 100 years ago. But no one still believes that social ownership is more efficient than private, or central planning than market allocation. The social science of socialism is equally discredited. Today, only anti-socialists, and to some extent ex-socialists, believe that they have charted history's course. Insofar as socialism is still the vehicle of the working class, that is now a handicap for socialist politicians rather than an asset. Partly because of all this, the secular religion has lost its power as well. The nominal socialism of today has zealous bureaucrats, faithful supporters, even loyal voters. What it does not have are true believers. The parties that espouse it still constitute a formidable reservoir of social decency and hope, but they no longer promise salvation to the elect or damnation to the unregenerate. They are, in Donald Sassoon's phrase, 'neo-revisionists'. They want to moralise, or mitigate, or humanise or regulate capitalism, but they no longer want to replace it. They have crossed the crucial dividing line that once separated the social liberalism of the early twentieth century from the democratic socialism of the same period. They have more in common with David Lloyd George or Woodrow Wilson than with August Bebel or Keir Hardie.

At this point, enter the second outstanding feature of the current conjuncture. In one crucial respect, the conventional wisdom points in precisely the wrong direction. The motor of the alleged new world of the 1990s and 2000s is new only in the foreshortened perspective of the last forty years. In the perspective of the last 200 it is not new at all. The post-war golden age, and the tamed, welfare capitalism that underpinned it, were aberrations from an older norm. They were the serendipitous products of a delicate balance, between capital and labour, left and right, socialists and conservatives, East and West, American pressures and European interests, embodied in hard-won social and political compromises. Now the wheel has come full circle. Partly (though not solely) because of the demise of socialism, the balance which made the golden age possible has broken down. Victorious capitalism is off the leash. Not surprisingly, it is behaving much as capitalism behaved before its tamers put it on the leash during the extraordinary burst of institutional creativity that followed the second world war. To be sure, its behaviour is not all of a piece. This is still a world of multiple capitalisms, marked by sharp variations of structure, culture and performance. Running through these variations, however, is a common theme. The heaving, masterless, productivity-enhancing, but inequality-generating and cohesion-destroying global economy of the 1990s may be a long way away from its benign and stable predecessor of the 1950s and 1960s, but it is uncomfortably close to that of the nineteenth century and even to that of the interwar period. Keynes may be dead, but Marx, Malthus and Ricardo have had a new lease of life.

The consequences lie all around us. The fundamental Keynesian (and Marxist) paradox of wasted resources in the midst of unsatisfied needs has returned. So has that old faithful of Marxian wage theory, the 'industrial reserve army' of the unemployed. In Britain and the United States, where capitalism's untaming has gone furthest, two other half-forgotten props of Marxist eschatology – the immiseration of the proletariat and the proletarianisation of widening swathes of the bourgeoisie – have returned as weft. The decasualisation of labour, which a generation of trade-union leaders saw as its life's work, has given way to its re-casualisation – and in what used to be the middle class as well as in the working class. Downsizing, de-layering, out-sourcing and re-engineering haunt the suburbs as well as the inner cities, mocking the commitments and hollowing out the institutions which were once the lodestars of the salariat. Capitalism has turned back on its tracks in less familiar ways as well. In most of western Europe, the great achievement of the second half of the nineteenth century and the first half of the twentieth was the creation of a public domain, ring-fenced from the pressures of the market-place. In the public domain, citizenship rights rather than market power governed the allocation of social goods. Now privatisation is narrowing its scope, while marketisation is twisting it out of shape – restricting the scope of democratic citizenship, devaluing the ethic of public service and even undermining the very notion of the public good.

Against that background, the third outstanding feature of the current conjuncture takes on a startling hue. Classical socialism, transformative socialism, the socialism that looked forward to a world re-made and that the Communist regimes of the eastern bloc claimed to embody, has fallen on evil days. But ameliorative social democracy – Sassoon's neo-revisionism' – has just experienced an unexpected rebirth. Social democrats are now in power in most of the member-states of the European Union, not least in France and Germany – the two leading member-states, which have provided the driving force of the European project since its earliest days. In itself, it is true, the social-democratic label is not very informative. In some moods, at least, the leaders of Britain's 'New' Labour Party describe themselves as social democrats, but everyone knows that their version of social democracy differs sharply from those of the ruling French Socialists and of some, if not all, of the key figures in the German 'red–green' coalition. In any case, it is not yet clear what social democracy can or should mean in practice in the economic era through which we are now living – or, for that matter, how the policy implications of the social-democratic tradition now differ from those of other traditions.

The rebirth of social democracy

Yet a beam of fight shines through the fog. Everywhere, the social-democratic rebirth of the late 1990s is a response to the social and moral dislocation that the new capitalism has brought in its train. The intensity of the response, and the programmatic channels through which it has flowed, have varied from society to society, according to the extent of the dislocation, the traditions of the society concerned and the resilience of the previous moral economy. That is only to be expected. The really striking feature of *fin-de-siè-cle* politics, however, is that, all over Europe, reborn capitalism and reborn social democracy have appeared on the scene, not simultaneously it is true, but at any rate in close proximity. First came the infection, then came the antibody: first the wound, and then the slow reappearance of healthy tissues.

This is where the fourth outstanding feature of the current conjuncture comes into the story. Fifty years ago, Karl Polanyi famously depicted the 'great transformation' of the nineteenth century as a kind of pendulum, that swung from 'planned' *laissez-faire* capitalism at the start of the century to 'unplanned' economic and social regulation later.[9] For him, the self-regulating free market of the early nineteenth century, and the commodification of land and labour that it logically entailed, was a 'utopia'. It was unrealisable, because land and labour are not in fact commodities like any other. It was also, in a profound sense, unnatural. It was not a spontaneous product of unfettered human instinct, as its apologists claimed. On the contrary, massive state interventions, pushed through by a ruthless and centralised bureaucracy, were needed to impose it on the Old Society and to uproot the old value-system that impeded it. The interventions did not succeed, of course. They could not, because the utopia they were designed to institute was an impossibility. But the attempt to institute it was a social and cultural disaster, provoking, in the end, a spontaneous reaction against it.

[9] Karl Polanyi, *The Great Transformation: The Political and Economic Origins of our Times* (Boston: Beacon Press, 1957).

David Marquand

As Polanyi put it:

> The road to the free market was opened and kept open by an enormous increase in continuous, centrally organized and controlled interventionism. To make Adam Smiths 'simple and natural liberty' compatible with the needs of a human society was a most complicated affair. Witness the complexity of the provisions in the innumerable enclosure laws; [and] the amount of bureaucratic control involved in the administration of the New Poor Laws ...

> This paradox was topped by another. While laissez-faire economy was the product of deliberate State action, subsequent restrictions on laissez-faire started in a spontaneous way. Laissez-faire was planned; planning was not. ... The legislative spearhead of the counter-movement against a self-regulating market ... in the half century following 1860 turned out to be spontaneous, undirected by opinion and actuated by a purely pragmatic spirit.[10]

Now Polanyi's pendulum seems to be swinging again only at a much greater speed. So far, the chief beneficiaries have been social democrats. But it does not follow that they will remain so for ever. Everything depends on whether the antibody eventually overcomes the infection. The peoples of Europe turned to social democracy because it was there: because it was the most obvious port in which to shelter from the neo-capitalist storm. If the shelter turns out to be illusory, if the infection continues unchecked, reborn social democracy will have no claim on the loyalties of electorates which are, in any case, more volatile than they used to be. The Polanyi pendulum can take a malign, as well as a benign, form. The German social-democratic pioneer, August Bebel, once described anti-semitism as the 'socialism of fools'. Today, the phrase has a wider application. In the world of the 1990s and 2000s, religious and ethnic fundamentalism, xenophobic nationalism, moral authoritarianism and the scape-goating of minorities might be called the fool's social democracy. They too offer escape routes – deceptive and dangerous ones, no doubt, but that does not make them less seductive – from the social fragmentation which is part and parcel of the current capitalist renaissance.

As Benjamin Barber puts it, 'Jihad' is the other side of the coin of 'McWorld': cultural tribalism of the global free market.[11] And although 'Jihad' is more prevalent in the former Soviet bloc and the Third World than in North America and western Europe, the moral

---

[10] Ibid., pp. 140–1.
[11] Benjamin Barber, *Jihad. vs. McWorld* (New York: Times Books, 1995).

majority in the United States, the Europhobic nationalists who control the British gutter press, the National Front in France and the Italian neo-Fascists and Lombard League all whistle essentially the same fundamentalist tune as Serbian zealots in Kosovo, Jewish zealots on the West Bank, Muslim zealots in Algeria and Hindu zealots in the Indian BJP. It would be wrong to exaggerate. London, Paris, Berlin, Milan and Naples are not Weimar. The political cultures and moral economies of present-day Europe are still, by the standards of past history, remarkably tolerant and generous. The current social-democratic rebirth is testimony to that. But if the reborn social democrats fail the peoples who have turned to them, if there is no end to the social and cultural disruption associated with the capitalist renaissance against which their victories were a protest, if nothing is done to halt the steady growth of inequality, anomie and alienation, a turn to darker forces could not be ruled out.

The open society in danger

The implications are plain. Polanyi's masterpiece appeared at around the same time as Karl Popper's greater masterpiece, *The Open Society and its Enemies*. Popper was a philosopher, not a historian or social scientist; and he said comparatively little about the social, cultural or economic prerequisites of the open society he celebrated and advocated. But the splendid peroration to volume one of his book contains a tantalising hint of how he saw them:

> [I]f we shrink from the task of carrying our cross, the cross of humaneness, of reason, of responsibility, then we must try to fortify ourselves with a clear understanding of the simple decision before us. We can return to the beasts. But if we wish to remain human, then there is only one way, the way into the open society. We must go on into the unknown, the uncertain and insecure, using what reason we may have to plan for both security *and* freedom.[12]

'[P]lan for security and freedom'. What, on *fin-de-siècle* assumptions, could be more old-fashioned or out-of-date? Yet the great achievement of post-war western Europe was to do just that. Tamed capitalism did ensure the symbiosis between freedom and security on which, as Popper foresaw, both depended. That, as much as – indeed, far more than – material prosperity was the true glory of the golden age. And in a Polanyiesque perspective, the

[12] Karl Popper, *The Open Society and Its Enemies, Vol. 1, The Spell of Plato* (London: Routledge and Kegan Paul, 1952), 2nd edn, pp. 200–1.

great challenge to modern Europe is to preserve that achievement: to make sure that untamed capitalism does not undermine the social and cultural underpinnings of the open society, and so destroy the security without which freedom cannot flourish.

It would be absurd to suggest that this is an easy task. In detail and in practice, the questions it poses are formidably difficult. Yet it does not follow that it is inherently impossible to define the broad outlines of a public philosophy from which detailed, practical answers might be drawn. Such a philosophy would be broadly social-democratic in economics and broadly social-liberal in politics. It is not difficult to delineate its central themes. The capitalist market economy is a marvellous servant, but a disastrous master. The task is to return it to the servitude which the builders of the post-war mixed economy imposed on it, and from which it has now escaped. To that end, the public domain of citizenship and service should be safeguarded from incursions by the market domain of buying and selling, from what Michael Walzer has called 'market imperialism'[13] In the public domain, goods should not be treated as commodities or proxy commodities. The language of buyer and seller, producer and customer, does not belong in the public domain and nor do the relationships which that language implies. Doctors and nurses do not 'sell' medical services; students are not 'customers' of their teachers; policemen and policewomen do not 'produce' public order. The attempt to force these relationships into a market mould merely undermines the service ethic which is the true guarantor of quality in the public domain, and in doing so impoverishes us all.

By the same token, enterprises should take account of stakeholders as well as owners. Wealth should be redefined to include well-being. Well-being should be defined to include, among other things, the social capital represented by, and embodied in, a diverse, pluralistic civil society, culturally and ethnically heterogeneous and rich in intermediate institutions. Crucially, the sovereignty of a federal Europe should countervail the sovereignty of the global market-place. But the point of European Union is to safeguard European values and ways of life, notably including the values of variety and autonomy. This means that European federalism should be based on the old Christian Democratic principle of *subsidiarity* – the principle that decisions should be taken on the lowest level of government appropriate to the issue concerned – and that authority and competence should be transferred downwards to regions and localities as well as upwards to the Union.

[13] Michael Walzer, *Spheres Of Justice: A Defence of Pluralism and Equality* (New York: Basic Books, 1983), pp. 119–20.

To repeat, none of this would be easy. But the greatest difficulties, I believe, are intellectual – perhaps emotional, one might even say spiritual – rather than practical. They have to do with a mind-set; with a nexus of largely implicit assumptions, held all the more tenaciously because they are rarely put into words and thereby opened up to challenge and debate. Two aspects of this mind-set deserve special attention. One might be called economism; the other, futurism. By economism I mean the notion that the economy is, in some mysterious sense, prior to society: that economic considerations should trump other considerations: that society should, so to speak, be tailored to fit the economy instead of the economy to fit society. That notion lay at the heart of the laissez-faire utopianisrn against which Polanyi's *Great Transformation* was a protest. A different version of essentially the same notion helped to inspire the inverse utopianism of the central planners of the old Soviet Union. It has surfaced again in the new-world discourse of today. I don't believe that untamed capitalism will be re-tamed until it is laid to rest.

By futurism I mean the notion, encapsulated in Tony Blair's Malmo exclamation, that we know what the future is going to be; that we have no choice but to embrace it; and that those who have embraced it are entitled, by virtue of their superior insight, to lead the rest of us towards it. The more I brood on it, the more I think that this is what, elsewhere in the essay from which I quoted, Isaiah Berlin called a 'theodicy'. It is an attempt to justify what might otherwise appear to be evil by an appeal to a higher power – no longer God, but history. It offers us a route out of the painful realm of choice and moral argument, and into the comforting realm of necessity. It implies that change is an exogenous force, operating on mere human beings from the outside; that there is only one modem condition which all rational people will recognise once it is pointed out to them; and that because of all this those who swim with the tide of history have no need to defend their decisions with moral arguments or to argue for their policies on moral grounds. Of the dangers inherent in that notion, the history of this terrible century is surely a sufficient warning.

Liberty's Hollow Triumph*

JOHN SKORUPSKI

1 Liberalism as an ethical ideal

The history of liberalism is the history of an ethical ideal as well as a set of political and social arrangements. In the latter sense liberalism entrenches the juridical equality of all citizens, their equal civil and political rights – including among those rights a set of liberties strong enough to restrict the authority of society over the individual in a fundamental way. How to express in institutions this politically fundamental restriction is an important matter of debate, but that debate will not concern us. For present purposes I assume I can refer to liberalism as a set of political and social arrangements without further examination. Our concern will instead be the liberal ethical ideal and its present prospects.

What is this ideal? The question is best answered historically, both because the ideal has gone through significant changes and because many people who think of themselves as liberals are now seriously unsure about what it is or should be. Or so it seems.

Undoubtedly a central element of the liberal ideal has been an ethical and not just juridical idea of equal respect. It has been of utmost political importance. For more than two centuries, one might say – that is since the French Revolution, but certainly with earlier roots in the growth of towns, trade and individualism – it has helped to generate a drive towards juridical equality in all spheres, abolition of all forms of social discrimination. Most of us would say that this has been pure gain. Yet even if the ethical conception which asserts that all human beings deserve equal respect simply as human beings has helped to bring about the juridical equality of rights which we approve, it seems in itself eminently questionable. Historically a kind of ground for it was found in Christian faith. As Alexis de Tocqueville (for example) put it, 'Christianity, which has declared all men equal in the sight of God, cannot hesitate to acknowledge all men equal before the law.'[1] But that hardly satisfies. What is it about human beings that makes them all equal in the sight of God? More generally, what are we to make of equal respect,

* I am grateful to Samuel Brittan, Geoff Cupit and Dudley Knowles for helpful discussion.
[1] Quoted in Larry Siedentop, *Tocqueville* (Oxford: Oxford University Press, 1994), p. 49.

if we find rest neither in the faith that all are equal 'in the sight of God', nor in a transcendental doctrine of absolute autonomy, nor an empirical hope that human beings can be equally worthy of respect if only society empowers them to become so?

Historically, however, equality of respect has certainly not been the only or the main ingredient in the liberal ethic. Its most significant element in the early nineteenth century was a determinate ideal which in fact stood in some potential tension with equality of respect. Liberty was justified as the condition which permitted the full and balanced development of human powers. This vision lay at the heart of the classical liberal ideal; but historically its force within liberalism has varied. Broadly speaking it was relatively great in the nineteenth-century phases of liberalism and small in the twentieth-century phases; while equal respect, in comparison, has played a significantly larger role in twentieth-century liberalism as the substantive ideal has faded. The change is striking and seems to require explanation. It is true that in general the nineteenth century is the century of ethical reflection *par excellence*, while twentieth-century ethical thought has at least until recently been in comparison thin, marginalised and largely inexplicit; but then this in turn seems to require explanation. At any rate after a hundred years of modernism in culture and socialism or social democracy in politics we find ourselves going back to Hegel, Mill and Nietzsche if we want to think hard about the viability of the liberal ethical ideal and the place of equal respect within it – in other words to a type of reflection which modernism and 'scientific' socialism combined to destroy, and which recent discussions of liberalism in moral and political philosophy are only just beginning to revive.

These two elements of the liberal ethic, their relative significance and the tension between them will be our subject. I shall distinguish four phases of the liberal tradition, two in the nineteenth century (early classical and late idealist), and two in the twentieth century (early modernist and late neutralist). I shall sketch the role the liberal ethical idea played in these four phases, as a preliminary to some questions about its current state.

2 Classical liberalism

To call the liberal thinkers of the first half of the nineteenth century classical liberals seems just, for it was in this period that liberalism first reached maturity. In response to political and spiritual revolutions in France and Germany it established its ideal and discovered its inner tensions and fears. Classical liberalism in this sense is represented at its earliest in Germany by Schiller, Humboldt and then later Burkhardt; in France by Constant, Guizot and Tocqueville; in Britain above all by Mill and in a later and more disenchanted way by Matthew Arnold. Mill was also a 'classical liberal' in the more common sense, that is, a believer in free trade. But he took pains to distinguish his qualified defence of free trade from his case for the liberty principle itself.[2] He defended free trade within certain limits,[3] on grounds of efficiency, but, in the great third chapter of Liberty which deals with 'Individuality', he grounded liberty on the ethical ideal of classical liberalism.

Classical liberalism got its vision of human good largely from a revival of hellenism and a response to Kant. It set a 'Greek ideal of self-development' (Mill's phrase) against the Kantian, or more broadly Protestant Christian, conception of human worth. For Kant the dignity of human beings and the respect owed to them rests on their capacity to give themselves the moral law. To act autonomously is to act from reason alone and not 'inclination'; only such action has 'moral worth'. But Schiller – a seminal thinker in this story – wanted to reaffirm a Hellenic conception of the culture of the whole human being, of feeling as well as of rational will: 'It will always argue a still defective education [*Bildung*] if the moral character is able to assert itself only by sacrificing the natural.' 'Wholeness of character must ... be present in any people capable, and worthy, of exchanging a State of compulsion for a State of freedom.'[4]

The issue is deep. To affirm the 'Greek ideal of self-development' is to place human worth on a basis of contingency. Beauty of character, the developed balance of freedom, intelligence and emotional spontaneity, are not wholly or even mostly under one's control. Admiration based on such excellence will be very unequally shared. Whereas what Kant calls autonomy is, at least according to his theory of transcendental freedom, not a merely contingent capacity of human beings. Kant thinks that autonomy, if it exists at all, exists non-empirically. Each of us is aware of it within ourselves, or at least we necessarily take ourselves to have it in deliberating how to act. Respect turns out to rest on something we must attribute to anyone we think of as a free chooser. Moreover that something,

[2] J. S. Mill, *On Liberty*, in M. Warnock (ed.), *Utilitarianism, On Liberty, Essay on Bentham* (Glasgow: Fontana, 1985), ch. V, para. 4.

[3] For an account of them see Pedro Schwartz, *The New Political Economy of J. S. Mill* (London: Weidenfeld & Nicholson, 1992).

[4] Friedrich Schiller, *On the Aesthetic Education of Man, in a Series of Letters*, edited and translated by Elizabeth M. Wilkinson and L. A. Willoughby (Oxford: Clarendon Press 1967), pp. 19, 23. These letters were written from 1793 to 1795; a revised version appeared in 1801.

'the causality of freedom', lies as firmly in the Beyond (to use Nietzsche's telling phrase) as does the Christian appeal to our equality 'in the sight of God'.

Not that classical liberalism repudiates the importance Kant and Christianity attach to this capacity of the individual. On the contrary, personal responsibility, the capacity to govern oneself, to recognise and act on good reasons – positive freedom – is central to nineteenth-century liberalism as a whole, both early and late. Nevertheless, liberals of the earlier period trod largely in the footsteps of Schiller not Kant. The important thing was to balance and fill out self-government by allowing due scope to human powers of emotional spontaneity. They agreed with Schiller that developed spontaneity is achieved by education of feeling. Spontaneity of feeling is no more incompatible with education of feeling than spontaneity of reason is incompatible with education of reason. A determinate potential or disposition is in both cases developed by self-culture. And the ideal is balance of the two.

In this same spirit, Mill does not straightforwardly reject 'the Platonic and Christian ideal of self-government'. Rather it represents to him the one-sided vision that Kantian moral worth represented to Schiller. 'There is a Greek ideal of self-development' which this narrower ideal 'blends with, but does not supersede. It may be better to be a John Knox than an Alcibiades, but it is better to be a Pericles than either.'[5]

A similar contrast is present in Matthew Arnold's well-known pairing of 'Hellenism' and 'Hebraism':

> The uppermost idea with Hellenism is to see things as they really are; the uppermost idea with Hebraism is conduct and obedience … The governing idea of Hellenism is *spontaneity of consciousness*; that of Hebraism, *strictness of conscience*.[6]

Arnold acknowledges the 'grandeur of earnestness and intensity' of hebraism as Schiller acknowledged the 'dignity' of acting from the moral law. But hellenism gets the fullest share of Arnold's eloquence. Hellenism has what Schiller called 'grace' and Arnold famously refers to as 'sweetness and light'. It has light because it sees 'things as they really are':

> To get rid of one's ignorance, to see things as they are, and by seeing them as they are to see them in their beauty, is the simple and attractive ideal which Hellenism holds out before human

[5] Mill, *On Liberty*, ch. III, para. 8.

[6] *Culture and Anarchy*, ch. IV, *The Complete Prose Works of Matthew Arnold*, R. H. Supe (ed.), (Ann Arbor: University of Michigan Press, 1960–78), vol. 5, p. 165.

nature; and from the simplicity and charm of this ideal, Hellenism, and human life in the hands of Hellenism, is invested with a kind of aerial ease, clearness, and radiancy; they are full of what we call sweetness and light.[7]

Yet Arnold belongs to a rather later part of this story and is not quite in the spirit of classical liberalism. He calls himself 'a Liberal tempered by experience, reflection, and renouncement'.[8] He affirms with classical liberalism that human good and worth lie in the balanced development of human powers, and that balanced development is also in harmony with the world – the capacity to see things as they are and thus to see them in their beauty. But classical liberalism aspires to give all human beings equitable access to this good. It believes in the realisability of an inclusive ethical community based on it. At least in more radical moments it still has revolutionary enthusiasm about the possibility of such a fully realised human community, living in equality and truth – in liberty, equality and fraternity. This radical optimism enables it to combine romantic hellenism with the 'desire to be in unity with one's fellow creatures' on equal terms – a 'powerful natural sentiment', as Mill says – 'a powerful principle in human nature',[9] and certainly a powerful principle in Mill's nature. It is memorably expressed in the revolutionary music to which Beethoven sets the words of Schiller:

Seid umschlungen, Millionen,
Diesen kuss der ganzen Welt![10]

From the beginning, however there was another and no less important moment in classical liberalism, a strain of apprehension as well a strain of enthusiasm: a sense of the danger posed to the human spirit by democratic mass culture. It was associated with a political sociology developed particularly by the French liberals,[11] which held that creative and progressive moral energies are released primarily through conflict and dissent. Democracy, just because of its equality and fraternity, threatened a spiritual if not political tyranny; the imposition of mediocrity, the stifling of great individualities and

[7] Ibid., p. 167.
[8] Ibid., p. 88.
[9] J. S. Mill, *Utilitarianism*, in M. Warnock (ed.) *Utilitarianism*, ch. 3, para. 10.
[10] 'O ye millions I embrace you/ Here's a kiss for all the world. The Ode to Joy continues: *Brüder! Über'm Sternenzelt/ Muss ein lieber Vater Wohnen.*' (Brothers, above the starry canopy/ there must dwell a loving father.) Compare Arnold's 5th 'Switzerland' poem:
'Yes! in the sea of life enisled/With echoing straits between us thrown/ Dotting the shoreless watery wild/We mortal millions live *alone*.'
[11] Siedentop gives a brief account.

dissenting voices on which moral and intellectual progress depends. I will call this *the worrying hypothesis*.

Freedom for individuals to develop in full diversity was the only prescription against this danger – hence the cardinal importance of entrenching negative liberty in democratic states. Another theme of the early nineteenth century also came to the rescue – a new faith in the historical progressiveness of human nature and society. The human spirit could yet flourish in democratic equality because there was virtually no limit to the eventual improvement of human beings in good and progressive states of society. This was the faith in which at least the radical end of classical liberalism placed its trust. It allowed long-term optimism as well as short-term pessimism. In a future good society the romantic-hellenic ideal would be reconcilable with equality of respect. Indeed even now it was possible to 'see things as they are' – without a Kantian or Christian Beyond – and yet still recognise the potential that is present if not actualised in all human beings. One could respect the *potential*. This was a naturalised equivalent of equality 'in the sight of God' – the promise of an inclusive this-worldly community of the future rather than a heavenly city or a transcendentally conceived kingdom of ends.

3 Criticisms

Like any ideal substantial enough to inspire, the romantic-hellenic ideal of classical liberals can also alienate. Objections come broadly from two sides. On one side is the moralistic – the side of 'hebraism', 'Christian self-denial', Kantian moral worth. Also on this side is the collectivist spirit of living for others. On the other side is the aesthetic. It finds the classical liberal's romantic-hellenic ideal in one or another way unattractive – anachronistic, or cold and inauthentic, unactual and imparticular. Both forms of criticism already arose in the nineteenth century.

From the moralistic-collectivist side comes the Hegelian objection that the classical-liberal ideal is too individualistic. It gives too much to free spontaneity and subjective conscience, and too little to the self-realisation which individuals achieve in the ethical life of the community. This objection must be stated with care. Classical liberalism's Periclean ideal certainly does not deny that virtue and civic contribution are a part of the realised individual. It recognises them as intrinsic elements in the balance of moral freedom and spontaneity. So its individualism does not lie in putting private self-culture, still less the pursuit of selfish material interest, ahead of public duty and disregarding the latter in favour of the former. That may be true of some liberalisms but not of classical liberalism. So where does its individualism lie? In Hegel's own hands the criticism is that the elements which the classical-liberal ideal seeks to balance, individual conscience and spontaneity of feeling, are *both* conceived too individualistically. He agrees with Schiller in rejecting Kant's one-sided valuation of conscience and devaluation of feeling, but thinks the antidote cannot simply consist in adding back in a revalued feeling and looking for a 'balance' between the two. For this accepts the dichotomy between them, instead of transcending it; whereas the drift of Hegel's argument is that it can be and must be transcended, in an ethical disposition which identifies itself with a social order. And this conclusion also implies the simultaneous overcoming of another dichotomy – that between individual and society. To this a classical liberal might robustly reply – in my view thoroughly plausibly – that there are untranscendable dichotomies of which these are two. But to leave it there, without exploring what dissatisfaction might lie behind the criticism, is unsatisfactory. The root of dissatisfaction (it seems to me) is that classical liberalism's developed individual is not an ideal to which most human beings can aspire – at least in actually existing societies, whatever one may hope about the Future Beyond. This ideal places too much worth in the accomplishment and satisfaction of the outstanding individual rather than in the trans-individual worth ('objective reason') embodied in the social order. In contrast an ethic which takes performance of the duties of one's social position, whatever they may be, as the condition of human worth places worth in something which all human beings can share:

> The *right of individuals* to their *subjective determination to freedom* is fulfilled in so far as they belong to ethical actuality; for their *certainty* of their own freedom has its *truth* in such objectivity, and it is in the ethical realm that they *actually* possess *their own* essence and their *inner* universality.[12]

Powerful words. In a properly constituted ethical order – one which is realisable in the human beings we know – *everyone* can discharge their role in ways that merit recognition.[13] Not that classical liberalism has to deny that in any way. Still, this is not the ethical insight which it distinctively brings to the fore. Rather it acknowledges and

---

[12] Hegel, *Philosophy of Right*, trans. T. M. Knox (Oxford: Clarendon, 1942), §153.

[13] Note that Hegel does not reject the modern principle of 'subjective freedom'; in that respect he regularly distinguishes his view of the state from Plato's, specifically rejecting the idea that social roles may be *allotted* to individuals – e.g., *Philosophy of Right*, §185, §262, addition.

John Skorupski

embraces a hierarchy of excellence in human attainment; it emphatically honours supreme human achievement without pretending that any and every kind of achievement is supreme. Moreover it presents its ideal of development and excellence as a universal ideal, not just the ideal of an aristocratic class. When an ideal is generally acknowledged as appropriate only to a certain class, then failure to achieve it in one's life damages self-esteem only if one is a member of that class. But the classical liberal presents the romantic-hellenic ideal as an ideal for humanity – while simultaneously affirming that 'the initiation of all wise or noble things' can come only from the few. 'The honour and glory of the average man is that he is capable of following that initiative; that he can respond internally to wise and noble things, and be led to them with his eyes open.'[14] This is honest – but it does not avoid the incipiently divisive character of the ideal. Were there a transcendental or divine backdrop on which the ethical equality of human beings was inscribed, and from which 'the initiation of all wise or noble things' could be held to come, then it would be that much easier to acknowledge the unequal performance of humans on the empirical stage. Failing that, it is still at least a little easier if one can believe in the approach of an equal yet fully human community in some Future Perfect. But what if we definitively recognise that the Future Perfect is a non-existent tense? Wholeness of character and excellence of achievement offer no salvation precisely to the poor in spirit.

Classical liberalism, the critic says, cannot overcome this diremption. This is the real shape of its 'individualism'. The ethics of autonomous conscience and the ideal of spontaneity cannot yield *Sittlichkeit*; objective ethical community and the ethical disposition. Let us next turn to the equally powerful aesthetic criticisms.

The first is that the romantic hellenism of classical liberals is anachronistic – it was so in their time and is even more clearly so now. We can recapture neither the primitive unity of the polis nor the 'aerial ease, clearness, and radiancy' of the Greek vision. In late nineteenth-century classicism (for example Lord Leighton) nineteenth-century people look wistfully out of classical kit, in an elegaic nowhere-land. There is a similar nostalgia about *Culture and Anarchy*. By the time Arnold wrote it, classical liberalism's ethical ideal had already come to seem problematic, not least to Arnold. Mill one might say still belongs to the world of Beethoven and Schiller, Arnold belongs to the world of Brahms.[15]

[14] Mill, *On Liberty*, chapter 3, para. 13.

[15] Brahms's personal motto, '*frei aber froh*' (free *but* joyful), expresses the distance travelled from that earlier liberal world. It was itself, apparently, a response to the motto of his friend Joachim – '*frei aber einsam*' (free but alone).

Why should the romantic-hellenic ideal seem anachronistic? Human suffering, conflict, finitude, etc. were as present for the Greeks as for us and are objectified and acknowledged in the clearness and radiancy that comes from seeing things as they really are. Or if they aren't, then this is a perennial limitation of the Apollonian spirit and not a problem of anachronism. The problem of anachronism is rather that the ideal relegates to the realm of means what most people in modern society must spend most of their lives doing – and these are free citizens not slaves.

This problem was recognised by Schiller – his answer was that full human freedom is possible only when specialisation is transcended.[16] But specialisation and the dynamism of constant change is the essence of modern life. Furthermore, although in modern society the realm of means is in a process of constant change (a fact which undermines the Hegelian ethical disposition as much as it challenges the romantic-hellenic ideal) it will never be transcended. Specialism and change must be embraced in our ethical life or we are alienated from modernity.

What is at stake is thus not purely aesthetic, in the sense that the aesthetic preference for the depiction of modern mass everyday life, or the affirmation of many unashamedly partial perspectives against some single fully balanced perspective which 'sees things as they are', is not *just* that. Behind the idea that the classical-liberal ideal is anachronistic we find again a rejection of its exclusiveness, or an increased pain at the sense of its exclusiveness on the part of those who continue to uphold it. This felt diremption pushes romantic hellenism into its elegiac Arnoldian or Brahmsian phase. It is not the only thing that makes the ideal seem anachronistic but it is an ingredient.

Nietzsche is the philosopher who sees most clearly the tension in classical liberalism between the hellenic ideal and the ethic of equality and fraternity. He is capable of representing this agonising tension with great sympathy – 'today there is perhaps no more decisive mark of the *"higher nature"*, of the more spiritual nature, than to be divided against oneself in this sense and to remain a battleground for these oppositions.'[17] But he is of course a critic of liberalism *in toto*, and not just a critic of the classical-liberal ideal from the stand-

[16] See Schiller's *Sixth Letter*. It is of course also the problem that Marx, whose ethical ideal of the developed human being is Schiller's, took very seriously.

[17] *On The Genealogy of Morals*, Douglas Smith (ed.) (Oxford: Oxford University Press, 1996), pp. 34–5. (First published 1887; Brahms' third symphony, for which '*frei aber froh*' provides the motto theme, was first performed in 1883.)

point of equality or fraternity, or of equality and fraternity from the standpoint of the classical-liberal ideal. Familiarly, equality and fraternity are for Nietzsche residues of slave-morality. But Nietzsche equally rejects the classical-liberal ideal – not however from the standpoint of 'modern civilisation', i.e. because of its inadequacy to the specialisation and dynamism of modern life. Rather Nietzsche finds it too Periclean, too Apollonian, cut off from pain, frenzy, life.[18] This is criticism from an equally 'anachronistic' standpoint of authenticity; it is still informed by Hellenic nostalgia, but now for Homeric society and pre-Socratic philosophy rather than Athenian democracy.

The ethic of authenticity is far more obviously incompatible with democratic equality than is classical liberalism; clear-thinking Nietzschean modernists have seen that. In affirming the necessity of a 'pathos of distance', 'discipline', 'breeding', the exploitation of the many for the perfection of the view and so on, Nietzsche is only being realistic and consistent to his ideal. In contrast, just because classical liberalism's ideal is Periclean, not Homeric, it is not evident that it is irreconcilable with the institutions of liberal democracy. On the other hand, the question of its inauthenticity remains. Nietzschean affirmation of life is anti-democratic but not anti-demotic. It may be incompatible with equality but it is not so obviously incompatible with community – the people can join in the dance. Whereas the ideal of realised balance, with its far-seeing philosopher–poet–statesmen and cold marble pediments, alienates the liberal from the people and indeed from his own demotic self. Affirming authenticity again turns out to be about the overcoming of diremption.

4 Moralistic or idealist liberalism

So in all these criticisms one can find a common strand. It is the difficulty of reconciling the liberal balance of moral freedom and spontaneity, the liberal ideal of 'seeing things as they are', in proportion and not one-sidedly – with one's authentic self, with the world of modern work, with the life of the community, with at-oneness with the people. The conflict with Nietzschean authenticity, important as it is, must be set aside here in that it was not a conflict experienced *within* the liberal spirit. But the other conflicts were.

[18] In *Twilight of the Idols* both Mill and Schiller appear on Nietzsche's list of 'impossibles', Mill for his 'offensive clarity' and Schiller as the 'Moral-Trumpeter of Säckingen' (*Twilight of the Idols and The Anti-Christ*, Harmondsworth: Penguin, 1990, p. 78).

How to overcome these diremptions? One way is through replacing the romantic-hellenic ideal with an ideal of service, and basing liberal equality of respect on that. Another is to cut off equality of respect from ethical grounding – either by grounding it instead on the denial of normative objectivity or by making it a 'political' rather than a 'philosophical' doctrine. These are respectively the communitarian, the populist and the neutralist directions in post-classical liberalism.

In Britain the prime exemplar of the liberal-communitarian direction is T. H. Green. On the one hand (unlike Hegel), he reaffirms Protestant/Kantian notions of personal responsibility at the expense of the classical liberal's hellenic ideal of individuality; on the other, he affirms the ideal of inclusion in an equal community in which selfhood is realised through pursuit of 'the common good'. This is a spirit that suddenly seems alive again. As others have pointed out, T. H. Green the New Liberal is also a spiritual forefather of New Labour. Compared to Mill and Marx, at any rate, he was the Third Way.

His object was to incorporate the working class into the moral community. He sees this project in Kantian terms, as an education into positive freedom, autonomy. Autonomy makes you a member of the kingdom of ends and is the only thing that has moral worth. For Green this has a well-known political implication. He argues that negative liberty can legitimately be limited by legislation which stabilises and builds individuals', and in particular workers', positive freedom. Thus he thinks, for example, that legislation to enforce temperance can be justified because alcoholic addiction undermines autonomy. But it can be justified only to the extent that it promotes moral growth. The exercise of autonomy is the one thing that has moral worth, so in so far as legal compulsion introduces heteronomous motives into the free pursuit of one's duty it is bad.

This reassertion of Kantianism against romantic hellenism is a telling difference between Mill and Green, but it is also important to see where they agree. As already noted, Mill did not reject the idea of positive freedom – the idea that a person's capacity to act rationally, to make and stick to a rational plan of life, is what makes that person *morally* free. He thinks that negative liberty develops this capacity as well as developing individual spontaneity of feeling. Both Mill and Green are teleological liberals; both must therefore recognise that the question whether we make people freer in the positive sense by interventionist legislation, for example by criminalising drugs, is one in which arguments can be made on both sides. And yet politically Mill is a more unqualified champion of negative liberty than Green. Why is this, given that neither of them thinks negative liberty is itself, in Mill's words, an 'abstract right'? What we see here is the strain placed on the connections between liberty, autonomy and equal respect as working-class enfranchisement, social as well as political, approaches. Mill does not think that each of us is equally possessed of moral freedom, and by our more populist standards he is far from reluctant to spell that out – but he thinks that in a good state of society we could all be morally free, and, for all his acknowledgement of historicity, his view of how quickly such a state might be attained retains a blithe enlightenment naivety, relying heavily on the enlightenment's associationist psychology. Green's sense of its imminence is tempered by social reality. He puts equal respect on the more abstruse horizons of idealist metaphysics and Christian religion. Each one of us in our highest self is identical with God; but in practice Green's willingness to see in everyone a potential to cultivate their *own* positive freedom, unassisted by law, is notably less robust than Mill's. Positive freedom, the foundation of equal respect and of membership of the kingdom of ends, turns out to be something that most individuals must be helped to attain.

As well as re-emphasising autonomy at the expense of expressive spontaneity Green takes another step against the diremptiveness of classical liberalism. Though he affirms autonomy he presents it as pursuit of the 'common good'. What belongs to common good is non-competitive – what does not belong to it is not truly good. 'The only true good is to be good' because this is 'the only good in the pursuit of which there can be no competition of interests, the only good which is really common to all who may pursue it'.[19] Freedom in the positive sense is freedom to make the best of oneself – but to make the best of oneself, it turns out, is to contribute single-mindedly to common good, and to one's own self-perfection as a harmonious part of common good. Even to have a right is only to have a claim on society 'in respect of a capacity freely ... to contribute to its good'.[20]

This is a liberalism impoverished by moralism and collectivism. Of course it is important to have a worthwhile role to discharge, but service is not the only or even the highest good. Likewise, it is profoundly true that some things cannot be properly enjoyed unless shared, or if others lack them. But then other goods are enjoyed at least in part because they are competitive achievements, and others again are neither competitive nor common but quite simply private. The sense of human diversity and individuality, which Mill fully

[19] *Prolegomena to Ethics* (Oxford: Clarendon Press, 5th edn, 1906), p. 288.
[20] *Works of Thomas Hill Green*, R. L. Nettleship (ed.) (London: Longmans, Green, 1885–8), vol. II, p. 463.

registers – with its acceptance of irreducible public-collective, social-competitive and private domains – receives at best notional recognition from Green.

In Green's hands self-realisation turns out to be self-transcendence – one of the deepest *fin-de-siècle* themes:

> sin consists in the individual's making his own self his object, not in the possible expansion in which it becomes that true will of humanity's which is also God's, but under the limitation of momentary appetite or interest.[21]

This elevates egoism into exalted spheres in another attempt to overcome a division. In free action, Green thinks along with Hegel, the self always makes *itself* its object – not a thesis Mill would have endorsed. But the object turns out to be something very different from what one thought; it is not a particular self among others but the universal 'self', God, the general will. Self-transcendence is one of the great human ideals – but it is a strange ideal to put at the heart of liberalism.

5 Modernist or populist liberalism

The *fin-de-siècle* revival of idealism was part of a widespread revulsion against the nineteenth-century liberal self: a heroically finite, self-propelling and self-cultivating item set in the actual, natural world. The culture of modernism which succeeded it contained an ideal of authenticity which undermined the liberal tradition even more powerfully than the earlier, shorter-lived ideal of self-transcendence. It is still with us (post-modernism is modernism gone populist), even though there is at the same time a revival of the ethics of character which is favourable to the classical-liberal ideal of self-culture and to which we shall return. For the classical-liberal ideal assumes a human nature of determinate if diverse and historically structured potential. I achieve individuality, or self-realisation, by *discovering* the particular life which is best for me. No doubt options and choices are involved but they are limited by my historical horizon, my own determinate powers, and the objective ethical hierarchy of human ends and ideals. In the modernist ethic of authenticity each of these – history, human nature, ethical objectivity – gives way (for many reasons and by many paths). To live authentically is to live by values that one chooses in some bafflingly radical sense. I do not discover myself, I make myself – from no materials and by no plan.

[21] Ibid., vol. III, p. 73.

John Skorupski

There is in fact a pincer movement in modernist ethical (or anti-ethical) thought – on the one hand, social determination eliminates an independently determinate self; on the other hand, existential freedom eliminates an independently determinate self. In this climate liberalism was always going to find it difficult to survive irrespective of other great political forces working against it. It survived by emptying itself of first-order content and withdrawing to a meta-level. In place of arguing for liberty and equality under the law from determinate ethical ideals – rational autonomy, diverse affective spontaneity – it began to argue for the institutions of liberalism by what I will call a *strategy of epistemological detachment.*

The populist version of the strategy is familiar. All 'values' are subjective – matters of choice. Thus the ends, ideals, moral principles of one individual cannot be regarded as more or less admirable than those of another. Since it is their 'values' that we judge people by, it follows that we have no ground for giving greater respect to one person than another, or imposing on anyone a way of life which they do not choose. Understood as a negative argument against unequal respect this is sound reasoning from the given premises. To make it an argument for a positive doctrine of equal respect or for liberal institutions based on such doctrine is unsound; nevertheless the unsound argument has been very influential, and inasmuch as it argues for liberalism from an epistemological thesis – in this case anti-objectivism about values – it exemplifies the strategy of epistemological detachment.

Popper is the modern liberal philosopher closest to populism. He also, it is true, inherits a large part of the legacy of classical liberalism. Thus for example, while the assault he launches on 'historicism' is quintessentially modernist, the story he tells of a transition, through the growth of critical rationality in Greece, from magical, tribal and collectivist societies to open societies in which criticism is free but the 'strain of civilisation' and the nostalgia for tribalism is acute – that is very much of a piece with the classical liberals' sociology of liberty. He sees the enlightenment as 'the greatest of all moral and spiritual revolutions in history'[22] and his admiration for Pericles equals Mill's. What he does not inherit is classical liberalism's Schillerian ethical outlook. For Popper the crucial attitude in an open society is 'critical rationalism'. It is, purportedly, an epistemological not an ethical attitude:

> very similar to the scientific attitude, to the belief that in the search for truth we need co-operation, and that, with the help of argument, we can in time attain something like objectivity.[23]

[22] *The Open Society and its Enemies* (London: Routledge, 1945), vol. I, p. ix
[23] Ibid., vol. II, p. 213.

Adopting it is however a 'moral decision'. Popper insists that a moral decision is not simply 'a matter of taste'; nonetheless his affirmation of the 'dualism of facts and decisions' has the moral fervour which one is used to hearing in some people's insistence that all ends and ideals are subjective. Proclaiming this dualism is, he evidently believes, an essential bulwark against authoritarianism.

Note the striking epistemological turn since Mill. Mill does argue, passingly but pregnantly, from fallibilism to liberty of discussion in the second chapter of *On Liberty* – in a manner somewhat similar to Popper's argument from critical rationalism to liberalism in general. But he treats fallibilism as a truth about finite human beings rather than a moral attitude that one 'decides' to adopt; and his argument is made only as part of a case for free speech. The main weight of his case for liberty in general lies in the classical-liberal analysis of human flourishing and the classical-liberal sociology of liberty which he propounds in chapter 3.

6 Value-pluralist and Neutralist liberalism

In the 1950s and 1960s liberal philosophy continued to pursue the strategy of epistemological detachment. Like Popper, Berlin inherits important parts of the legacy of classical liberalism – in his case, the very parts with which Popper has least sympathy: the German counter-enlightenment, its appreciation of historicity, its sympathy for a variety of values and its liberality of mind. The value-pluralism on which Berlin's liberal argument rests reflects this source. There are incompatible systems of value which cannot be put on to a single scale. Berlin does not see this as a form of subjectivism, and thus his argument is not as close to the populist argument as Popper's. Nonetheless value-pluralism, however one interprets it,[24] is apparently an *epistemological* doctrine about values, and not just a classical-liberal affirmation of the objective value of diversity. The idea that objectivism about value leads to authoritarianism in politics is present in Berlin as it is in Popper. Perhaps it was not a misguided thing to say in its time. There can be such connections in specific historical contexts and the context then was the struggle against totalitarianism. But that context has passed some time ago and the supposed connection between objectivism and authoritarianism has become a will-o'-the-wisp.

The most recent period in the discussion of liberalism, at least in

[24] I examine value-pluralism in Skorupski, 'Value-pluralism', in David Archard (ed.) *Philosophy and Pluralism*, (Cambridge University Press, 1996).

academic philosophy, has been dominated by John Rawls. No doubt one main reason for this has been his success in focusing liberalism on the theory of justice – a topic which had never played such a salient role in liberalism before. That in itself is telling. But there is another side of his thought which is just as important and has become increasingly so – his neutralism. In his more recent work Rawls places a new degree of emphasis on his distinction between 'comprehensive' and 'political liberalism'. Comprehensive liberalism is one of a number of philosophical and ethical positions, liberal and non-liberal – Rawls cites Mill and Kant as developing comprehensive forms of liberalism. 'Political liberalism' refrains from endorsing any one comprehensive position, liberal or other. Thus in particular it eschews the classical-liberal ideal. As a further refinement on the epistemological detachment of Popper and Berlin, it does not even take a view on meta-ethical questions about the existence and nature of truth in ethics, since these are philosophical questions which should not be dragged into the political domain:

> Once we accept the fact that reasonable pluralism is a permanent condition of public culture under free institutions, the idea of the reasonable is more suitable as part of the basis of public justification for a constitutional regime than the idea of moral truth. Holding a political conception as true, and for that reason alone the one suitable basis of public reason, is *exclusive, even sectarian, and so likely to foster public division.*[25]

Political liberalism restricts itself to assessing which comprehensive positions are 'reasonable' and then arguing to constitutional proposals from an 'overlapping consensus' of such reasonable positions. Moreover Rawls, with the mainstream of recent American liberal theory, puts forward a very strong doctrine of state neutrality. The state must not favour any conception of the good, *either* (1) by prohibiting any individual from pursuing his or her conception (within just limits) *or* (2) by acting as a persuader in favour of some conception. But while (1) was also a central tenet of classical liberalism, (2) was not. The classical liberal had a definite conception of the good and was ready to accept in principle that the state had a role in fostering, as against enforcing, that ideal through educational and cultural policies such as the curriculum of state schools, the setting up of free museums, the pub-

---

[25] John Rawls, *Political Liberalism* (New York: Columbia University Press, 1993), p. 129 (my emphasis). Rawls has again set out his conception of 'public reason' in 'The Idea of Public Reason Revisited', *The University of Chicago Law Review*, **64** (1997), pp. 765–807.

lic funding of the arts, conservation, scholarship or scientific research.[26]

7 The hollow triumph

This brings the story up to the present – admittedly at a breakneck pace! What can be learnt from it? Classical liberals feared that democracy would produce a culturally or spiritually levelling conformism. It might not take the form of a political tyranny, though democracy without the institutions of liberalism might easily produce that. However even a liberal democracy with constitutionally entrenched freedoms might, they feared, still tend towards effective imposition of mediocre consensus through social rather than political means. The triumph of liberty would then be hollow, in that political emancipation of individuals would have destroyed the individual.

The combination of idealism and foreboding can be tiresome. Nevertheless it is one of the classical liberals' strengths. Their analysis of the dangers attendant on their own political programme was penetrating in both ethical and sociological terms; it gives us a well-considered measure against which to set the liberal democracies we know.

The evolution in the philosophy of liberalism which we have considered in previous sections already seems to go some way towards confirming the classical liberals' fears. Classical liberalism's central tension was between its ambitious hellenic ideal of human excellence and its wish to live with others in community on equal terms. This tension – contrary to classical liberalism's critics – was a strength not a flaw. It registered an ineliminable conflict in human aspiration which must come into the open whenever people escape hierarchy and mythical social charters. So a truly liberal society, committed to escaping these things, has to accept the conflict and try to find ways of coping with it – as does any individual to whom the liberal ideal means something. And yet, as it turned out, the reality of the tension was soon lost or denied within the liberal tradition itself. After a brief interlude of moralistic idealism, liberalism in this century has moved with increasing firmness towards the

[26] I argue this point with reference to Mill in Skorupski, 'The Ethical Content of Liberal Law', in John Tasoulias (ed.), *Law, Values and Social Practices* (Aldershot: Dartmouth, 1997), pp. 191–211. Obviously there can be and was debate about how useful it is for the state to get involved in such things; my point is that it was not conducted at the level of a philosophical thesis of state-neutrality.

strategy of epistemological detachment. The most influential liberalism of the 'post-modern' period, that of Rawls, confirms this in a striking way: by its division between the political and the comprehensively ethical, its strong doctrine of state neutrality and its preoccupation with developing a 'theory' of justice – of rights as against goods – which can emerge from an overlapping consensus. I think it is fair to say that in practice the most influential liberal philosophies in this century concede ground (in more or less subtle ways) to the populist version of the ethic of equal respect. And this is at least *consistent* with the classical liberals' worrying hypothesis.

On the other hand, caution urges that even now we still have very little material to test it. For the century and a half since they wrote has turned out to be one of the great periods of conflict in Western history and simultaneously a period of immense cultural revolution and renewal. We are hardly well supplied with data to test the idea that peaceful and prosperous liberal democratic states destroy individuality. Perhaps only with the end of cold war and then the collapse of the socialist model have we reached the right laboratory conditions, so to speak, for testing it.

Let us fix more clearly where, according to the worrying hypothesis, the problem is supposed to lie. It is not a problem of liberty or material affluence, nor quite a problem of morality or intellectual attainment. Improving the freedom and material security of individuals is always possible and important, but it does not diminish its importance to say that these are not crisis areas in modern liberal democracies. Nor is it the case, at least from any liberal point of view (including the classical), that there is a crisis of morality in the West. Any liberal must reckon the softening of the traditional ferocity of the moral, the elimination of sheer moral prejudice and irrational taboo, as a great gain for the human spirit. This can be acknowledged even by those liberals who feel a need to pull back from 'liberalism' in the current loose and unphilosophical sense of 'permissiveness' – for example, in the irresponsibility with which we now bring children into the world and shuffle on to others the complex and demanding charge of bringing them up. (Such unpermissive thoughts would not of course have seemed at all outrageous to a Mill or a Green.)

Similar remarks apply to the intellectual domain of science, philosophy and scholarship. They are at unparalleled levels of development and support. Maybe here some worries about mediocritisation and conformism begin to seep in. Still these collective activities continue solidly, and in doing so, underpin rationality steadily – which is their pre-eminent indirect social function. They expand and solidify mentality, 'objective spirit', just as technical progress expands and deepens its material base. More: we see striking reversals of strong modernist trends. Philosophy witnesses a restoration of normative objectivity, a revival of interest in the ethics of character and excellence, while history and biology gradually unravel the modernist illusion that human beings are blank canvases, on which either they themselves or atemporal 'social structures' paint.

In short there is no evident crisis of liberty or material security, nor of intellectual culture or morality. If there is a crisis it is a crisis of ethical and aesthetic self-identity. Which takes us back to Schiller. The problem, it seems, is not the corruption of the right, or the weakening of the true, but the coarsening or diminution of the good. It is a problem of our art, our ideals, our aspirations for our own improvement as human beings, not of our cognitive inquiries or moral commitment. We lack powerful and inspiring models, whether in art or philosophy, of a life worth living. So much recent art seems to fall on a spectrum between sheer childishness or vacuous gimmickry and alienation or inner exile. Is this the 'weariness' which Nietzsche thought would afflict modern life?

If so, what is its cause? The worrying hypothesis is not the only available one. The cause could be the intellectual decline of faith and thus of serious as against wacky or folksy religious ideals. Or it could be that we are at the end of the modernist and socialist century – which just because it was one of the greatest cultural and spiritual flowerings (and traumas) of the West could understandably produce a period of spiritual weariness in its decline.

All three hypotheses could be true. However the worrying hypothesis is the one we are considering. It says that liberal democracy has an inbuilt demotic drift which eventually cuts down all great ideals to a 'tolerant' equality of standing, removes public and objective acknowledgement of their grandeur, and instead gives public reinforcement only to those emotions strongly ('profoundly') felt by the Many. It also explains why equality of respect has flourished even as the religious and metaphysical bases for it have been removed. Older liberals sought to give the ethical doctrine of equal respect intellectual support. But it is now quite obvious that when equal respect catches the demotic tide it no longer needs such support. At that point it becomes an obfuscating anti-ideal, a golden calf around which one must dance (or if dancing is not one's *forte* supply philosophical rationalisations). Nietzsche was right to locate modern 'weariness' here.

But to agree with his diagnosis is not to accept his prognosis or prescription. We can reject the ethical doctrine of equal respect as demotic ideology without throwing out anything liberalism needs.

John Skorupski

1. We do not need the thesis of equal respect to affirm juridical equality, of civil and political rights and duties, for all citizens. Juridical equality in liberties, claims and duties remains the keystone of the arch of liberal institutions. But the arch can bridge a void without support from the wooden scaffold of metaphysical or religious ideas which was needed while it was being built; the keystone ties together the structure of liberal democracy and that structure keeps the keystone in place.

2 We retain the sentiment of our common humanity; an emotion of fellow-feeling and companionable understanding which requires no intellectual support and no belief in equality of powers.

3 Given these two firm bases, we can and must still have civility – easy to recognise but hard to define: not treating people demeaningly, as though they and their views were of no account, or they were inferior just because of what they do, where they come from or who they are. 'The first law of good manners (*des guten Tones*) is: *Show respect for the freedom of others; the second: Show forth freedom in yourself.*'[27]

4 We can still accept that the quality of moral agency, and its character as 'autonomy', that is, personal responsibility, is the basis of a certain distinctive *respect* (something separate from civility as such). Kant was right in that, and right to emphasise that moral respect can be gained irrespectively of one's place in society or one's achievements in life. Yet it is also true that people differ deeply and irremediably in the quality of their moral sensibility, their force of will, their self-restraint, their independence of mind, etc. There is no level, empirical or other, at which those differences are annulled; a liberal democracy is rightly committed to applying the standard of moral responsibility, so far as possible, to every mature human being but in doing so it must find ways of recognising this difficult fact.

5 Finally we can recognise, irrespective of equality of respect, that the well-being of all must be impartially taken into account in the making of policy, that is by all of us in our role as citizens. This ethical imperative of impartial concern does not rest on any thesis of equal desert.

Consider again then the 'desire to be in unity with our fellow creatures' on equal terms. Is that a desire which can be satisfied if (1)–(5) are fully realised? If so, it is concrete and finite and could be

---

[27] From Schiller's *Kallias* letters, quoted by the editors in Schiller, *Aesthetic Education of Man*, p. 297.

satisfied without coming into conflict with any other aspect of the good. On the other hand, if it requires the ideology of equal respect then it is not in that way concrete and finite: it is abstract and infinite, it does not determine its own limits and so must ultimately become inimical to the pursuit of any great ethical ideal, in particular to the pursuit of the liberal ideal.

The desire of classical liberals to be in unity with their fellow creatures was abstract. They did not know their fellow creatures. Or rather they thought they did not know them because they believed in their unknown potential. To know the people (they would have agreed) you have to emancipate the people – that has been the work of this century not the nineteenth. But in this century knowledge of the people has been distorted by revolution, dictatorship, genocide, global and civil war, passages of crisis which reveal the depths to which people can fall and the heights to which they can rise. In the last three or four decades in the West the character of the people in conditions of stable liberal democracy has begun to emerge. No doubt it is still far too early to draw any firm conclusions, but it would just be sheer complacency to deny that what is emerging provides some confirmation of the worrying hypothesis.

The antidote is not to be found in the moralism of Green. On the contrary, moralistic liberalism, which we are in some danger of returning to, is part of the problem rather than part of the solution to spiritual weariness. Moreover moralism and populism can all too easily combine: there are worrying signs that that is happening. On the other hand, it is even less helpful to go on affirming the ethical neutrality of the state as a fundamental liberal principle, or searching for ever-more ingenious and unconvincing bases on which to affirm equal respect. The best to be hoped for from that approach is a situation in which ethical and aesthetic seriousness is maintained in elite enclaves, but insulated from the common culture and preserved on condition of presenting a suitable outward face. That may be a path along which modern liberal societies are going, and from a liberal point of view there are worse paths, but it cannot be the best path for anyone who shares the hopes of classical liberalism.

If one shares those hopes then, on the contrary, one must do what one can to resist demotic-liberal ideology, while affirming the true bases for living together in freedom, the bases given in (1) to (5): equality under the law, the sentiment of common humanity, civility, respect for moral worth, acceptance of the responsibilities of citizenship, that is, of impartial concern for the well-being of all. Beyond that, however, though philosophy and policy can do much to remove the obstacles in the way of public affirmation of great ideals, there is little they can do to give such affirmations life, attraction, influence. The classical-liberal ideal of wholeness and balance between moral freedom and spontaneity could be philosophically stated but its aesthetic substance and hence main influence on public imagination and sensibility was realisable only in creative works of art. To the limited extent that nineteenth-century art attempted to express it, it tried to do so, more often than not, through the literary and visual invocation of the hellenic world. But the aesthetic substance given to an ideal must fit its time, and nineteenth-century hellenism flowed into academicism and nostalgia: there is scant reason to think that hellenism is the aesthetic substance (as against the philosophical idea) to which classical-liberal ideals must always return.[28] Whether they can still be given authentic aesthetic substance, or what shape and historical resonance that substance requires – what strands of aesthetic modernism or contemporary multi-culturalism it needs to draw on for example – depends, as ever, on how the possibilities to hand can be worked on creatively by the aesthetic inspiration of the Few.

[28] The Schillerian element in classical liberalism's ideal – spiritual freedom embodied in honest aesthetic semblance – is better expressed, for example, in those paintings in which Cézanne achieves it, or perhaps by the enigmatic classicism of Seurat, or in some high modernist architecture, than in any of the nineteenth century's exercises in hellenic nostalgia – Lord Leighton, say (for all the power with which he conveys that nostalgia).

Politics, Religion, and National Identity

GORDON GRAHAM

This essay is not a further contribution to the debate about liberal individualism, the chief topic of discussion in political and social philosophy for the last twenty-five years or more. Nevertheless it is necessary to begin by rehearsing some features of that debate, claims that will be very familiar to contemporary political philosophers. Inspired largely by John Rawls, the modern version of political liberalism has tried to make coherent a conception of politics according to which political affairs should be separated, or at least seriously distanced, from the various moral and religious loyalties and programmes of individuals and groups of citizens. This central contention of Rawlsian liberalism has been expressed in different ways, but according to one of the commonest versions, it is to be interpreted as the view that the right must take precedence over the good. That is to say, in the political sphere, the implementation and application of impartial rules of social justice and civil liberty (the right) must take precedence over competing conceptions of what is or is not a valuable way of spending a human life (the good). Another familiar way of expressing the same doctrine says that the state must be neutral with respect to the moral alternatives with which a modern pluralistic society presents its members. This claim about state neutrality is most easily illustrated by a notable example; whether homosexuality is morally wrong or not is not the business of the legislator, and thus the goodness or badness of a gay lifestyle is a matter on which the law should be neutral.

Many subtle avenues have been explored in elaborating, defending and attacking the doctrine of the priority of the right over the good, but if it is true that it is not in essence distinguishable from a doctrine of state neutrality, then the contemporary debate is to a large extent a re-run of a subject with a much longer history, namely the theory of church-state relations. This is confirmed indeed by Rawls who, in his second major assault on the subject, *Political Liberalism*,[1] does not disguise the fact that his aim (all along, one is inclined to say with hindsight) has been to articulate the underlying

---

[1] John Rawls, *Political Liberalism* (New York: Columbia University Press, 1993).

principles of toleration that emerged from the religious wars of the sixteenth century. Arguably, these principles found their clearest endorsement in the strict separation of church and state that eventually became such an important element in the constitution of the United States. (I say 'eventually' because some of the founding states, Massachusetts for instance, had established churches for a time.)

There is thus an important continuity between contemporary political philosophy and a much older issue. There are also notable differences, however. First, it would be highly unusual for a contributor to the contemporary debate actually to describe its concern as being that of church-state relations. Second, it would not even be true to say that the contemporary debate is primarily about religion in politics; in general the attention of both liberals and their critics has been focused more on morality than religion. Indeed, it has been extended from morality to systems of value even more broadly construed, to include for example the aesthetic. In short, it is not the relation of politics to religion as such that is under discussion in modern political philosophy, but its relation to what Rawls somewhat vaguely, if familiarly, calls 'conceptions of the good'. Third, and this is perhaps a more important difference, in its modern version the argument for the neutrality of the state with respect to things moral and religious is essentially political, a form of social contractualism in fact. It is supposed that the rational agent deliberating about the terms of political association will seek personal liberty, acknowledge the fact of pluralism and recognise the dangers of sectarianism. Such rational deliberators, the Rawlsian picture holds, will thus only agree to a political system which embodies what we might call a mutual hands-off approach—I am willing to be prevented from using the power of the state in promotion of my favourite cause, if you are also prevented from using it in favour of yours. This sort of argument contrasts quite markedly with the older arguments of Martin Luther, John Locke and others in favour of religious toleration. They argued that the interests of true religion required toleration and that it was the requirements of politics which set limits on how far that toleration could go. Locke, for example, thought toleration could not be extended to Roman Catholics, not because of their religious beliefs, but because their political loyalties lay beyond the state of England. Similarly, the oaths of political loyalty which atheists made had to be suspect because, by implication, they denied the possibility of oaths. In other words, Luther and Locke defended political toleration from the point of view of religion, whereas the modern argument defends religious toleration from the point of view of politics. This is a point of difference to which I will return.

There have been many critics of Rawlsian liberalism, mounting their challenges under different labels, most familiarly of course, 'communitarianism'. Communitarianism is not one thing, however, and these critics differ amongst themselves on many points. Nevertheless there is, as it seems to me, a recurrent and fairly wide-spread theme in all their criticisms. This might be expressed as the thought that liberal individualism of the Rawlsian variety rests upon a mistake about human motivation. The precise nature of this mistake, and its philosophical depth, are themselves both matters of disagreement and matters of consequence. For the moment how-ever, it is sufficient to state the basic charge in a relatively vague form. It is this: liberalism cannot explain why, faced with a Rawlsian-type argument for preferring the right over the good or the neutrality of the state, the individual to whom some conception of the good is already enormously important, should agree to give that conception second place. In reality, individuals often have too much invested in their value systems (to use an ugly term) to allow them to relegate them to the (alleged) requirements of the political order.

What does this talk of 'investment in a value system' amount to? Some, such as Michael Sandel[2], have given it a strongly metaphysi-cal interpretation, and linked the idea of personal investment with the concept of personal identity itself. To require someone to rele-gate his or her most cherished beliefs, they argue, is to undermine *who they are* in a very strong sense. Thus to ask, say, devout Roman Catholics to distance themselves from their religion in the way that Rawlsian liberalism does, in its attitude to laws on abortion for example, is to ask them to relinquish a part of who they are, to sac-rifice something of their very identity. In effect, it asks them to con-done what in the depths of their hearts they believe to be murder for the sake of political neutrality.

Phrases alluding to a 'sense of identity' are familiarly and easily used in this context, but actually to make good the philosophical claims which employ them turns out to be a very ambitious under-taking. Personal identity strictly understood need make no essential reference to moral or religious belief—the same person may under-go a radical conversion, after all—and understood more vaguely it lacks the fundamentality upon which the anti-liberal argument relies for its power. For this reason other critics of liberalism have adopted a less metaphysical, more psychological approach and claimed simply that it is unrealistic and hence unreasonable to

[2] Michael J. Sandel, *Liberalism and the Limits of Justice* (Cambridge University Press, 1982).

expect people with a particular upbringing, education, and acculturation simply to suspend their strongest loyalties. To do so is to require them to ignore their own psychological history to a large degree. But this involves abandoning the set of reasons and attitudes which customarily move them to action. How, then, can the liberal's abstract conceptual argument be expected to motivate them to follow its conclusions?

There will be reason to return to the ideas of history and identity which these objections invoke. For the moment, however, the differences between these two kinds of criticism can be ignored since both may be seen to advance the same general point. It is one easily illustrated by a much discussed example—the emergence of Islamic fundamentalism. Let us suppose that a good argument can be made for liberal neutrality on the part of the state. An enthusiastic Muslim could in fact accept the validity of such an argument. But its validity does not supply an answer to this question: why should he prefer its liberal conclusion to the non-liberal beliefs with which it competes? What the argument in defence of liberal neutrality requires, if it is to command his allegiance, is not just that it be valid so far as it goes, but that it give him grounds to prefer civil right over the religious good for the promotion of which, we may assume, he also has reasons. Now it seems evident that human beings can as a matter of fact be more strongly attached to the moral and religious causes they espouse than to anything else, including the belief in impartial justice and civil order. Where this is the case, and where the religious affiliation in question is not one of simple blind obedience, it seems that the argument for neutrality will inevitably fail one way or the other. Either, it will have to recognise that there are conceptions of the good whose adherents are unwilling to submit to the priority of civil right, or it will claim for itself the status of 'supreme' conception of the good. If it takes the second line of defence it becomes the claim that liberal toleration constitutes a better system of values than any religious or moral exclusivism which competes with it.

If the the first of these approaches is adopted, the liberalism it can be made to defend enjoys no rational advantage over competing doctrines, and hence can at best be thought of only as making explicit political principles which are adhered to in some places and not in others. This seems to be Rawls own understanding of what, in the end, his intellectual project amounts to—the uncovering of the underlying principles of an historically contingent liberal society, namely that of the United States. If, on the other hand, the second approach is taken, what emerges is a robust, nineteenth century style liberal progressivism, which may have much to commend it, but sits very ill with the ideal of the neutral state since it amounts to the recommendation not that the state be neutral, but that there is reason for every and any state to embody the principles of liberalism in preference to any competing moral or political conception.

All this, I take it, is very familiar ground, and of course there are replies that the liberals can make which I shall leave unrehearsed. It is not my intention to add to the arguments and counter-arguments for two reasons. First, though the debate cannot be said to have been concluded, there is reason to think that it is exhausted. If this is true, if the position between modern liberalism and its critics is indeed one of stalemate, what is needed are not more arguments on one side or the other, but a new approach from a different angle. Second, in the debate as hitherto conducted it is quite unclear whether the issues under discussion are those of political philosophy properly so called, or questions of moral philosophy more broadly construed. On this second point it is worth observing that a recent attempt, by Onora O'Neill[3], to arrive at a *rapprochement* between the two positions broadly described as liberal and communitarian is construed and conducted as an exercise in moral theory very generally conceived, one concerning the relations between the moral concept of justice on the one hand and the moral concept of virtue on the other. O'Neill does not directly mention politics or the state at all, and it is not evident that in failing to do so she is failing to engage in the debate between liberalism and its critics.

In developing an alternative, and clearly political, approach an initial point to be made is this. Liberalism generally, and Rawlsian liberalism in particular, is a doctrine about the internal organisation of society and, by derivation, of the state within it. It says nothing about the international order, relations between states. This is not to say that there have been no attempts to extend Rawlsian principles to questions of international justice and right. In fact there have been a good many. But the result is inevitably what has come to be known as a global ethic. That is to say, principles of liberty and justice conceived along traditional liberal lines have nothing to say about where the boundaries *between* political communities are to be drawn. Their logical conclusion is a liberal world state within which subdivisions are (at most) to be justified on pragmatic or utilitarian grounds. As far as liberal theory is concerned, in themselves, national boundaries are of no more moral significance than are divisions between local authorities within a single nation state.

By contrast, nationalism, a doctrine or set of doctrines that has been hugely influential in international politics but which until recently was

[3] Onora O'Neill, *Towards Justice and Virtue: a constructive account of practical reasoning* (Cambridge University Press, 1996).

largely ignored by political philosophers, has just the reverse character. Nationalism is concerned with the international order, and has
nothing to say about the internal organisation of the state. It holds,
very roughly speaking, that every nation ought to constitute its own
state, and hence the world should consist in nation states, but it is
silent on whether these states should be liberal or otherwise.

It is not my purpose to defend, or even explore the principles of
nationalism, but only to use the contrast between nationalism and
liberalism as a way of pointing up what I think is a genuine hiatus
in liberal thinking, and hence also a hiatus in the broad communitarian critique of it; though it has a lot to say about the internal constitution of the state it has nothing to tell us about where state
boundaries should be drawn. For anything which aspires to be a
political philosophy this must be a serious deficiency.

In the face of such an assertion, it might be questioned whether
this really is a hiatus, whether that is to say, the failure of liberalism
to provide grounds other than purely pragmatic ones for deciding
where the boundaries between political communities are to be
drawn is truly a deficiency. Someone who raised this doubt might
have something like this in mind. Normative relations are relations
between groups of people—rulers and subjects, for instance, or fellow citizens. But if relations between countries are a *purely* political
matter, then there *is* no special normative relevance to national
boundaries, and a philosophical theory can hardly be faulted for
failing to explain it.

To appreciate the point at issue here something needs to be said
about what it means for political boundaries to have normative relevance. Consider this imaginary case. Peru (say) arbitrarily annexes
part of Colombia, and the Colombian government successfully
recovers it by means of military force. It seems wholly appropriate
to say that Peru had no right to the territory, and Colombia was justified in using arms to recover it. Conversely, had the government of
Colombia through inefficiency or indifference failed to take steps to
recover the lost territory, it could plausibly be accused of failing in
its duty. But these terms—right, justification, duty—are employed
here in describing relations between states with respect to their territorial integrity, from which it seems to follow easily enough that
the invasion and protection of territorial integrity is in part at any
rate a normative, and perhaps a morally normative issue.

It might be supposed that international law covers all such examples, and that there is consequently no reason to regard them as
moral in any interesting sense. I do not think this is so, and in any
case even if it were this would not show that international law does
not itself rest upon some essentially non-legal norms. But to avoid

protracted discussion about the nature and basis of international law, it may be easiest to consider another case. Imagine that flooding leaves people homeless in Kent. It seems clear that the British government has an obligation to provide assistance and in doing so it will be spending money raised by taxation from the other citizens of Britain. Now if flooding leaves people homeless in Bangladesh, the government of Bangladesh has a parallel obligation to its citizens. However, since Britain is so much richer than Bangladesh, most people would agree that there is *some* obligation on the British people through the British government to offer a measure of assistance in this case also. But the nature of the obligation is not the same; it is, we might say, an obligation of charity rather than justice. Another way of putting it is to say that British citizens collectively have a *special* obligation to each other that they do not have to the citizens of other countries, towards whom they only have *general* duties.

Political communities are not the only communities with special obligations. A yet plainer instance can be found in families. Although from a normative (in this case moral) point of view I cannot wholly disregard the vital needs and special predicaments of other people's children, I do not have the same obligations to them that I have to my own children. I cannot leave other people's children to starve, for example, but I do not have the obligation to nurture them that I have with respect to my own children. If this is true, family boundaries are normatively relevant, and if the parallel holds, so too are political boundaries. The question now is: what explains their normative relevance?

In the case of families we can, for present purposes, rest content with simply naming the basis of normative relevance as 'kinship'. Kinship is a topic upon which anthropologists have written extensively, but I do not propose to conduct any exploration of it here. I refer to it only to ask what the equivalent of family duties and responsibilities might be in the case of states. According to nationalism the answer lies in the special affinity that exists between people of the same nationality. Indeed, at least one nationalist writer, Neil MacCormick[4], has argued that nationality is a kind of kinship (though his reason for doing so does not relate directly to the topic under discussion here). But even if it were true *both* that nationality is a kind of kinship *and* that the similarity is close enough to lend political boundaries the moral relevance that family boundaries are usually thought to have, this would not be enough to demonstrate the moral relevance of political boundaries in general. This is because, despite the aspirations and efforts of nationalists over the

[4] Neil MacCormick, 'Nation and Nationalism' in *Legal Right and Social Democracy* (Oxford: Clarendon Press, 1982).

last 150 years, relatively few political boundaries mark clear lines between distinct nationalities.

The cogency of this claim rests in part on what is to count as a nation. Early nationalist theories favoured language as the key criterion—the Germans are a nation because all and only they speak German, for example—but this quickly proves too strong a test of nationality since only some national groupings have their own distinct language. More importantly it is a criterion that would undermine the claims of many nationalistic causes. In several prominent instances—Ireland being a striking example—campaigners for national self-determination precisely made a point of the fact that though their distinctive language had been almost eliminated by alien oppressors, the national spirit none the less remained. But if a single language is too strong a criterion, alternative weaker criteria of nationhood—'cultural identity' for instance—which can be made to encompass such cases are necessarily vaguer, and in large part subjective. They thus introduce a high degree of uncertainty as to what is and what is not to count as a nation. Is a body of people a nation if it believes it is, or is persuaded so to believe?

These questions, and the issues surrounding criteria of nationhood are interesting but highly intractable. Fortunately, we do not need to go too far into them in order discover an important range of cases which will reveal that national boundaries and political boundaries cannot be the same. It seems plain that a state cannot have a single national character if it encompasses more than one nationality, and equally plain that there are many states of which this is true—Australia, Britain, Canada, the Netherlands, the US, Switzerland. *Ergo*, the normative relevance of political boundaries cannot be explained entirely on the basis of a nationalistic conception of kinship.

In what then is the normative relevance of a political boundary rooted? It is here, as it seems to me, that we can profitably return to the concepts of history and identity alluded to at an earlier stage in the argument. The crucial point relating to *political* identity (and political history), I think, is that it has to do with territorial integrity. What the imaginary example of Peru and Colombia shows is that the state has (some sort of) obligation to preserve the integrity of the realm. (This is its *chief* obligation according to Machiavelli and some other political theorists.) This is not an overriding duty in all circumstances. Political communities break up, not infrequently because of deep internal dissent. But this possibility itself serves to underline the nature of the normal case where there is a duty on those charged with political responsibility to preserve the realm of a single people as a central aspect of their political identity. Given the failure of nationalist theory to supply a satisfactory explanation of this sort of identity, we must turn I think to common history and a shared understanding of political unity. A people makes a political community, whatever differences there may be within it, if those who live within it understand themselves as sharing a common identity and history.

A very plain example of what I have in mind here is the United States of America. Both pride and mockery have surrounded the idea of 'the American dream'. Whatever else is to be said about it, however, the conception of the United States as a refuge and new beginning has so regularly informed its history and played such a prominent part in the lives and aspirations of the various major waves of immigration which have marked (one might say made) that history that it can be said to have formed a people, a political entity. It is an entity, a political community which finds expression in a set of symbols and shared values and institutions. To be an American is to own those symbols as one's own, to respect those values and to appeal to those institutions. The United States in short, even though it is on any account a multinational state, has a recognisable identity formed by and in turn informing its history.

If this is true, and if it is a duty of the state not merely to secure a morally well ordered society within its boundaries (as Rawlsian liberalism contends) but to protect the integrity of those boundaries, then it will the duty of the state to promote and protect the symbols, values and institutions which sustain its unity. Just what these are in any given case is an empirical question, a function of a particular history and a contingent identity. This is a point of difference with nationalism worth stressing. We are concerned here not with an abstract political theory, but with the realities of political history. Now the very fact that there are (when there are) such unifying symbols, values and institutions shows that there is a limit on how far the state can pursue the idea of neutrality. Since some values and institutions lie at the heart of its integrity as a political community, and since it is one duty of the state to preserve that community, there will be at least some values and institutions which it cannot regard as being on a par with all others.

On this analysis it is no surprise that Rawls in the end has to abandon the abstract strategy of *A Theory of Justice* and revert to the contingencies of history in *Political Liberalism*. In advocating the primacy of the right over the good, and with it a certain sort of state neutrality, he is not defending personal liberty and religious toleration as universal values, but as the central values of one political community—that which was formed out of European factionalism, namely the United States.

Gordon Graham

This conclusion has at least one important implication in the present context. The separation of church and state is a cardinal political value in the US. The arguments, both traditional and contemporary, for religious neutrality on the part of the state, on the other hand, are always presented as universal, as applying ideally to all states, and not merely those with a particular history. To secure this universality against the background of the account of political community that I have been offering, we would have to show that there is something special about religious values and institutions which legitimately denies them the same respect that is to accorded to other values, like those of the democratic process, for instance (a parallel which would in my view repay close examination). What might this difference be? Is there any?

Faced with the contention that matters of state should be sharply separated from matters of religion, and with those who reject this contention, it is hard to know where the burden of proof lies, but there are I think at least three important observations that are worth making. First, the history of Europe has influenced thinking on this point much more widely than merely the theorising of Rawls and other contemporary liberals. The religious wars in Europe, and elsewhere for that matter, have left a widespread and abiding impression that religious fervour is deeply divisive. What is less frequently noted, nowadays, though for a very long time it was a central tenet of British conservative thinkers, is that religion can also be profoundly unifying. Religious disputes have indeed driven political communities apart, but religious belief has also formed and preserved them. The most striking example of this is Judaism whose power to bind was still strong enough after almost 2000 years of Diaspora to call into existence the state of Israel. Something similar might be said about the role of Roman Catholicism in the chequered history of Poland. Or to take another example closer to (my) home, it is arguable that a continuing sense of Scotland as a political entity after the Act of Union in 1707 was preserved by the unifying character of the Presbyterian Church of Scotland and its General Assembly in particular, a political entity often referred to at the time in fact as 'the Church and Nation of Scotland'. Correspondingly, it can plausibly be argued that the serious decline of distinctively Scottish institutions is to be dated from the Disruption of 1843 which split the Church of Scotland for over eighty years. It follows that if we allow the state a legitimate role in preserving the integrity of the political community in its charge, history shows that there will be occasions when the state can legitimately give special protection to a religion or a church.

The second observation to be made about religion and political life is this. In many parts of the modern industrialised world, for whatever reason, religion has come to be seen as a purely personal matter and religious observance as something like a hobby or leisure time occupation. From this point of view, religious values are no more plausible as objects of government oversight and protection than are particular fashions of dress. Now there is no doubt that this is indeed how religion is viewed by many people, including not a few who would declare themselves to be religious devotees, so much so that there are societies in which a really serious religion affiliation is scarcely possible any longer. But it would be a modernistic, and Western, prejudice to generalise from this to a view of the possible role and character of religion in all times and places. For most people at most times, and for many still I am inclined to say, religious aspirations and institutions are amongst their most deeply held values, and those which most inform their sense of communal belonging. Only a deep ignorance of history could make us doubt it.

A third important point is that the excesses of some modern Islamic states has distorted our idea of what a state protected religion must look like. To accord one religion or church special status does not automatically imply religious persecution or the existence of an enforcing religious police such as can be found in Saudi Arabia. The millett system which operated in the Ottoman Empire is one device by which minority religions have been accommodated within a religious state. In England there is an established church with special duties and privileges. These are less extensive and significant than they once were, but as long ago as 1688, when the Established Church enjoyed real power and social pre-eminence, the Toleration Act provided for dissenters from this establishment. Similarly, the attempt in Russia to give some religionists special status over others, refers to *four* traditional religions, and not exclusively to one. Established religions do not inevitably mean oppressive states, as the Lutheran countries of contemporary Northern Europe testify. These are countries in which there are established churches supported and protected by the state, and in which religious persecution, or even intolerance, is unknown.

These observations do not show that there is nothing about religion which makes it intrinsically inimical as one of the unifying factors which the state is justified in protecting in the interests of political integrity. What they do, to my mind, is to show that the onus of proof is on those who, while accepting the necessity, desirability and justifiability of state protection for some unifying values and institutions, wish to exclude religious values and institutions from the list. They also serve to undermine the usual motivations for wanting to do so—love of liberty and fear of persecution. This second effect can be strengthened by returning, briefly, to Locke and Luther. The special interest attaching to their arguments, in contrast to those of modern liberalism, is that they combine a belief in the seriousness of religion with a defence of toleration, arguing that any adherence worth winning from a religious point of view must be largely uncoerced. Such arguments show, in fact, that religion, far from being the enemy of freedom, can on its own account give us reason to put limits on the powers of the state. If what concerns us, in the end, is how to secure both a free and a stable society, perhaps we would do better to consider carefully the claims of the political friends of religion rather than the abstract, and I would say indefensible, neutralism of the liberal theorist.

Contemporary Art, Democracy, and the State

GEORGE WALDEN

Not long before the change of Government in Britain in 1997, the then Heritage Secretary, Virginia Bottomley, made a speech in which she praised British contemporary art, describing it as the most exciting and innovatory in the world. Unexciting as it seemed, her observation was profoundly innovatory, indeed in its small way historic. To my knowledge no British Cabinet Minister, still less a Conservative, has ever given an official seal of approval to what is conventionally regarded as avant-garde art. The Labour Government has echoed its predecessor's praise at a higher volume, as if determined to out-do it. The sanctification by the state of works of contemporary art has now become part of the discourse of officialdom.

At this stage I am not concerned with the aesthetic qualities of the works in question. Whether our contemporary art deserves the prestige and official approval it enjoys, or whether it represents to a large extent the incoherent ramblings of modernism in a state of advanced senescence, has no bearing on the point. That point is that the state through its Ministers has begun to confer unqualified praise on works of art that are habitually referred to by critics as, at the very least, 'disturbing'. It is not possible for Ministers to praise contemporary British art while excluding the best known work of its most acclaimed practitioners. In saying what she did Mrs Bottomley was pronouncing herself excited by the spectacle of sections of animals pickled in formaldehyde by Damien Hirst, by the concrete cast of a desolate house by Rachel Whiteread, and by the private parts of Gilbert and George. I am not being satirical, or pedantic: her words of blanket approval—and those of other Ministers since her time—bear no other sense. Both major political parties are now on record as warmly recommending what are invariably presented as 'challenging', 'shocking', or 'controversial' works of art to the British people.

In the case of Mrs Bottomley especially, much of the art she was referring to portrays itself not just as avant-garde but as antinomian, and thus subversive of her view of the world which—unless she is a closer and more sympathetic student of modernism than I give her credit for—can be safely assumed to have less in common with

Duchamp and Tristan Tzara than with Ms Joan Hunter-Dunne. The full import of her words can only be seen in historical context. It is as though Napoleon III had commended *Les Fleurs du Mal* to the French bourgeoisie, Czar Nicholas II had nursed a private passion for Malevich, or (begging Mrs Bottomley's pardon) Hitler was a surreptitious collector of Nolde, Kirchner, or other so-called decadents of the time.

It seems unlikely that she said what she did by accident: she must have known full well that much of the art in question was dubbed 'controversial.' Why, then, did she say it? The reasons seem to me to tell us a great deal about the current relations between art and the state, and the nature of allegedly avant-garde art in a late twentieth century democracy.

The most obvious explanation of her remarks and those of her successors is bureaucratic reflex. As Ministers with cultural responsibilities, they are *ipso facto* patrons of the arts. That is to say that it is their function to patronise British art, in both senses of the word: to assist it financially, and to pronounce it good. Just as Health Ministers are obliged to defend the taxpayers' money they disburse as well spent—for example by commending the efficacy of new drugs or the work of nurses—so Ministers of Culture must uphold the value of the art whose creation or display they directly or indirectly subsidise. The alternative—a Minister denouncing art which has benefited from millions of pounds of expenditure on art schools and galleries, as worthlesss, or seriously lacking in quality—would be similar to a Minister of Health saying that doctors are quacks. To that extent, all state-assisted art must by definition be good. Now that we have a Minister of Culture, the British authors of films, plays, novels, works of art or music will increasingly be said to be 'of the first rank', or 'world class'. Some might deserve the praise, but that is incidental. At the same time it will be tirelessly repeated that the 'arts industry'—a very twentieth century solicism when you think of it—is one of our major tourist and export earners. Already the very existence of the Ministry and the lottery is fuelling appeals for more investment in the arts, on exactly the same premise that calls are made for more investment in the infrastructure. Such calls are seen as evidence of a commitment to the arts themselves, and therefore attractive to politicians—a class of persons often suspected of congenital philistinism. The philistinism implicit in the notion that more cash produces more and better art goes largely unnoticed. As early as the Twenties, Walter Sickert attempted to dissuade painters and critics of the notion that the future of British art depended on a fund secreted somewhere in the Treasury; to no avail, it seems.

Contemporary Art, Democracy, and the State

The Government is of course bound to defer to whatever the art Establishment of the day—by which I mean the Arts Council, directors of public galleries and the like—deem to be outstanding. Till recently it has not however felt obliged explicitly to endorse the work in question: if challenged on an allegedly 'controversial' work it could easily say that aesthetic judgments were matters for independent experts—perhaps with a wry smile—much in the way that Governments defend the independence of the BBC. Yet Ministers have taken to making what are implicitly aesthetic pronouncements, invariably of a positive nature, thereby underwriting the quality of individual works as well as such government expenditure as is incurred in their production and display.

It is a crucial shift, moving the state from the sidelines into the mainstream of whatever happens to be the style of the day. In the case of contemporary art, Ministers are especially keen—as we have seen in the case of Mrs Bottomley—to demonstrate the breadth of their tastes. It is possible of course that these tastes are genuinely broad—perhaps to the point of lack of discrimination—but the primary reasons for the demonstrative open-mindedness of politicians are for the most part fear, ignorance, or political pressures. The fear is that by failing to endorse what is said to be 'new' and 'challenging' in the arts they will appear reactionary or elitist, so forfeiting the sympathies of the young. Ignorance can be suspected as a motive since, when you do not know or care enough about the arts to make discriminating choices, indiscriminate enthusiasm is the safest bet. The political pressures are best seen in insistent demands to endorse popular culture in all its forms. In the last election I recall a single brave exception: asked for the names of the *Spice Girls* Donald Dewar dared to say that he didn't know and he didn't care. Given the audiences he or she has to satisfy and the lobbies at work on him, a genuinely discriminating Minister of the Arts becomes a contradiction in terms. Discrimination involves selection and rejection, and in no major art form can the British be officially pronounced to be deficient in talent, potential or creativity, or to be doing a poor job. To say or imply this would be an affront to the people.

That in itself, it seems to me, is an important truth about the state and the arts in an advanced democracy. Democratic peoples must be more creative than non-democratic ones, if only because the notion that the opposite might be the case is intolerable. Whatever the merits of the contention that repressive or authoritarian regimes have produced the finest literature or most brilliant artistic movements, it would be a bold man who took the next logical step in the argument. A democratic public also have their right to art, to which they contribute through their taxes and lottery tickets, and a plentiful supply must be forthcoming. Like health and education art is a public good, a commodity whose provision must be officially guaranteed and overseen.

The quality of contemporary work in any particular genre may or may not be high; either way it must be officially lauded. To imply that we are in any way inferior to previous generations in any field of creation would be more than an insult to the people; it would be a slur on modernity itself. Hence the oft-heard claims that if Shakespeare were alive today he would be writing for television, the comparison of our artists with the Masters of the Renaissance, and the growing insistence that we are living through a renaissance ourselves. With our commitment to the notion of progress, our claims to a steadily improving system of education, and the release of the creative potential of the masses, logically speaking modern democratic societies must perforce be living through a permanent cultural renaissance: in a free, secular democracy the creative spirit of man is infinite by definition.

All that is needed are the bureaucratic and financial mechanisms to bring this spirit out. Hence the emphasis on new facilities for the arts and our expanding arts bureaucracy, who invest in and nurture art much as they would an enterprise zone. Provision for the arts must also be forward-looking. Theatres or galleries of contemporary art are therefore relentlessly expanded or—in the case of Bankside—newly constructed, as an act of democratic faith, with scant discussion of what might be put in them. The assumption is that works still to be conceived or executed will merit the distinction of being displayed, in much the same way that governments build schools for children yet to be born, or prisons for criminals yet to be convicted.

Patriotism is another powerful force at work on Ministers of Culture. One reason Ministers speak as they do is that British contemporary work is highly rated on the international art market, and today all Ministers have a great respect for markets. That of course is no guarantee of its lasting aesthetic qualities, any more than Jeffrey Archer's global sales indicate an enduring contribution to literature. Nor should we overlook the 'market distortions' that result from state support for what might be described as the closed shop of contemporary art. The more state institutions buy, the higher the prices.

What this patriotic boosterism tells us is that behind their universalist pretentions the arts, like the sciences, are frequently a field of both nationalistic and financial competitiveness by artists and governments. Proud claims by Ministers that British contemporary

art is in high demand by collectors and galleries abroad are note-
worthy, since they illustrate the degree to which art has become both
commodified and quasi-nationalised. It it the function of Arts
Ministers to praise the advanced nature of British contemporary art
in precisely the way that it is a function of Defence Ministers to
boast of the most advanced British-made tank or missile. Over-sen-
sitive politicians—assuming the genus exists—would be wise to
avoid either job: whether in the arms or arts industries, squeamish-
ness about the ethical or aesthetic viability of the product they are
promoting would be a non-affordable luxury. Like an unduly purist
attitude towards defence contracts, an over-rigorous attitude to the
quality of some of our artistic exports could be ruinous.

On the face of it, the boosting of some categories of contemporary art might appear to pose special problems for the state. British
Governments of the left or right tend to be composed of prudent,
conservatively-minded people, who reflect the broad sentiments of
the electorate, who in turn are broadly committed to the social and
political status quo. Why then should Governments risk propagat-
ing that aspect of contemporary art that is frequently described as
'shocking', 'nihilistic' or even 'subversive', and which often appears
derisive of conventional social mores, not to speak of officialdom
itself? Here we come to the heart of the matter. In talking up contemporary art as they have taken to doing Ministers run no risk. If
the works in question were a genuine affront to the public, or a
threat to the established order, prudence would prevail: they would
not do it. As it is governments intuitively sense—correctly in my
view—that contemporary British art poses no such threat. How can
this be, when the power of art is seen as limitless? The reason our
contemporary art has little or none of the power attributed to it is
that it is art of a low order.

Personally I do not believe that British contemporary art is either
exciting or innovatory; indeed, I do not find it of much value or
interest at all. Some of it is capable of affording entertainment or
distraction, but if those are the criteria, in terms of wit, intelligence,
originality, social commentary or philosophical undertones, it rarely
rises to the level of the most accomplished American TV shows,
such as the Simpsons. Popular art forms at their best are genuine
and alive. Works invested with the title of fine art can frequently
leave us unmoved and indifferent because they are in every sense
inauthentic.

In so far as our contemporary art enjoys the support of an all-
party parliamentary consensus, and is vociferously championed by
public bodies such as the Arts Council and the BBC, I am conscious
that my views may appear arrogant, undemocratic—even subver-

sive. I can only hope that, in the arts as in other fields, our democracy feels confident enough of its stability to tolerate dissenting voices. This is not the place to elaborate on my reasons for declining to accept the guidance and authority of the state and of government appointed organs on aesthetic matters. I do not intend to go through the various schools of pop art, minimalism, installations and suchlike. Though capable of infinite scholastic refinement in the hands of their votaries, they can be seen as adding up to a single, continuous movement. My criticisms may appear broad-brush, but one of the problems of conceptual art is that it leaves itself open to conceptual criticism. Of the characteristics of contemporary British art I shall say three things which I believe are pertinent to the argument.

First, much of it appears to me to be both derivative and residual: pallid or gaudy offshoots of genuinely exciting and innovative artistic movements that flowered in Russia, France and later America in the first half of the twentieth century. Second, I believe that the tardy adoption of these styles in Britain, far from being proof of our openness to the 'new', is an aspect of our national conservatism in the arts: only when a style has lost its power to sting do we feel ready to espouse it in safely diluted, popularised versions. In that sense British contemporary art is akin in spirit to the genteel imitations of Cezanne by painters in the Bloomsbury circle: his noisiness notwithstanding, conceptually speaking, Damien Hirst is Duncan Grant. (It may be more than coincidental that Mrs Bottomley is, I understand, a distant relation of Bloomsbury.) It must also be confessed that in our less fruitful periods of art, as a country we have frequently shown a weakness for the mimetic and backward-looking in our artistic styles. In the nineteenth century we had the mock Gothic of the Pre-Raphaelites, the mock Japanese of Whistler, and the mock classical of Lord Leighton. Today we have mock revolutionary art. Third, I believe that it is this same conservatism that has led us into a situation where state-modernism—for want of a better term—has become the official academy: which is to say the primary medium for conformism in the arts.

Official patronage of the arts has always existed in one form or another, though in the past the donor tended to call the tune. The Popes did not commission or subsidise portraits or tombs in which they risked being depicted like creatures from Gilbert and George. The Victorians did not build museums and galleries to be filled with socialist propaganda. And the Soviet Union confined its considerable largesse to artists who produced nothing else but socialist propaganda. In modern democracies all that has been stood on its head: the elected authorities frequently find themselves financing works of art in which their beliefs are vilified or caricatured—which does not prevent them from applauding the artists in question. The modern patron, it seems, has turned masochist—though again it would be a mistake to take things at face value.

Comparisons have been made between British state-modernism and socialist realism. There is truth in the analogy to the extent that, in both cases, a closed market is established, complete with an enforcing bureaucracy, from which dissidents are excluded. Yet the comparison is essentially a rhetorical distraction, leading us to lose sight of what is most important in the argument. The point is that Britain is not a totalitarian country. How is it that a democracy can voluntarily acquire a quasi-official artistic style at all, let alone one that portrays itself, and is accepted by a majority of critics, as 'revolutionary', 'anarchic', or 'subversive'? How, in other words, has the state come to embrace its own opposite in the arts? And how is it that artists fail to see that they are being asphyxiated in the embrace?

The answer, I believe, lies not in a conspiracy, as some of the beleaguered opponents of modernism suggest—the art world can be a paranoid place—but in the far more familiar human failings of make-believe and self-deception. The key word is mime. Artists go through the motions of biting the hand that feeds them, while the state, rich collectors, critics and the media go through the motions of wincing at the pain. The art in question—a mimicry of older styles—induces mimetic responses amongst its apologists and promotors. Defenders of state-modernism insist that it tells us much about the contemporary world, not least through its powers of irony. It certainly does, though—ironically—not in the sense its defenders like to think. One irony, like one train, can hide another—and it is the hidden irony that does the damage. What inauthentic modernist art tells us about contemporary life is the inauthenticity of society's artistic critique of itself, even at the level of irony, and about the collusive myths of advanced democracies.

This is not to say that the artists or their work are frauds in the usual sense. Like method actors, they have entered into the spirit of the style they are impersonating. Even as they lay claim to originality they are miming, in all earnestness, a defunct tradition: striking the bold or anarchic stances of early modernism for all the world as if their work were not taught as orthodoxy in art schools financed by the state, and with approved curricula. And just as actors sometimes continue to mime their favourite character off-stage, and to that extent become the character, think of themselves as the character, so artists play out their mimetic role in all sincerity. They genuinely see their work as being a challenge to society and its values, as if they themselves were not part of a sophisticated and well-established enterprise from which they show no disinclination to profit. Supposedly free, antinomian spirits accept prizes at dinners graced by Ministers whose subsidies keep the awarding institution afloat, and where speeches are made solemnly pronouncing their offerings to be ground-breaking, whereas they are mostly in a style that will soon be a century old. It is not so much the art that is surreal and disturbing, as the dinners.

Ministers and the arts officials they appoint have their appointed parts in the mime, behaving as if contemporary art were indeed excitingly 'subversive'. It is a role they are fated to play. If they did not, there would be no virtue in their ostentatious tolerance. Again the mimicry is, as it were, unaffected. Politicians are entirely genuine in the warm sincerity of their condescension to the arts. It comes, as we must now all learn to say, from the heart. It is a game Ministers are well suited to play. In treating the 'challenge' of contemporary art as if it were real, they are mimicking the democratic process in Parliament itself, with its set-piece jousts and stagey confrontations, while the business of the House is fixed through the usual channels by amicable agreement.

It could be argued that this element of sham and simulation, far from being lamentable, is progressive. To have reached a stage of democratic tolerance where governments subsidise 'oppositionary' art much in the way that the salaries of the opposition who abuse them in the House of Commons are paid from official funds, is evidence of an advanced civilisation. In this state of affairs it is tacitly understood by everyone that, with the artists as with the opposition spokesmen, the denunciation of the authorities and all their works is largely for the form, that their bark is worse than their bite, and that their underlying respect for the institutions of the state, democracy, the workings of the market, and conventional social mores is not in doubt. Yet that would reduce the creative artist to the position of mere participants in a system of checks and balances: at best to the role of a kind of loyal opposition, at worst to that of court jesters trained by the state for the delectation of the authorities and the public. Hardly a role that an authentically disturbing artist would wish to play.

So it is that the state has enfolded its artistic opposition. By unwritten agreement old notions of approved and non-approved, conformist and non-conformist, academic and innovatory art have been stood on their heads. There is no doubt as to who has got the best of the bargain. Artists cannot expect to enter such agreements and to preserve their fire power intact. As the erstwhile *refusés* have been ushered into the official *salon* by nervously deferential authorities, in accordance with convention, they leave their weapons at the door.

A striking aspect of British contemporary art is the low level of the critical exegesis that surrounds it. One might have thought that, if the art were as outstanding as is claimed, its critical language would be on a similarly elevated level. Yet with the possible exception of Tim Hilton, people of the calibre of Clement Greenberg, Robert Hughes or the former *New York Times* critic, the British-born John Russell—whatever one thinks of their views—are conspicuously lacking. It is characteristic of semi-official orthodoxies that the writings of their supporters should be obscure, jargonised, and defensive, and in relation to contemporary British art, that, largely, is what we get. (The discourse of progressive educationalists, another elderly orthodoxy, is remarkably similar). The response of artistic power-holders to adverse comment is reminiscent of the nervy reactions of a fragile regime. The mildest doubters are treated as out-and-out reactionaries, on the principle that if you are not with us, you are against us.

This polarisation has its own, internal logic. Depending as it does on a synthetic conflict between art and authority, state-modernism encourages a Manichean approach to criticism, in which disputes are dramatised as those between elitism and egalitarianism, between constraint and liberation, between the old and the new. The smaller the opposition, the more stagey the polarisation. Despite occasional flurries of publicity contemporary art is suffering from a lack of hostility. Critical indifference, or the tepid enthusiasms of conditional supporters, is insupportable. Hence the stubborn attempt to provoke an argument, whether it be by a display of human excrement, or a portrait of Myra Hindley. As energy drains away in a closed, entropic system, increasingly laborious means are necessary to bludgeon the adversary into reacting, to give at least a semblance of reality to the mime.

Smothered in official approbation, praised by compliant critics, established as orthodoxy in art schools, cosseted by indirect subsidies of every description, and with the lure of financial success for its most successful practitioners, late modernism finds itself in the position of the classic academic schools of art—but with a major difference. In the past reigning styles were challenged, or obliged to re-invent themselves, by new, more dynamic movements. State-modernism faces no such challenge. Exhausted as it is, there seems nothing to replace it. No one seriously suggests that a new an vibrant style of art is waiting in the wings. If the Tate, the Royal Academy and the Serpentine gallery (of which the late Princess Diana was a patron (note the collusion of royalty in the game) were to be taken over by insurgents, and a show of exclusively figurative art staged, with the exception perhaps of Lucian Freud, it would be a wan, pallid thing. A full-scale counter-revolution involving a return to pre-modernism is both technically impractical and aesthetically undesirable. Short of a general collapse of the market—predicted some years ago by one of modernism's most discriminating critics, Robert Hughes, but yet to come about—I see no chance of an aesthetic re-evaluation. I believe Mr Hughes underestimated the institutional underpinning for what I have called a closed system. In that sense the comparison with socialist realism is valid: it took the collapse of communism to get rid of that.

As for us, in our democracy as in our art, we appear to have reached a sort of stasis. The mime of democracy must go on, if only because no one can think of a better piece of theatre. Art has become caught up in the game of fictitious oppositions. In the short and medium term, I do not see how this situation can change. What we are seeing is an arts cartel in the process of formation—the first of its kind in history. It is as if society had taken a major holding in a hostile enterprise, on the understanding that that old products and brand names will be retained. The strategy—albeit unconscious—is working brilliantly.

Public protest—such as it is—is increasingly handled by the arts establishment in the same way as Government departments. When inflation leaps or the trade gap widens the Treasury says 'Not too much weight should be placed on a single month's figures'. Should the figures be good, it insists that they indicate the underlying strength of the economy. Illogicality has never troubled Ministers' press departments, and shows no signs of troubling our public galleries.

If a new exhibition is ignored or heavily criticised, then that is proof of its worth. The avant-garde is, by its nature, in advance of its time. And should a controversial show draw the crowds, the attendance figures are quoted as proof of its worth as well. In other words the art is good when it is popular, but being unpopular doesn't make it any less so. Hostility validates art, as does popularity. Like all Groucho Marx logic, the position is impregnable. In its public relations as in its mimetic conflict with authority, like some quasi-privatised public utility, from whom you are forced to buy whether you like it or not, state-modernism has cornered the market.

'Accessibility' is important in the theatre of British contemporary art—a theatre based, like much of democracy itself, on a solemn fiction. The reaction of the contemporary art theorist to the protest that 'anyone could do it' is a beaming affirmation. The new canon is easily learnt. Nothing could be further removed—to take an extreme example—from the complex skein of mythology, religion, classical references of Poussin, or the intricate, hard-to-read surfaces of a Titian or Degas.

Duchamp's ready-mades have been invested with a democratic, egalitarian ethos as the art of the everyday—the very opposite of what was essentially an intellectual jeu d'esprit. His black, destructive humour has been lightly ironised, playfulness being a democratic virtue. As we enter some contemporary exhibitions, the words 'jolly' and 'larky' frequently come to mind—Ms Joan Hunter-Dunne again. Here is a palace of harmless fun—a word increasingly found in the prospectuses of galleries. Alternatively the exhibits are of the plaintive or anarchistic variety, appealing to the kind of inchoate resentment Rousseau and others warned would be a concommitant of democracy. That is the 'subversive' element. There can also be the quirkiness and cult of originality dear to the British sensibility. In other words, like a fairground with its sexual raucousness, its distorting mirrors and House of Horrors, something for everyone.

Yet however 'disturbing' the object, the key word is *play*. Just kidding. Contemporary art falls four-square into the bread-and-circuses aspect of modern democracy, best summed up in the advertising business. It is fitting that the biggest private collection of contemporary art in Britain belongs to one of the Saatchi brothers—a name that conjures every aspect of late modernity: the ephemeral, quick-money world of virtuality and make-believe, in which everything from art to Conservative politics can be turned into hot properties—though some sell better than others.

Like commerce itself, we are unlikely to see an end to the process. Democracy is a settled state. Apart from a few adjustments here and there, it is not something we strive to move on from. We have got what we wanted and are stuck with it. In this sense contemporary art is a true mirror of the times. All we can do is make faces in the glass: amuse ourselves, frighten ourselves, distract ourselves. The alternative is to turn aside, close our eyes, and analyse the situation. The trouble about doing that is that, in thinking about art and society in a late twentieth century democracy, we shall begin thinking thoughts we would prefer not to hear. Perhaps because they are genuinely, rather than factitiously disturbing.

Popular Culture and Public Affairs

BRYAN APPLEYARD

Recently I saw a corporate TV advertisement for the American television network ABC. It showed brief shots of people in other countries—France, Japan, Russia and so on. These people were doing all kinds of things, but they weren't watching television. Americans, the commentary told us, watch more TV than any of these people. Yet America is the richest, most innovative, most productive nation on the planet. 'A coincidence', concluded the wry, confident voice, 'we don't think so'.

ABC pursued the same theme in an advertisement on the back of the magazine *TV Guide*. It is worth quoting in full.

> For years the pundits, moralists and self-righteous, self-appointed preservers of our culture have told us that television is bad. They've stood high on their soap box and looked condescendingly on our innocuous pleasure. They've sought to wean us from our harmless habit by derisively referring to television as the Boob Tube or the Idiot Box.
>
> Well, television is not the evil destroyer of all that is right in this world. In fact, and we say this with all the disdain we can muster for the elitists who purport otherwise, TV is good.
>
> TV binds us together. It makes us laugh. Makes us cry. Why, in the span of ten years, TV brought us the downfall of an American president, one giant step for mankind and the introduction of Farrah Fawcett as one of 'Charlie's Angels'. Can any other medium match TV for its immediacy, its impact, its capacity to entertain. Who among us hasn't spent an entire weekend on the couch, bathed in the cool glow of a Sony Trinitron, only to return to work recuperated and completely refreshed? And who would dispute that the greatest advancement in aviation over the last ten years was the decision to air sitcoms during the in-flight service?
>
> Why then should we cower behind our remote controls? Let us rejoice in our fully-adjustable, leather-upholstered recliners. Let us celebrate our cerebral-free non-activity. Let us climb the highest figurative mountaintop and proclaim, with all the vigour and shrillness that made Roseanne a household name, that TV is good.

I was startled by these ads. They are so knowing. They are also, in their brazen patriotism, surprisingly politically incorrect. But I suspect this is regarded as acceptable because of the proletarian values they appear to endorse.

At their simplest level these ads are based on the long American economic boom, now twenty years old. Even though people dependent on wages and salaries may have done poorly relative to those with investments, the feeling that American is triumphant runs deep. Not only have they won the Cold War, they have also won the hot economic peace. This view has recently been reinforced by the economic problems in Asia. With the tigers now reduced to dependent cubs, American exceptionalism is once again the unchallengeable ideology. It is not just that they must be doing something right, they must be doing *everything* right. Watching TV must be part of the triumphant mix that is America.

There is a carefree slobbishness about the idea that spending a weekend in front of the television is virtuous. Perhaps this is a reflection of the Clinton years in which a President continuously embroiled in sexual scandals manages to retain a huge approval rating in the polls. It reminds me of some lines from a song of Randy Newman's— 'He may be a fool, but he's our fool/ And if they think they're better than him, they're wrong'. He's a slob, but so what? We win.

But all of that makes the ads only locally predictable. What really startled me was the realisation that a global change I had vaguely noted myself over a number of years had finally and fully penetrated the imagination of corporate America.

For these ads would have been unthinkable five, ten or twenty years ago. In those days television would not have dared say anything like this. The unspoken consensus then was that TV was definitely not good for you, that there was, beyond television, something better—higher culture, books, sport, whatever. Television was seen not as a distinctive culture itself, but rather a parasite on other cultures. Its one claim to seriousness was that it was a 'window on the world', a means of enlightenment and enrichment. Simple TV entertainment was, in this view, merely necessary froth. True quality resided in the news and documentaries. In this country and, I think, in America, it remains a snobbish boast that 'I don't watch television except for the news and documentaries'.

What has changed? At one level there has been a highbrow elevation of popular culture. This began in Britain in the early fifties when pop artists like Richard Hamilton and Eduardo Paolozzi established the imagery of advertising, fashion and films as suitable material for high art. Pop was then embraced by the Americans— most notably by Andy Warhol. This, said Warhol's work, was the real surface of the real world, it was not inferior to the guitars, wine bottles, madonnas and saints of the past.

Conspiring with this approach was the spread of new ideologies within the universities. Structuralism and post-structuralism encouraged scepticism about the claims of high culture. They stressed the aesthetic neutrality of the text or the image. The words on a can of soup might have as much cultural 'depth' as *Anna Karenina* and, of course, Warhol painted cans of soup. Students infected by these ideologies then appeared in the arts and media industries. In the magazine *Modern Review* but also in new types of writing for newspapers and magazines, the products of mass culture were analysed as earnestly as Shakespeare or Titian. This was a diverse phenomenon with many different approaches, but there was a common underlying attitude—there was no acceptance of the idea that any one genre, form or content was intrinsically superior to another.

Accompanying this was an acceptance of the forms of the modern media. If you watch any decent Open University programme, it is at once clear that you have stepped out of the genre of mainstream television. These OU programmes are driven by the need to convey a certain amount of information. The medium itself is rendered as transparent as possible. There is only a minimal requirement to make you watch since you are, if you are taking one of these courses, a captive audience.

Plainly, if one of these programmes was being made for prime time television, the approach would have to be utterly different. They would have to be dramatised to keep our interest. The style of the OU programmes implies a phase of boredom. In order to attain C—understanding, appreciation—you have to get through A and B. There is no other way. The result is earned and an authority is present—the person who, you know, will get you from A to C.

But, in prime time, boredom and authority are intolerable. Rather there is only the effect, which must be all but instant or it will simply be disregarded. The contemporary approach of using pop culture as an occasion for serious analysis does not work up to the effect as the crown of the effort. Rather it starts from the effect and works back from it. An Arnold Schwarzenegger movie has its visceral impact and then you say clever things about it, either to explain this impact or to place it in a wider cultural context. There is no necessary depth to be examined within the thing itself. The effect is all.

I don't think this is a marginal phenomenon. It may have begun in the studios of artists and spread out of the universities into relatively high brow publications. But it was very attractive. It made life easier. You need no longer be ashamed of what would previously have been seen as 'low' pleasures. Note how the ABC ads insist on the virtues of spending a weekend inert in front of the television. And, as a result of the intellectual elevation of the easiest pleasures of all, I would guess that most people are now persuaded. For now the attractions of the culture are laid before people with deliberate neutrality. There is no reason to choose one thing or another. Therefore why choose the thing that requires effort. There is no point in making the journey.

You may say that it was ever thus. Most people have not felt the need, or had the opportunity, to make the effort to get from A to C. The few that still do may well be exactly the same proportion who made the effort before. The elite remains constant, the masses simply evolve their justifications.

Even if that is true, there has been an important shift of power. The new confidence of popular culture in its own significance is not being expressed by people who really think of themselves as the masses. These are the new elites. They are as rich and powerful as the old elites ever were—indeed, they are a lot richer and more powerful than the current academic and high art elites. Their power base is the media, including, of course, the new media of computers and the Internet, and they owe little or nothing to the culture of the old elite. They can , in any case, buy it at hugely inflated prices. Bill Gates of Microsoft recently paid $40 million for a painting by Winslow Homer. Nothing wrong with Winslow Homer, but you could get a couple of good Velasquez canvases for that. What this says is: a) Gates is hugely rich, no great revelation there, and b) that his wealth gives him the power to inflict his taste on the old high art categories. I have spoken to Gates about art and he understands it, essentially, as a code to be cracked. He is, in short, a philistine, but a proactive philistine who wishes to neutralise what he does not understand.

But the real point is that the Homer—even at $40 million—is a very small part of Gates's world view. His real concern is with the popular culture that he believes will drive the multi-media world of the future. He has spoken of how 'cool' it would be if, while watching the film *Top Gun*, you fell in love with Tom Cruise's aviator sunglasses. You could pause the film, find out about the glasses and order them over the Internet. There would be a direct connection between aesthetic effect and consumption.

Of course, the fact that Gates bought his Homer for such an inflated price indicates that conventional high culture still exerts some kind of a grip on him. But I suspect that is as much to do with the sort of things rich people decide to buy as it is with an intrinsic awe he feels for the idea of traditional painting. Elsewhere the grip has gone. The claim of high art as something to which one aspires or struggles to understand has gone. And, because it has gone, there is no shame attached to wallowing in low culture—hence the ABC ads.

The wallow, in this case, is not endorsed by sophisticated cultural theory, but by the mere fact that America is the 'richest, most innovative, most productive' nation on earth. If you are not a slob you lose by being poor. Maybe this is irony. But, in a way, that's the point as well. For it is irony that will not produce any significant howls of outrage from concerned parents. Rather it is irony that is intended to draw howls of agreement. The reference to Roseanne in the last sentence is no accident. She is a slob's heroine and she is good. Her cynicism is seen as strength. It is what gets her through the reality of her flamboyantly ordinary life.

So what I am saying is not simply that popular culture is in the ascendant. It has been for a long time. But, rather, that it is now triumphant. It does not regard itself as a part of the culture—as indeed a small parasitic part of the culture, it regards itself as the whole of the culture. Anything outside this realm is the province of geeks and fanatics and it certainly cannot hope to excite the aspirations of anybody within the pop culture.

This is, I think, a turning point. For anybody committed to anything other than pop culture, it asks some awkward questions—for example, what's the point? The realm of, say, art or of philosophy has long accepted its own uselessness in the real world. But, at the same time, it has secretly been convinced that it is very useful indeed, or, at least, important, that it stands in a certain relation to all other human activities.

This can no longer be taken for granted. There was always a faintly mystical assumption behind this superiority of high culture —even when it was not explicitly religious. It assumed that the people knew that Giotto—or Kant or Wittgenstein—was important, even though they might not know why. But this assumption, like so many others, has been subjected to a form of scientific analysis.

For that is, in fact, what is happening here. The structure of the ABC ads is crudely scientific. They point to a cause and effect relationship between watching lots of television and being successful. Remember that line 'A coincidence—we don't think so'. The point is that there appears to be a strong case for correlating TV watching and success. So strong, indeed, that it would be absurd to suggest it was a coincidence.

You may bridle at calling this an appeal to science. But I do not think you should. The structure of the thought is clearly formed by a culture which expects this kind of clear cause and effect narrative. And the conclusion is that it works. Doing what you like doing best makes you a member of an economically successful culture. So why worry? What's the problem?

This is not merely an American phenomenon, first, because a

global culture is, overwhelmingly, an American culture, and, secondly, because we have seen some recent spectacular examples over here. Most obviously there was the death and subsequent secular canonisation of Princess Diana.

These events have been thoroughly discussed just about everywhere. I do not need or wish to go through all that again other than to point out that one clear theme persistently emerged. The death of Diana, it was accepted by critics and fans alike, was a mass cultural event. She was, said the Prime Minister or rather his press secretary Alastair Campbell, 'the People's Princess'. This was an explicit protest against the guardians of old cultural hierarchies whether they were the Royal Family, the ecclesiastical authorities who ran the Westminster Abbey service, or those who found something disgusting in her entirely shameless manipulation of the media and her celebration of the low cultural world of pop stars and fashion designers in which she liked to live.

For, the people asked via their tribunes, was this disgusting? She could pour out her heart in an interview on BBC's *Panorama*, but this was justified by the fact that she visited Aids patients and campaigned against landmines. Seeking publicity is now seen as a necessary aspect of the process of doing good. Pop culture, which is at the very centre of this publicity machine, is sanctified, a process that began with the Live Aid concert at which rock 'n' roll ceased to be a hedonistic, socially dissident form and became a moral force more effective than anything controlled by the old religious, social or artistic forms. Diana thus further justifies the elevation of pop culture by providing it with a moral as well as an aesthetic foundation.

Now I am a child of pop culture myself. I think that Andy Warhol was, in his way, a fine artist and I yield to no one in my admiration of Bob Dylan. The world of pop, of mass, youth culture, has, perhaps inevitably, nurtured a thin but significant layer of genius. But there is an enormous difference between Warhol and Dylan and Damien Hirst and Elton John. The former are transforming and elevating their material in ways that are recognisably related to the art of the past. The latter are neither transforming nor elevating, rather they are merely sustaining the easily assimilated form of their material. You can study Dylan, I defy anyone to study Elton John. Warhol and Dylan imply a higher realm; Hirst and John do not.

The question thus becomes: what happens if the higher realm is abandoned? This is happening all around us, what if it continues? What if America continues to be hugely successful and continues to throw off the useless metaphysics of high culture? What if the world, as it inevitably will, follows suit? Will this then prove that high culture was a waste of time, that the difficult journey from A to C was futile. You can get straight to C—the experience. Giotto will not then be at C, but Elton John will be.

The problem for the defenders of high culture is that all arguments in this area tend to be entirely utilitarian or even political. The present Labour Government of Great Britain, for example, is plainly afraid to associate itself with anything that might remotely be regarded as elitist. It is afraid because it sees no votes—indeed, it sees a loss of votes—in anything that might imply that there is something better than the simple wallow, the weekend spent in front of the TV.

This is a utilitarian calculation that is reinforced by a straightforward economic sum. The 'Cool Britannia' phenomenon, for example, was all about selling Britain as a creative—in pop cultural terms —country. Fashion and pop make money, they encourage exports by making the Union Jack seem as fashionable and hip as it was in the sixties. Many have come to resent Cool Britannia and the Government is now plainly embarrassed by the whole affair. But they are not embarrassed and Cool Britannia is not resented because people feel they should be doing something better. Rather they see it as a betrayal of the authenticity of pop culture itself. And, for the few occasions when pop culture is authentic, they are right.

This means, I think, that the idea of excellence and coherence embodied in high culture is seriously threatened. We know, in terms of GNP, marketing and electoral success, it is all but useless. And we know from the ABC ads and the pop bias of New Labour that low culture is now seen as distinctly useful. The world of pop and the slob works, so what is our problem? Why agonise over Tolstoy or Wittgenstein when life can be so good without either?

Perhaps this is what happens at the end of history. Once the great systemic conflicts are over, once we know the broad rules of how to get richer in a secular, liberal democratic society, then the difficult issues simply becomes redundant. We become as happy as pigs. And why not?

One answer may be that, once you have experienced Mozart, then Elton John is not enough. This is true but it avoids the issue. For it does not answer the question: why bother experiencing Mozart? What is it about the condition of having listened to Mozart that is so superior to the condition of not having listened to Mozart? After all, it is routinely said at this point, the concentration camp commanders listened to Mozart. George Steiner has always insisted this is a particularly serious problem and, after years of disdain for his argument, I think I now agree with him. For the problem presses upon us the demand to know exactly what is happening at these peak high cultural experiences. Whatever it is, it does not stop people killing Jews, so what does it do? Knowing at least some kind of answer to that question is the one way we can be sure of passing the high cultural tradition on to the next generation.

I have been trying here simply to explain a cultural change that I think is now happening globally. It seems to me to be a change to a deadened culture of consumption and endless self-indulgence in which difficulty—either of appreciation or of attainment—has been eliminated. Defining the virtues of high culture against this wasteland is not my concern, largely because I suspect I am not capable. But I will say that I think the idea that difficulty can be eliminated from human life is nonsensical. We are thwarted in our desires, we rub up against other people, we make mistakes and we die. None of this is changed by listening to Elton John and it is not concealed by the bright, colourful surface of mass culture. If anything, it is emphasised. Watching the inanities of the *Big Breakfast* is as sure a way I know of experiencing intense loneliness.

Art and philosophy—real, difficult art and philosophy—are the most trustworthy ways of, if not resolving these difficulties, then at least rendering them coherent and, finally, bearable. They are not therapeutic because they do not cure, but rather they construct a high perspective from which to view the chaos below. They don't 'work' in any utilitarian sense, but they provide a place and a time that is not simply here and now. And the virtue of that is that 'here and now' is the very nightmare into which the mandarins of officially-sanctioned pop culture and the economically successful TV-watching slobs are trying to drive us.

Welfare and the State

MELANIE PHILLIPS

1 Introduction

Once upon a time, there was a consensus in this country that the welfare state was the jewel in the crown of the post-war settlement. It was a national badge of moral worth. It was held to embody certain virtues that people told themselves were the hallmark of a civilised society: altruism, equity, dignity, fellowship. It defined Britain as a co-operative exercise which bound us together into a cohesive society. Or so we told ourselves.

Now, however, the mood is very different. We are told that we can no longer afford the welfare state we once took for granted. People are increasingly being told they will have to pay for themselves – student fees, second pensions. The reason we cannot afford it, we are told, is a combination of rising demand – people living longer, new medical interventions – and the fact that people will not pay higher taxes any more. The question, though, is surely not whether we can afford the welfare state, but whether we want to spend our money in this way.

Overall, there is no crisis. Welfare spending has remained pretty steady as a proportion of GDP. What has changed is that, within that, more is being spent on means-tested benefits. This helps explain the paradox that although the total is the same, more people are dissatisfied.

There are several separate problems: pockets of high unemployment; a steep increase in the number of lone parents dependent upon the state; and a shortfall in the value of pensions, with a growing minority of pensioners needing expensive long-term care for the last years of their lives. The health service is in crisis; but it has always been in crisis, surviving only by means of an enormous rolling debt. That crisis becomes visible whenever governments attempt to balance the books, because they have never balanced.

Of course, we could pay more in taxes. But the crisis of welfare is not so much financial as moral. The current uncertainty is not just about whether we can or should afford it. It is about what kind of values we think should govern our society, and what the proper relationship should be between the individual and the state. In particular, there is an anxiety that the welfare state may hurt some of the very people it was designed to help. We have become confused about the values we think should be driving it along. We have had the collectivist model. The deficiencies of that sent us to Mrs Thatcher for rescue. The local state in particular was delivering grim old people's homes, sink housing estates, a health service teetering on bankruptcy and schools instructed by local authority advisers to implement quack theories that left hundreds of thousands of children functionally illiterate. We then had the freedom model, which did nothing to help the problems of health and education and which gave us old people selling their homes to pay for care they had understood they had already paid for through taxes and national insurance; and mass home ownership which produced even worse sink ghettos of public housing for those left behind by the home-owning revolution. The quasi markets in health, education, and social services offered advantages in breaking up monopolies, offset by the disadvantages of tendering for service contracts where driving down costs was the only consideration.

The sense that public services were at breaking point, the welfare contract was broken and social cohesion dangerously threatened sent the British electorate to Tony Blair for rescue from the politics of selfishness and greed – even though Blair was promising to restore public services and social cohesion without raising a penny more in taxes to bring it about. In other words, he believed the public wanted to retain the gains of selfishness without adverse consequences.

But now Blair intends to end the 'something for nothing' society, requiring unemployed people to do some kind of work or training in return for welfare benefits, encouraging welfare mothers out to work, imposing student fees and compulsory second pensions. Leave aside the ambiguities and contradictions in policy. The underlying message is clear. Everyone's going to have to start paying for themselves in more and more parts of the welfare state.

This is provoking unease and opposition. We are told such an approach will abandon the virtues of decency and social justice which promoted social cohesion. In fact, the welfare state embodied muddled values, which allowed it to be quickly redirected away from some crucial principles, while others which were too little regarded were abandoned. I shall argue that the doctrine of equality in particular undermined its founding ethic of personal responsibility, and promoted a state role which encouraged the rise of a clamorous rights culture and irresponsible individualism. The old choice between altruism and self-interest, collectivism and individualism, was too narrow. There is a middle route, promoting the common good and a collective interest in which we all have a share.

2 Beveridge's vision

Welfare systems reflect a country's values and the image of itself that a country wishes to promote. European welfare systems were designed to reflect an image of social solidarity, although in different ways appropriate to those cultures. Thus Sweden promoted an egalitarian social democracy; Germany promoted social solidarity not through egalitarianism but through a hierarchical system in which everyone knew their place. America's approach, by contrast again, reflected rugged individualism and social mobility.

As the sociologist Robert Pinker has outlined, notions of welfare in Britain have been caught up in a flux of conflicting ideas: freedom and security, individualism and collectivism, self-determination and the pursuit of the notion of the common good, commutative and distributive justice.[1] The defence of the welfare state is held to be a liberal position. But the history of welfare reveals a shift from classical liberal principles to an increased role for the state, which contradicted those principles and thus enabled neo-liberal Conservatives to claim them as their own.

Both the liberal and ethical socialist ideas which lay behind the creation of the post-war welfare state embodied the classical liberal assumption that moral improvement was the dynamic of social progress. As the twentieth century wore on, however, the role of the state assumed ever greater importance, unravelling that rich tapestry of voluntary associations, mutual aid schemes, philanthropy and self-help which had characterised nineteenth-century liberalism.

Nevertheless, individual responsibility and personal morality through self-discipline remained central to the thinking behind the establishment of the welfare state. No-one then foresaw how positive liberty in the form of the rights culture, in the absence of firm moral boundaries and the collapse of organised religion, would come to erode those moral codes that were then still taken for granted.

William Beveridge's famous plan laid down the post-war welfare settlement. The mistake made by subsequent generations was to assume that this settlement was a blueprint for social cohesion. This followed from its claim to be a universal system. It is wrong, though, to think universality necessarily promotes social cohesion. Under the influence of Marxist thinking, the goal of universality later became synonymous with equality – which was certainly never Beveridge's intention. If the system not only provides something for everyone but seeks to provide the *same* thing for everyone, then

[1] Robert Pinker, 'New Liberalism and the Middle Way' in Robert M. Page and Richard L. Silburn: 'British Social Welfare in the 20th Century', (Macmillan Press, 1999).

that automaticity destroys social cohesion. Equality promotes a culture of entitlement, which means people stop thinking they have a duty to put *into* society and believe instead they have a right to take out. That is why state provision and individualism are symbiotically linked. In the decibel auction of rights and entitlements, everyone is out for himself. Far from producing equal provision, far from bringing about social cohesion, those with the sharpest elbows win.

Moreover, Beveridge's plan was not a bottom-up exercise, getting everyone to pull together for a common objective. It was imposing a vision from the top down, a vision of building the New Jerusalem, constructing the peace on the same principles with which Britain had won the war. There were fresh enemies to be defeated. This was not a mere bureaucratic exercise to tidy up the existing insurance schemes and the Poor Law. The peacetime enemies were the five giant evils of Want, Disease, Ignorance, Squalor and Idleness. Inspired by the spirit of national unity released by the war effort, the plan embodied unrivalled optimism about social progress and a faith in the benign power of the state to change people's lives for the better. It was utopian and transformative and thus entailed a high degree of social engineering. But above all, it meant imposing a view. It was designed to correct deficiencies in individual human experience. It was a highly paternalistic vision, born not so much from the English tradition of liberalism as from Christian romantic idealism, heavily overlaid by the English class system. It could not promote social solidarity because at its core was the arrogant presumption of the English upper classes that the masses needed 'good' things to be done to them. What was missing from the start was a concept of a shared national project of mutually supportive individual endeavour.

3 What was wrong with Beveridge's vision.

From the start, there were glaring contradictions in Beveridge's vision. It boasted cradle to grave provision for all, including a completely free national health service. Warnings from the beginning that it could not be afforded were brushed aside. Kingsley Wood, the Chancellor of the Exchequer, pointed out in 1942 that although it was supposed to be contributory, it actually depended on the bottomless purse of the taxpayer to fund an open-ended deficiency grant. The principles of universality and free provision were instantly undermined. The government abandoned Beveridge's promise that national insurance benefits would cover subsistence, and prescription charges were introduced. The immediate difficulty of providing equally for everyone prompted *The Times* to run an article headlined *Crisis in the Welfare State* as early as 1952.

Even more serious were the intellectual inconsistencies. The root of the problem was the yoking together of individualism and collectivism – defined by Dicey as 'government for the good of the people by experts and officials' – within the same scheme. Beveridge's plan embodied simultaneously the desire to enhance individual freedom and responsibility, *and* the belief that poverty was not the responsibility of every individual.

He was not an egalitarian. He wanted the scheme to be based primarily on the contributory principle, requiring individual responsibility. And he was clear that the universal safety net provision of national assistance for those falling out of the contributory scheme would assist those he deemed to be 'less eligible', in language from which we would today recoil. This basic minimum was to be reserved for the 'feeble minded', 'cripples' and the small number of mothers with illegitimate children. The problems with his scheme were financial and practical. Not only could Britain not afford it, but huge numbers came to depend on that basic minimum, not least because national insurance was set below subsistence levels from the start and more people were forced to depend on means-tested national assistance. He also made certain assumptions about society which as we all know did not survive the test of time: that there would be full employment, and that families would be supported by breadwinning males.

But as great if not a greater problem was his intellectual catch-22. Under a contributory system, how can a basic minimum provide for subsistence if that is what national insurance provides? There has got to be some clear advantage to make people contribute. Yet, if the safety net does *not* provide for subsistence, how can it be a safety net? Beveridge was trapped by this conundrum, as has every welfare thinker ever since. His scheme did not abolish the 1834 Poor Law with its 'less eligibility' criteria as much as nationalise it. The Poor Law assumed poverty was the result of individual failings. If you were poor it was either your fault or the responsibility of your family to look after you. It therefore operated on the deterrence principle, that by making poor relief as awful as possible it would force people to change their behaviour.

But because so many were forced to depend on the Poor Law's successor of national assistance – people who represented a broader cross section then fell within Beveridge's criteria of less eligibility – the contributory principle was undermined and automaticity given greater emphasis. So deterrence could no longer be justified. Other principles came into focus. Notions of 'charity', 'dependency' and moralism were replaced by the language of universal rights. It was universality as opposed to selectivity, social insurance instead of the

Poor Law, impersonal entitlement instead of moralistic discretion and benefits paid not through discretion but as rights of citizenship. Universalism became the hallmark of citizenship and social solidarity. Except that, in practice, this rhetoric was a con. As Jose Harris has observed, real universality was provided not by the means-tested welfare state but ironically by the detested Poor Law.[2] Despite attempts to limit entitlement, under that law some poor relief was available to everyone by right as a citizen.

But revulsion against the Poor Law principles of discrimination and judgementalism was very strong and gained in strength. One might say that the whole history of social policy has been the attempt to move away from the Poor Law principles of fault to an acceptance of structural causes of poverty which preclude judgement upon individuals. But in junking those principles, thinkers junked moral responsibility as well.

4 How Beveridge's vision was distorted by individuals

Setting conditions for those claiming unemployment benefits was always part of the original plan. Conservative theorists, particularly in America, have emphasised its deterrent effect. There, where conditionality is now being applied, the policy is punitive in intent. But there is another way of looking at it, which is that it is in the best interests of unemployed people themselves. As the welfare specialist Alan Deacon has pointed out, conditionality was integral to the thinking of Beveridge, Temple and Tawney, the original architects of the welfare state.[3] Their original vision was highly moralistic and very much bound up with both the good and bad likely effects of welfare upon behaviour. There was also a view that certain types of character were deficient – impulsive, reckless, feckless and so on – which led to the harshness of Bosanquet's Charity Organisation Society with its distinction between the helpable and the unhelpable. Beveridge wrote: 'The plan is not one for giving to everybody something for nothing and without trouble, or something that will free the recipients from their personal responsibilities. The plan is to secure income for subsistence on condition of service and contribution.' There was anxiety about 'demoralisation' or the moral isolation of the long-term unemployed if they were given benefits. So

[2] Jose Harris, 'Contract' and 'Citizenship', in David Marquand and Anthony Seldon (eds), *The Ideas That Shaped Post-War Britain,* (London: Fontana, 1996).
[3] Alan Deacon, 'Re-reading Titmuss: Moralism, Work and Welfare', *University of Leeds Review*, 36 (1993).

Beveridge proposed unlimited unemployment benefit, but that after six months it should be conditional on attendance at work or a training centre. This was rejected by both the Coalition and Labour governments. Benefit and training were separated for decades. Welfare was thus separated from its consequences for behaviour and character.

Beveridge's vision was further skewed by later thinkers who recoiled from anything that smacked of Poor Law distinctions. Alan Deacon and Simon Robinson have pointed out how the ethical position held by Richard Tawney was undermined by Richard Titmuss, Tawney's intellectual heir and a thinker whose ideas dominated the post-war development of the welfare state.[4] Tawney believed man was sinful as well as capable of compassion. This meant altruism was unreliable, leading to a stress on duties and responsibilities rather than rights. Titmuss, by contrast, was much more optimistic about human nature and thus emphasised the obligations of the state *to* the individual, rather than the obligations *of* the individual.

This paved the way for an increasing economic determinism which deemed it immoral to suggest that the poor might in any way be responsible for their plight or be expected to get themselves out of it. This was blaming the victim and therefore morally wrong. Worse, it was held to typecast individuals according to supposed character defects, which appeared to suggest an intellectual conveyor belt from the Poor Law to Nazism. Yet this non-judgementalism was to undermine the honest and industrious poor. Their own judgementalism is still very noticeable; married couples struggling to feed and clothe their children adequately will single out never-married mothers as non-deserving, and will complain they are deliberately fleecing the system by jumping the housing queue and so forth.

Of course, character is not fixed. No-one is unhelpable. But behaviour and character are surely linked. We learn principles like personal responsibility, duty to one's children, the work ethic, the need to defer gratification. Our characters are formed by experiences; our moral character is formed by our experiences in childhood. Clearly if that process goes wrong it is very difficult to put it right later. But people can still be helped by being taught that society operates by certain principles. If they expect their wants and needs will automatically be provided by others, they will not learn the same moral lessons as if they are taught things are expected of them. Behaviour helps create character. And welfare and behaviour are undoubtedly linked. Welfare, as part of a complex web of cul-

[4] Ibid. Simon Robinson, 'Tawney's Theory of Equality' unpublished Ph.D. thesis, University of Edinburgh, 1989.

tural references, signals, incentives and influences, helps create a set of assumptions and expectations. No-one is induced to have a baby or run away from home if the state pays income support and provides accommodation. It is rather, surely, that the fact the state pays benefits and provides housing means the prospect is not so terrible as to make people stop and think twice. It removes a disincentive. Removing the benefit which removes that disincentive will not necessarily prevent the pregnancy or keep the teenager at home. Other factors may simply be too strong. But it seems wrong nevertheless to use taxpayers' money to remove a disincentive to antisocial behaviour.

Christian ethical socialism, such an important force behind the welfare state, believed in personal responsibility under virtually all circumstances. To deny that is to demean human beings. This does not deny the importance of structural considerations. The two have to be held in balance with each other. Yet the fact that welfare has *any* effect on behaviour is still widely and vehemently denied. Frank Field's analysis of the way the welfare state has promoted dishonesty and dependency through means-tested benefits and exacerbated family breakdown is held by some to be class treachery.[5] Yet all he is doing is returning, as it were, back to basics, back to the liberal view that morality is the motor of social progress.

The downside of our welfare system, however, is about more than means tests. Altruism, the governing shibboleth which excluded judgementalism, has become a euphemism for state charity. But why is impersonal charity thought to be any more civilised than personal charity? State charity, after all, is attractive to those who seek control over very large numbers of people, not in itself an attractive feature. The paradox of state charity has been that, although it set out to replace the demeaning dependence on others by universal entitlement, it made its recipients passively dependent on the bounty not of philanthropists but of bureaucrats.

5 Poverty, equality and redistribution

With questions of behaviour and discrimination deemed to be *infra dig*, equality took over as the defining motif in welfare. Earlier this century, however, the goal of equality had a different meaning from today. Then it was all to do with the equal dignity of persons, fellowship, shared experience, mutual respect. Now it has been

[5] Frank Field, *Stakeholder Welfare* (London: Institute of Economic Affairs, 1996).

debased into identical material ends. And it has become all but ineradicably confused with poverty.

As the sociologist Norman Dennis has written, by the early sixties the consensus was that poverty had been all but eradicated.[6] In *The Affluent Society* in 1958, J. K. Galbraith wrote that the defeat of poverty as it had traditionally been conceived meant that people's concerns had to be raised above material things. In this, he reflected Tawney's own emphasis on a common good far beyond material possessions.

Yet by the seventies, we were being told that poverty was a national scourge, widespread and increasing. In his scathing analysis of this phenomenon, Norman Dennis illustrates how this came about through intellectual sleight of hand. Welfare analysts were pressing to remove the stigma from means-tested benefits by treating them as non-discretionary entitlements and unconditional rights. It was a crusade to remove any embarrassment at not being able to manage on your own. This resulted in the happy discovery of new and clearly deserving groups in poverty, both the old and the young. One could say that such analysts wanted to keep their own intellectual welfare empires intact by making sure that the poor were always with us. More likely, though, they were simply part of the growing wider cultural revolt against any kind of judgementalism, as the climate of possessive individualism roared into top gear.

Meanwhile, the idea of poverty itself was being reshaped. The benefit rate was redefined not as the sum keeping people out of poverty but as proof they were in poverty. That was connected to another development. In the sixties, poverty was redefined from a concept related to subsistence to one related to average income. It became inextricably confused with inequality and the redistribution of wealth. As Robert Skidelsky has written, demand had risen faster than national income.[7] The solution to this newly reformulated problem was to get growth to rise faster and to meet demand for redistribution of income through the growth dividend. Poverty suddenly became defined arbitrarily as half the national average income. At a stroke, as Norman Dennis has observed, this discovery caused the proportion in poverty between 1979 and 1996 to shoot up from seven to 25 per cent.[8] Absolute poverty was dead. Poverty was redefined as relative. The suggestion that people who had freezers and videos and central heating could not be poor was regarded as further proof of heartlessness.

[6] Norman Dennis, *The Invention of Permanent Poverty* (London: Institute of Economic Affairs, 1997).
[7] Robert Skidelsky, *Beyond the Welfare State* (London: Social Market Foundation, 1997).
[8] Dennis, *The Invention of Permanent Poverty*.

Melanie Phillips

The intellectual chicanery behind the concept of relative poverty occasionally produced comical results. As Norman Dennis recounts, research published in 1992 claimed that the average family needed £21,000 a year for the basic necessities of life.[9] Yet this was some £5,000 above the national average income! So even people earning considerably more than average were 'in poverty'.

Despite the absurdities, eradicating inequality has become a shibboleth of social policy. The Rowntree Inquiry into Income and Wealth in 1995 reported that income inequality had hugely increased during the eighties.[10] This great and growing gap between rich and poor was blamed for social exclusion, itself a major cause of problems such as crime, drug abuse, political extremism and social unrest. This can hardly be true, when crime rocketed up in this country in the sixties, the decade when poverty had been officially abolished and inequality was greatly reduced. The same phenomenon has occurred in egalitarian Scandinavia, while some countries with massive inequalities are reasonably law abiding places. In other words, social breakdown has other causes. Rowntree and other welfare analysts single out as a product of poverty young men with no take in society. But this is a back to front analysis. The undoubted problems of young men are related to the collapse of fatherhood and jobs, the two primary means of socialising young men, not income inequality. Such welfare analysts only think in terms of economic determinism. Issues of personal responsibility and the contribution of behaviour to poverty, and the fact that it is above all a moral and cultural issue, are simply absent from the script.

But behaviour and welfare are inextricably linked. As Frank Field and Robert Skidelsky have written, the massive increase in means tested benefits ensnaring people in the poverty traps have brought rationality and morality into direct conflict.[11] Why work if you can get more on benefit? Far from taking personal responsibility for one's situation, the system encourages others to pay for the consequences of one's own behaviour.

Inequality is seen as unfair. Equality is often linked to the notion of social justice. But the pursuit of equality has redistributed money from the productive to the unproductive, regardless of whether they can help being unproductive or not, which is much more unfair. It cannot be just if everyone gets the same regardless of their contribution or behaviour. That is why the aim of equality of income is unjust, not to mention unattainable in a free society.

[9] Ibid.

[10] Income and Wealth: Report of the JRF Inquiry Group (London: Joseph Rowntree Foundation, 1995).

[11] Field, *Stakeholder Welfare* and Skidelsky, *Beyond the Welfare State*.

And that is in large measure why people do not want to pay higher taxes. At the same time, people do worry about inequality. They think it is wrong – even while they play the lottery in the hope of becoming millionaires with no more effort than scratching a card. They worry about its effects because they think it means social exclusion. This is surely muddled thinking. Social exclusion is caused by snapping the social bonds that link us to each other. Money does not bind us to each other; relationships of empathy and reciprocity do. Absence of work weakens those bonds; family disintegration tests them to breaking point; the combination of the two shatters them.

The state originally stepped in to fill the gaps in welfare provision. But the intention to eradicate need was soon overtaken by the intention to eradicate poverty and reduce inequality by redistributing income and opportunity from the haves to the have-nots. David Blunkett has said that the idea of financial redistribution is now dead and buried and that equality of outcome, that false goal of egalitarianism, is also dead and buried. In fact, government thinking so far embodies considerable confusion and inconsistencies. The education programme appears wedded to equality of outcome, with modular qualifications reducing the distinction between A-level and vocational qualifications to provide the illusion that more and more young people are able to fulfil their equal 'entitlement' to higher education, regardless of whether this equality is in their or the country's best interests.

Both left and right criticise the welfare system. The right hates its collectivism which it says has undermined the family and altruistic values, and eroded individual initiative and responsibility. The left blames it for failing to eradicate either poverty or inequality. The dilemma of the welfare state is that it could not increase security and equity except at the expense of responsibility and community.

6 How can we square fairness with personal responsibility?

This dilemma remains unresolved. It is personal responsibility versus the universal safety net. Justice versus compassion. Self-interest versus altruism. Charles Murray versus Richard Titmuss. Yet we do not have to choose between these opposing concepts. There is, I would suggest, profit in developing a middle way, going back to the liberal principles of the earliest founders of the welfare state – and by liberal, I mean moral – but which sloughs off the illiberal statism and Marxist-inspired drive for equality which all but submerged those principles. It would uphold the principle that most people should take personal responsibility and contribute, while those who cannot will not be left to fend for themselves at the whim of private charity. But it would widen the definitions of those who should be expected to take responsibility for themselves. And those who cannot should be provided for by a mixture of public and private provision, with active encouragement of the not-for-profit sector.

There is talk now of a move in the direction of personal responsibility, of a shift from rights to duties in welfare. We are hearing about home-school contracts, an emphasis on parental responsibility, action against unruly tenants, curfews restricting children at night. We are hearing about making unemployment benefits conditional on taking up work or training schemes. What we are hearing less straightforwardly about is perhaps the most important responsibility of all and one whose dereliction has had untold consequences for welfare. That is the progressive disintegration of the family.

7 Feminism, family and the impact on poverty and ill-health

The welfare state has been deformed by the impact of a culture of individualism which has fuelled family breakdown and the widening phenomenon of fatherlessness, to a degree that is simply not acknowledged. A huge amount of poverty is now caused by family breakdown through both divorce and the increase in the numbers of never-married mothers. The poverty lobby never acknowledges this causal connection. Instead, the state is blamed for allowing lone parents to remain in poverty. It is regarded as the duty of the state to provide for them. But it is not the state which caused their poverty. It is the fragmentation of their family life which has caused it.

The impact of family breakdown on our welfare state, and indeed on our whole civic culture, is hard to overstate. It has fuelled a great deal of our housing crisis, for example; people living separately need separate houses. The phenomenon of young people begging, which causes so many to blame 'income inequality' for this distressingly visible symptom of social exclusion, is actually caused in large measure by young people running away from home; and the most significant reason for that is family breakdown and in particular the hatred of step-parents. Poverty is said to be the cause of crime; but what causes that poverty in the first place is usually family fragmentation, which in itself is also a major factor – probably *the* major factor – behind juvenile criminality. The health service is under ever greater pressure from the increasing depression and illness caused by divorce, particularly among men. Social workers' child abuse caseloads are dominated by households where the biological father is absent. Children from fragmented households generally do worse at school and in every single area of their lives than children from intact homes.

Yet the response of the welfare state to the manifold ill effects of this phenomenon of family disintegration is to try to mop up the effects, while running as fast as possible in order to stick heads in the sand. Whatever the Prime Ministerial rhetoric about supporting strong families, a number of taboos are still preventing family breakdown from being tackled at source. So apparent solutions are at best peripheral and at worst are implementing the anti-family agenda of extreme feminism. For example, we are told that lone parents will be encouraged to go out to work. Assuming this will amount to more than a cosy chat with a lone parent adviser, this policy may reduce the benefits bill but it will not address the phenomenon of lone motherhood. Indeed, it may make that even worse. It may exacerbate the problems of the children by causing them to be dumped in unsuitable substitute care or indeed with no care at all. It may displace young men from the workforce, thus reducing their marriageability and increasing the number of never-married mothers. This would be all part of the extreme feminist agenda which seeks to bring about unisex parenting and the reinvention of men. But it would not tackle family breakdown, regardless of its antisocial consequences. Why not?

Politicians are fearful of this issue because of the Back to Basics fiasco. They fear comparison between policy upholding family values, on the one hand, and ministers who are wrecking their own families, on the other. In other words, it is now more important to prevent hypocrisy than irresponsibility. The suggestion that ministers should no more be excused revelations of adultery, with its retinue of lies, betrayal of trust and harm to others, than they should be excused, say, revelations of stealing or drunk-driving strikes them as preposterous.

Partly, this is because they are frightened of being thought not to want to uphold the rights of women, now defined as being able to throw out their husbands whenever they want to. But mainly, it is because they are overwhelmingly signed up to the prevailing non-judgementalism of the age, in which it is far worse to criticise a lifestyle than to criticise the person who has wrecked someone else's life.

And that is because of the split between public and private behaviour. Family life is deemed to be a private matter (except of course where the agenda is to demand child care or other benefits). The fact that if it breaks down on a large scale this has huge consequences for society is dismissed. Mill's dictum that interference with individual liberty is justified only to prevent harm to others is a modern article of faith. Although Mill qualified this with exceptions for the protection of children and other non-responsible dependants, the caveat has been rather lost. Harm, that subjective and slippery concept, has been redefined to mean not what is wrong but, as Jonathan Sacks has written, 'what is right for me and what I can get away with'.[12] Morality has been redefined as merely another consumer lifestyle choice.

But is it possible to put the family genie back into the bottle? Are not politicians helpless before such massive cultural change? Clearly, the state is limited in what it can do. But the state also intersects with behaviour. What it does and what it says help create a climate. The signals it sends out are very important in fuelling cultural change. The great liberalising Acts of the 1970s – divorce reform, homosexuality, abortion – all led public opinion and behaviour rather than responding to demand. Now the state should lead again to restore the notion of the common good in family life by promoting and privileging marriage. The tax and benefits system should make it more advantageous for couples with children to get married than not. The state should reverse by statute law the changes quietly promoted by heavily feminist family lawyers eradicating distinctions between cohabiting and married couples. The government should stop the Family Law Act from coming into force. There is no other area of law where a legal contract is so utterly meaningless that one party to it can unilaterally tear it up without having to justify such an action. The government should no longer fund so-called value-neutral sex education or marriage guidance which in fact legitimise promiscuity and marriage collapse. That would be a start. And it must be attempted because stable families are essential for emotional health, moral responsibility and economic independence. A welfare state which runs away from this responsibility is not concerned with welfare.

Family breakdown is, however, but one illustration of an individualistic rights culture which has produced a spiral of demand, fuelled by science and secularisation. When people believed in acts of God, they thought nothing could be done about fate and there would be a better life hereafter. As soon as the state said it would eliminate risk, insecurity or hardship, its anonymity and collectivist nature turned such a prospect into an entitlement. In health, as science forged across hitherto unimaginable frontiers, every new advance became everyone's justified demand. We have developed a

[12] Jonathan Sacks, *The Persistence of Faith* (London: Weidenfeld and Nicholson, 1991).

culture of escalating and never realisable rights which have not promoted but destroyed social cohesion by setting up competition between interests and eroding our duty to take care of ourselves and our families. Our free health service has helped turn our children into commodities, objects to further our individual need for fulfilment and satisfaction, either by producing them regardless of their own interests in genetic or biological continuity, or terminating them according to whether or not their arrival would make us happy.

So what should we do? We do not want to return to the punitive principles of the Bosanquets or Beatrice Webb. Nor should we return to state provision on the basis that individuals are powerless before circumstances. Nor surely do we want to abandon people to their own resources. There has to be a balance of mutual and reciprocal undertakings in which everyone plays their part. It is right for the state to be involved, as the custodian of the common good and promoter of social solidarity. But with that aim in mind, the state must enable people to help themselves as far as possible. It should also make moral choices, helping promote pro-social behaviour rather than behaviour which has anti-social consequences. What it cannot do is pretend to embody value neutrality. Such a thing just does not exist.

People should be brought to acknowledge that their behaviour may have consequences, the burden of which should not automatically be shouldered by the state. Unemployment and family breakdown are our contemporary twin giant evils, eroding not just the welfare state but the civic fabric in dislocating individuals from the network of social ties and obligations towards each other. But the state has a primary duty to create the economic conditions that will promote employment.

We should try to unpick the confusion of needs and wants. If everyone is entitled to a university education, then not surprisingly the state cannot afford to pay for it. But a university education is not appropriate for the vast majority. They need instead high-quality vocational training in partnership with employers. The illusion of university degrees for all hits three ways: it dilutes the value of university education itself, it stokes up unfulfillable expectations and it fails to meet the real needs of individuals and the country, ensuring a less-productive economy which cannot afford to provide services. In health care, to provide equal access to every development on the basis that everything that is invented becomes everyone's entitlement is the rights culture gone mad. As in other areas of welfare, we should agree on a basic minimum and then encourage individual contributions through both private and voluntary bodies.

Welfare has to be paid for. We can do it in ways that promote social cohesion or social dismemberment. Until now, politicians have told people they will deliver whatever people demand of them, either through state provision or consumer choice. They should instead exercise political leadership and stand for a concept of the common good. People should no longer be treated as consumers with an inalienable right to obtain whatever they desire.

However, the welfare state can only be reformed in ways that truly will work with the grain of British culture if the fault line running through that culture is repaired. This fault line is a despair about Britain's identity and future. Such despair helps explain the education disaster; it explains the collective self-destruction of full-blown individualism; it explains the ambivalence and uncertainty about the welfare state. Among some of our most influential intellectuals, there is no commitment to the British national project. A kind of cultural nihilism has taken over, a rejection of the very idea of transmitting the culture at all. Among these elites there is a stoicism about the decline of a nation, the value of whose national identity can be measured by history teachers who resist the very idea they should teach British history at all as a cultural irrelevance or as a racist and elitist plot. The nation can never pull together in social solidarity or provide a framework for the civic ethic through welfare if its citizens have lost belief in the nation itself.

Questions of Begging

TONY SKILLEN

It has always seemed to me that one of my father's great contributions to monarchical practice was the manner in which, without apparent design, he managed to resolve the internal contradictions of monarchy in the twentieth century that requires it to be remote from, yet at the same time to personify the aspirations of the people. It must appear aloof and distant in order to sustain the illusion of a Monarch who, shunning faction, stands above politics and the more mundane allegiances. At the same time it must appear to share intimately the ideals of the multitude, whose affection and loyalty provide the broad base of constitutional Monarchy. My father, with the instinctive genius of the simple man, found the means of squaring the apparent circle within the resources of his own character.'¹By the force of his own authentic example – the king himself in the role of the bearded paterfamilias ... he transformed the Crown as personified by the Royal Family into a model of the traditional family virtues, a model that was all the more genuine for its suspected but inconspicuous flaws. The King, as the dutiful father, became the living symbol not only of the nation, but also of the Empire, the last link holding these diversified and scattered communities.¹

Thus did the Duke of Windsor describe his late father, King George V. The account and the sense of political values that inform it sit uneasily with the aspiration to rationality and interest-security that seems inherent in professional political philosophy. I am not focusing here on the claims of monarchy; after all we could find analogous terms and iconography in republican nationalist or internationalist discourse. Rather I am talking about a cluster of values which relate to sensibility more than to sense, to matters of the style, quality, density and intensity of social relationships and the feelings and sense of personality and identity that are reflected in them. We might, over-rationalistically, forget that there are rich and grounded intuitions and counter-intuitions here: think of the sense of snobbery, pomposity, condescension, servility, coldness; and of the fact that any one who values things along such dimensions must have a sense of what is true and appropriate as distinct from what is phoney, inadequate or over-the-top. Thus, for example, it is worth

¹ *A King's Story*, *Memoirs of Duke of Windsor* (London: Cassell, 1951).

121

remembering that the dynastic paternalism celebrated in his father by young Edward appeared exposed as cruelly and frigidly authoritarian by the circumstances of his own abdication. So it was to be with Margaret and Group-Captain Townshend and so it was to be with the late Princess of Wales. For what she represented was a 'principle' of beauty, erotic grace, empathy and creaturely humanity that has been a dimension of the romance of royalty and of higher personages throughout the history of states. The young Duke of Windsor had discovered this in 1920, during his period as Governor General of Australia:

> The touching mania, one of the most remarkable phenomena connected with my travels, took the form of a mass impulse to prod some part of the Prince of Wales. Whenever I entered a crowd, it closed around me like an octopus. I can still hear the shrill, excited cry, 'I touched him'. If I were out of reach, then a blow on my head with a folded newspaper appeared to satisfy the impulse... God help the Prince of Wales if in the noisy press of a public reception. I missed the mild little woman in black who had lost her only two sons in the war. Next day might bring a letter reproving me for being a *Thoughtless Prince.*[2]

If George V's image, resisted by his errant son, was of an inclusive 'father of us all' touching from above the heads and shoulders of his family's lesser members throughout the empire, Princess Diana extended the areas and depths 'included', and altered the register of what 'inclusion' meant. She hung out in glamorous-regal touch with deviants, marginals, losers and, it might be added, parasites, by virtue of a reciprocally felt participation in their pains and joys, weakness dependency and courage. She appeared as the embodiment of graciousness and charity in a way that, at face value, retrieved those concepts from their coldly deontologised condition in the uniforms of humiliating hierarchy, the habits of piousness and the overalls of Sheer Bloody Hard Work.

It is worth keeping this dodgily mythic figure in mind when thinking about beggars and vagrants and what they mean. It will help us not only to seek a humane system but to avoid thinking that everything human can be put into a system, let alone a 'policy'. There is something in the 'genius' of a person, parish or people that bespeaks and enacts itself in everyday generosities and attentions – or their absence or opposites. These embodiments are inevitably subject to 'iconic' representation and modelling, more, or less, conspicuous. And thus it can always be that icons are subject to assessment as hypocritical, misrepresentative or diversionary.

[2] Ibid., endnote pp. 155–9.

Dianaphobia can thus be seen as the understandable prejudice that grace, like beauty, can only be skin deep in a world where every corroboration seems to be of cynicism and where a person's known vices are felt to characterise their apparent virtues. This cynicism is dynamic in its inhibitiveness: if my act is only an act, then its performance, being only a performance is vicious in its hypocrisy: I can preempt that by inaction. But my inaction has no tendency to supply an unimpeachable alternative to the forgone 'token gesture'. Instead of an act which at least pays its respects to the genuine response to need, my inaction 'acts' as an expression of indifference and helps to cement that indifference as the everyday norm. And so, the colder the moral climate, the more the act of humanity is vulnerable to representation as hollow, hyprocritical, deceitful or at best futile. So do we reinforce our spiritual privatisation, taking comfort from the exposé of do-gooders as no better than the rest of us. We can lament the fact that royal personages have the iconic status they do have; but it may be well to remind ourselves of the tragic protagonists of the theatre – they represent humanity far beyond the palace walls. They represent, in the context of this essay, those with something of themselves to give or withhold – humanity.

At the other end of this human transaction, beggars are, arguably, iconic personages – bottom rather than top dependants – 'portraying' both their own predicament and that of those of whom they beg; they make a 'claim' on us and our responses to such claims represent both ourselves and our sense of where we situate ourselves in relation to the begging self. This is not a thing that is specific to the relations of higher and lower, or inside and outside. The busy workers of the city-mart-state of Singapore have a characteristic air; they seem, even by the grumpy standards of the British, 'pissed-off'. Periodically, the regime, aware of the bottom-line consequences of such moroseness, mounts a 'Courtesy Campaign' – 'It Pays to Smile', and so-on. But somehow, such campaigns seem only to augment the aura of onerousness. As Thomas Carlyle harped, once something ceases to be 'unconscious', the attempt deliberately to reinsert it into the pattern of everyday life takes on the character of a 'mechanical' grappling with 'mechanism'. It partakes of the vices it seeks to remedy. The style in which we do the things of which we are expected indicates the existential truism that we are always on the line; but the beggar in the street, while certainly sensitive to styles of grants and refusals, puts us on the line through the very freedom we have even to recognise his or her presence.

Three snatches from three formerly popular songs glimpse at the many aspects of begging and beggars that make them difficult to think and feel clearly about. Getting clearer in all this may be as

much a matter of patiently sorting out paradigms and images as of
constructing one argument:

> So long to you, gotta get on the road again.
> So long to you, gotta hitch up my load again.
> It's been great to meet you here;
> Right good company and right good beer.
> Now then my lads; any one like to come with me?
> A wanderer's life is free!
> As I go, rain or snow, wandering the King's Highway.
>
> Nights are cold; maybe I'm getting old –
> Yet I thrive;
> And the pals that I meet make it good to be alive.
> So then my lads; any one like to come with me etc.

> I went to a house and I knocked on the door
> And the lady said 'Bum-bum, you've been here before!'
> Hallelujah! I'm a bum! Hallelujah! Bum again!
> Hallelujah! Give us a handout to revive us again.
>
> Now, I don't like work, and work don't like me.
> And that is the reason why I'm so hungry.
> Hallelujah, I'm a bum. Hallelujah, bum again.
> Hallelujah give'us a handout to revive us again.

> Once I built a railroad, made it run;
> Made it race against time.
> Once I built a railroad, now it's done
> Brother can you spare a dime?
>
> In our khaki suits, gee we looked swell;
> Full of the yankeedoodly-dum.
> All those muddy boots, marching through hell
> And I was the kid with the gun.
>
> Say, don't you remember, they called me Al.
> It was Al all the time.
> Say, don't you remember, I'm your pal!
> Buddy can you spare a dime?

Perhaps a different diversion from seriousness, but one with its
own instructiveness, could be provided by a train of thought along
lines of the English 'ordinary language philosophy' of the 'fifties:

Despite its regular conjunction with them, the verb 'to beg', does not function grammatically like 'to borrow' or 'to steal'. You can say that John Doe borrowed the money from Richard Roe, or that he borrowed the axe from him. But you do not say that John begged the money, or for that matter the axe, from Richard. It is a moot point whether Doe can borrow from Roe without his at least tacit permission, and I guess he could not steal from Roe without the absence of permission. If the verb 'to beg' takes an object, it is 'Richard Roe' that is in the objective case: as 'John D. begged Richard R.' to give or to lend him money, an axe, or whatever. Begging is a kind of asking; not, so to speak, a kind of taking or even a kind of demanding. (We really ought to resist talk of 'aggressive begging' as mind-numbing oxymoron – to beg or implore is not to demand. At the other extreme one might note that Jeremy Bentham urged that all begging was 'extortion' since its intention was to extract goods by means of inflicting 'the pain of sympathy';[3] a case of the logician chopping himself, through indiscriminate zeal, in the foot since Bentham's hammer would crush the nut of virtually any voluntary interaction.) There are exceptions to this transitivity rule. Doe might beg pardon of Roe, but this is an interesting deviation, because he would beg *for* mercy. It may be that this is a mere matter of idiom, but it seems plausible that idiom here tracks the fact that beg-pardons are performances with appropriate performatives: 'I beg your pardon', and also that pardons are themselves signalled by at least implicit performatives, no material action or refraining is required. And let us not forget that whereas money borrowed or stolen is money received, pardons begged remain to be granted.

Borrowing and stealing are, in a technical sense achievements: the client is trying to borrow the money, the breaker and enterer is trying to steal. But the man in the street is begging: he is not trying to beg, when he asks you for some spare change. Begging goes on, while borrowings and stealings take place after some goings on. To refuse or ignore the beggar is not to stop him from begging, whereas the armed homeowner and the mean bank-manager prevent theft and borrowing from taking place. Of course the police might stop the man in the street from begging, just as he might stop him from standing there. This is like a bouncer stopping one from asking questions or even from being present at a meeting. Or the man in the street might be unable to beg because he is too ill or exhausted – he's just there.

Begging, borrowing and stealing all imply some framework of entitlement, some notion of yours and mine. But this institutional-

[3] Jeremy Bentham, 'Pauper Management', in P. M. Bowring (ed.), *Collected Works*, vol. VIII (New York: Russell & Russell, 1962), p. 401.

isation is least essential to begging, since one might beg for help or food or attention in very 'basic' contexts. Infants can beg from those on whom they are dependent before they are sophisticated enough to borrow or steal from them. Hobbes' account of the parent-child relation is essentially one of a begging relationship. Regarding this, I commend to you the anecdote about John Dewey in Alan Ryan's biography, when the great man, having given money to a boy who had approached him, complained of the ubiquity of such child beggars, only to be informed that the lad was his own son.[4] In begging, I do not claim something as of right; I put myself at your mercy. But it does not follow either that I do not have that right or even that I might not be aware of such – consider those who beg for their possessions or lives from robbers or killers.

Unlike another fellow-traveller of the verb 'to beg', the verb 'to wander', begging has an internal goal: to obtain some more or less determinate good. One begs by doing or saying something that, in the context, signals that one is begging and what one is begging for. Materially, as Bentham hisses, 'dumb show may be as expressive as words'.[5]

These pickings over the bare bones 'grammar', may come back to haunt us. The truth is that I allude to them only because one of my more analytical colleagues wanted to know how there is anything of conceptual interest about begging. But, when, on the day after Tony Blair told the *Big Issue* that there should be zero tolerance for begging in the streets and that he did not give 'personally' to beggars but rather to 'certain charities', I was invited by the officer of Warwick's Philosophy Society for a paper on Aesthetics or Political Philosophy, I thought that the then Opposition Leader's, to me ugly, mean and insidiously damaging remarks must merit a philosopher's attention, one which might stretch to the theme of 'squeegee-merchants'. And this, of course involves a conceptual enquiry that, while it might include analytical logic-chopping, must attend to the character and context of what is, after all, a nest of big issues. As one who, having hitchhiked a couple of hundred times in my life, has begged in the streets, at least as I understand what I have done, I feel I have a personal 'interest'. Not of course, being in receipt of proper grants, scholarships and salaries for doing what I largely loved, that I was to be categorised as a 'beggar'. But let me counterpose to the introductory abstractions, a concrete predicament of mine. In Canterbury, there is a pleasant young man, Lawrence, from Belfast. He sits for much of the day at the end of the foot-

[4] Alan Ryan, *John Dewey* (New York, London: Norton, 1995).
[5] Ibid., vol. 8, p. 402.

bridge from the station over the ringroad to the City Wall. As I ride my bicycle to work, and as the cycle path includes this junction, I pass him every day. No; this is not quite true; I pass him about twice a week. I generally take a slight detour, which is in fact quicker but more hazardous. Partly this speeds my journey but partly it causes me to avoid Lawrence from Belfast. What I tend to do is to stop and have a brief, sometimes perfunctory chat – he's not very talkative in fact and, though friendly, makes no effort to be more than civil and pleasant. He has a nice dog and his relationship to the dog has affected my feelings about supporting the existence of these apparent luxuries. I reckon I gave this bloke on average about a quid a month. I feel fully happy neither about that, nor in it. It is unnecessary to note that, notwithstanding various ordinances and cleanup campaigns, there remains a large number of people of all ages and both sexes begging in the City of St. Thomas a'Beckett's shrine and that these conflicting facts have to do with the tourist trade. Colleagues of mine advise people charged with begging under the Vagrancy Act of 1824, a date in the interval between the Napoleonic Wars and the Poor Law Act of 1834, when begging and vagrancy were seen as a critical problem despite all sorts of institutions for their suppression. In Canterbury at this time it is common for vagrants to be banned by police or magistrates from the city, by deeming their presence there as demonstrative of begging intent, hence in violation of bail conditions.

> Diogenes the Cynic was, it was said
> 'A homeless exile, to his country dead.
> A wanderer who begs his daily bread.'
> (D. Laertius, II, p. 39)

Plato, both in *Republic* and *Laws*, gave begging less than the zero-tolerance granted to the hopelessly infirm. His love–hate object, Homer, gives a different model: in Book 13 Odysseus, having been transfigured by Athena into a wrinkly and bald old tramp, is saved from the dogs by his very own swineherd Eumaeus, who responds to his thanks as follows:

> Sir, my conscience would not let me turn away a stranger in a worse state even than yourself, for strangers and beggars all come in Zeus' name, and a gift from folk like us is none the less welcome for being small.

Aristotle seems to have had no normal place for beggars, and his magnificently liberal man was not disposed to give to any Tom Dick or Harry, as the translator happily dubs them. (I note here that it seems to be assumed that the bourgeois shopper or flaneur is incapable of discerning the difference between the needy Tom, the profligate Dick and the nefarious Harry in the street, whereas the bureaucrat in the office is.) For a contrasting ancient culture, it is well, if need be, to be reminded that the Old Testament is replete with injunctions and commandments of open heart, hand, gate and door to destitute neighbours and brethren. Job's protesting account, in chapter 29, of his own virtues is dominated, for example, by a proper sense of his unstinting charity towards those bereft.

How do more modern political moralists help? Utilitarians have to tread this pavement warily. On the one hand, as Bentham and Chadwick show, they devote unbounded energy to the project of extirpating mendicity. Bentham's *Pauper Management*, for example is concerned to construct sanctions such that it is more eligible for the masses to work for a wage than to work in the workhouse; but more eligible to work in the workhouse than to work in prison or be executed. (Yet Orwell was to report in *Down and Out in Paris and London* that the best bedding in the 'spike' dosshouses was said to be almost up to prison standard.) All this presupposed a policing mechanism sufficient to create the certainty of these graduated sanctions operating. A more relaxed Utilitarian might have urged on behalf of begging, not only the literal absence of overheads, but the desirability of indigents preferring begging from their betters to mugging them or generally resorting to crime. But Bentham and the intelligentsia generally were concerned with two externals; the first a fixed one: labour is painful drudgery, which any rational utility-maximiser would prefer to avoid; thus they did not consider the possibility that an eligible life of idleness could function as a spur to the amelioration of working life. The second external was an all too variable one: the liability of 'indiscriminate alms-giving' to inconsistency and to sentimental excess. As it seemed to many that this maleficently promiscuous benevolence was as much an instinct of the affluent as the tendency to breed was among the poor, it was considered by many desirable to outlaw, not just those who took the addictive drug of indiscriminate alms but those who pushed it. Helen Bosanquet, doyenne of the Victorian Charity Organisation Society favourably quoted one Dr Guy as hyperbolically advocating the 'handcuffing' of these tender souls, these addictive pushers, on the charity supply-side. Bentham had opposed this idea on the grounds that such legislation would make it more difficult to convict 'dumb' loiterers.

Whatever his quirks in arriving at his definition, Plato conceived of justice in terms of an equilibrium of give and take, of benefit and burden; a balance upset as much by the poor as by the rich non-contributor. Capitalism may have rendered Adam's curse, through industrialisation, an abstraction in concrete and iron. But it did not take capitalism to invent the necessity of arduous and often dreary labour. Think of slavery and serfdom. When Ralph Waldo Emerson wrote à propos 'Wealth' that 'every man is a consumer and ought to be a producer' he was only saying what in effect is proverbial. In other words, there is a problem about the parasitical activity of begging in terms of fairly basic notions of justice. Among contemporary political philosophers, I do not recall John Rawls on the subject of begging. I think he assumes, barring accidents and disablements, that a just society would need its 'worst off' to be in the worst and worst-rewarded jobs, not excluded from a position to earn their keep. Perhaps he takes structurally involuntary unemployment as manifestly incompatible with justice and perhaps he thinks also that it is manifestly unfair that any one should simply choose to live dependent on others' good will. Nor can I find anything in Rawls' right-wing critic, Robert Nozick. But he must allow begging, for he wants to insist on an 'entitlement' view of justice and, unless he is a Scrooge as well as a Gradgrind, he would better have on the left hand people at liberty to receive the charity which those on the right hand are free to bestow or withold. Nozick would surely take the line that both the request and the donation of alms is properly a private matter – caveat donor. So, Political Theorists, do you/we allow begging in your just society or not? Sir Thomas More did not. Indeed, his *Utopia* of 1516 begins with the scandal of mass beggary and vagabondage. Those who steal and beg, he argued, cannot be restrained by any punishment if 'they have no other means of getting a livelihood'. Thus did he put forward the proposition that unemployment, far from being the choice of the dispositionally idle parasite, was itself a predicament that needed to be extirpated so that no one had that reason not to labour, hence, with exceptions, no excuse. (As I understand him, More deems pride and not sloth the cardinal vice.) If you want to see this late-medieval early modern idea perverted into a savage onslaught on the poor during the Tudor period, I commend to you the writings of one Nicholas Ridley, the architect of Bridewell, with its hopeless mission of graduated deterrence through imprisonment, labour, flogging and hellfire threats. But do not forget to look over the Channel where things were as grim; so that in Amsterdam's Rasphuis, for example those among the mainly teenage vagrants who failed in their workhoused labours were subject to confinement in a cellar which they could prevent from filling with water only by peddling like hell.

Would you allow voluntary unemployment in your Utopia? Until Newlabour's constrictings, premised on the delusion of

Tony Skillen

omnipresent work opportunities in a cycle-free capitalism, it has been a feature of the post-war Welfare State, to the extent that living on the dole, receiving housing benefit and so on was considered a sufficiently eligible condition to reduce begging to subliminal levels. It was possible to be, in the Australian expression, a 'dole-bludger' without living in destitution and without resort to the activity of scrounging off anyone in particular. Whereas 'signing on' had been a step which risked one's liberty and public dignity, the post-war SS office, despite its hassles, churlishness and temporary humiliations, was, even in times of low structural unemployment, endured by many in preference to what was with often accurate contempt called the shit-work available through the labour exchange or its informal equivalents. You more or less had a situation where you could go on the SS and choose not to earn your living, at the cost of straitening circumstances. That is an aspect of the Welfare State that Beveridge, who wanted to extirpate both Poverty and Idleness as two of the Seven Giants, would not have welcomed. To-day Newlabour ratchets up the Thatcher-Major attempt to push the young into work or college by tightening up on the conditions of dole-reception for young people especially, with a requirement to enter classes or 'training' or work programmes paid for out of windfall taxes. At the same time, by tightening up on vagrancy, begging and squeegee-merchandising, Newlabour seems intent on closing off access to the informal economies and sub-economies, categorised as 'Social Exclusion', a term whose connotations should ring not just Orwellian alarms but also bells connecting with my earlier invocation of the royal embrace in its more generous meaning.

Now, I have lost many of my comrades' esteem by advocating that community work, which I define as work 'constitutive' of community membership and not reducible to a commodity, should be a normal expectation of citizens young and old in a modern society. I have criticised the idea that such work should be the preserve, on the one hand, of the especially virtuous volunteer, on the other hand, of the especially vicious parolee. In *Down and Out in Paris and London*, having tried on the argument that begging is as real and as arduous work as any other:

> Beggars do not work, it is said, but then, what is work? A navvy works by swinging a pick. An accountant works by adding up figures. A beggar works by standing out of doors in all weathers and getting varicose veins, chronic bronchitis, etc. it is a trade like any other; quite useless, of course – but, then, many trades are quite useless.[6]

[6] G. Orwell, *Down and Out in Paris and London* (Harmondsworth: Penguin Books, 1974) p. 174.

Orwell goes on to compare favourably the ethics of his mendicant acquaintance with those of more harmfully parasitic professions. The latter is a more profitable line of thought. For, although begging typically involves effort (by contrast with opening an envelope with money in it), it is not work that is describable independently of the activity of getting remuneration; you do not get paid for begging.

Orwell advocates at the end that the able needy could reasonably be asked to do something 'useful' and 'beneficial' and 'productive' both to themselves and to others as part of, as well as in return for the means to a decent life.[7] Thus he draws a series of comparisons and contrasts: between work and idleness, between work and what costs pain, between useful work and treadmill toil, between 'honest' work and hack-huckstering business. There is something else, a sort of subtext, in Orwell's whole account: what he is confronting his fellow-bourgeois readers with is precisely their own shameful shame about the reality of life on the sunless side of the street: the sort of attitude that does not want to allow one's children or their chauffeur to be confronted by beggars or squeegee-merchants en route to school. This confrontation would need a different angle in to-day's more cleaned-up context, when state institutions have swept poverty, at least for a few decades, away from the streets. But it is a confrontation that was made directly in 1797 by Wordsworth in '*The Old Cumberland Beggar*', opposing an earlier fin-de-siècle clean up:

> Many, I believe there are
> Who live a life of virtuous decency,
> Men who can hear the Decalogue and feel
> No self-reproach; who of the moral law
> Established in the land where they abide
> Are strict observers; and are not negligent
> In acts of love to those with whom they dwell,
> Their kindred and the children of their blood.
> Praise be to such, and to their slumbers peace!
> – But of the poor man ask, the abject poor;
> Go, and demand of him, if there be here
> In this cold abstinence from evil deeds,
> And these inevitable charities
> Wherewith to satisfy the human soul?
> No – man is dear to man;

So, I want to say, with a sort of sub-Aristotelian striving for a balanced view, that we should take a generous attitude, both to the inertly idle and the active mendicant, meanwhile enhancing the

[7] Ibid., p. 208.

quality and democratic dignity of working life, both in and outside the market. Then, not only can we reasonably expect the life without work to be less eligible, we can assume, unlike Bentham and his slave-driver fellow-travellers, that in opening our hearts and hands to the scrounger, we are not opening the floodgates that resist the torrent of idleness consequent on the aversion to labour alleged to be part of human nature. Utopia can permit begging and is repressive to the extent that it does not permit this uncoercive exploitation.

You may recall that Jesus Christ, while silent on the slavery and slaughter of the Roman era, urged the rich to give away their wealth, for it was the poor who would inherit the earth. The apostles, it seems, were to espouse a 'primitive communism' among themselves, pooling the fruits of their labour. Those who invoke Christ's saying 'the poor are with you always' had better look at the context of what was said in the house of Simon the Leper. First, the disciples were shocked that Jesus didn't do the expected thing and hang on to the alabaster box and its precious ointment, in order to sell it to raise money for the poor. Second, Jesus, knowing the imminence of his death, defined the woman's offering as funereal anointment. Better to regard the story as drawing on the image of precious personal tribute than as an incitement to tell beggars to bugger off. How many humanitarians are chucked into a pit in a paper bag so that the money saved can be sent to Oxfam?

Not only did the mendicant orders of the 12th and 13th centuries place a positive value on poverty, they did so in the context of its place in a sort of spiritual ecosystem along with Charity. Now, every one knows that Martin Luther excoriated the Mendicant Orders, their corrupt ways and their corrupting example. In 1520, he wrote to the Christian Nobles of Germany: 'It is of the highest importance to extirpate beggary entirely from the Christian world. No Christian should beg for alms'.[8]

But the Protestants did not invent the Work Ethic. From the start, the Mendicants' ideology was attacked and pulled, like the Tories over Europe, apart. In any case, it tended to involve a tripartite division, susceptible of infinite refinement:

1 The voluntary poverty of apostleship – 'The Poor with Peter'- the definition was of sacrifice of worldly goods and the stigmata were marks of high birth or wealth status or power foregone, signified in rituals of renunciation and abjection. The mendicant is so to speak honoured for accepting the Christlike humiliation of abjection and paltriness in the eyes of 'the world'. At the same time, with greater

[8] See *Luther's Works*, vol. 44, James Atkinson (ed.) (Philadelphia: Fortress Press, 1966).

perceived clout than the common vagrant, the friars were able to offer prayers on behalf of their benefactors in an economy which transcended that of earthly honour or wealth. The Beatnik is the secular twentieth-century's homage to this tradition.

2 The involuntary poverty of misfortune – 'The Poor with Lazarus' – the starving, the injured, the wounded, the aged, orphaned, the widowed, the infirm, the mad, the imprisoned. These are the proper 'objects' of charity, whose proper subjective state is resignation and, if graced by charity, gratitude. The spiritual economy here allowed for the parameters of climate, trade-cycles and technological or proprietorial change as propelling people involuntarily into poverty. Moreover, by reducing the pains of poverty, it maintained the society's stability in what was assumed to be a cyclically unstable climatic flux. In this respect, the Medievals were ahead of their successors' times. The stigmata of need were signs and evidence of one's condition and its causes. Thus one might have at some time to beg, or one might, with legitimacy, be a beggar.

3 The voluntary poverty of idleness, insubordination, lasciviousness, imprudence – the poor with nothing much going for them in a spiritual sense: the needy through sin and the sinful pretenders of need or beatitude. The stigmata? Here the epistemologists among you can wake up because, from time immemorial, the third category has contrived to appear in the guise of the second or first. (And vice versa, think of Odysseus and of how cunning Tristan makes an honest woman of Isolde and of the strange shifts in Edgar's status in *King Lear*.)

These categories and their institutionalisations and discourses constitute a fascinating if gruesomely interwoven pattern through time and space. At one time we feel the force of the idea of the saintly mendicant witnessing for a life of naked spirituality and providing an image to mock the world of status, wealth and power. At another we are aware of the shock of beggars, living as well as their labouring fellows and threatening to function as witnesses for a life of masterless idleness.

We are surely entering an era of the functional replacement of human labour by machines. In that era, it seems to me, the function of jobs as we now understand the term will shift from the technical-productive to the social-disciplinary. The activity of begging provokes the question 'why work?', not just in individuals but in structures. The Newlabour idea of a workaholic utopia is as untimely as it is oppressive.[9]

[9] My thinking on begging has been helped by Roger Hewitt's 'The Beggar's Blanket' in U. Meinhof and K. Richardson (eds) *Representations of Poverty in Britain* (Singapore: Longman, 1994), pp. 122–146; and by Bronislaw Geremek's *Poverty, A History* (Cornwall: Blackwell, 1994).

Philosophy and Educational Policy

ANTHONY O'HEAR

There is a country where teachers have high status, and in which they have qualifications on a par with members of other respected professions. Parents and children have high aspirations and high expectations from education. Children are fully aware of the importance of hard and consistent work from each pupil. Schools open on 222 days in the year, and operate on the belief that *all* children can acquire the core elements of the core subjects. It is not expected that a class will have a tail. Those in danger of becoming part of an incipient tail have to make up work in their breaks or after school. If the worst comes to the worst poor pupils have to repeat a year, while those who are exceptionally able will move up a year. In the primary schools, children are kept as one large group whatever their individual ability. The teacher teaches the whole group, largely from a text book, though interspersing exposition with focused questioning and discussion, so as to ensure the matter in hand has been properly assimilated by all. Lessons last 40 minutes each, with frequent breaks for letting off steam, after which it is down to work again. Pupils are frequently tested and the school Principal makes a couple of unannounced checks on homework books each term. Secondary schools are selective (grammar, technical and secondary modern), allowing whole class teaching and whole class progression to predominate up to the end of schooling. The teacher indeed is in contact with the whole class for up to 80 per cent of the lesson time. While the school certainly does have non-academic aims, the focus is clearly on academic work. There is a conviction, shared by all involved, that the social and moral dimensions of the curriculum will tend to look after themselves and emerge as by-products of a properly conducted academic study.

Where is this country? Many will immediately and not incorrectly conclude that we are describing Japan and Korea, the Pacific Rim, and with perhaps a bit of Germany and Switzerland thrown in for good measure. We know, too, that achievements in all these countries are frighteningly high in measurable subjects such as mathematics and science, compared with those in England, Wales and (contrary to popular belief) Scotland. Indeed the profile in the previous paragraph is actually based on the English schools inspectorate report on maths and science in the Pacific Rim countries.[1] In

[1] D. Reynolds and S. Farrell, *Worlds Apart* (London: OFSTED, 1996).

this report it points out that in schools in England, by the age of seven, in contrast to the Pacific Rim schools, there is already a wide gap in achievement between the able and less-able pupils, a gap which gets greater year by year. Teachers typically spend 20 per cent of lesson time in contact with the whole class, so for three-quarters or more of the day children are pushed back on their own naturally limited resources. Teachers do not rely on textbooks and have to spend considerable effort in devising their own worksheets, often geared to small groups within the class. In general there is what the report politely refers to as 'complex pedagogy', which combined with constant changes and movement within the class-room, a stress on small group work and poor use of auxiliary staff. All this may go a long way to explaining our poor results in number and mental arithmetic in primary schools and the fact that by the age of 16, 20 per cent of English pupils fail to get a grade 'G' in GCSE English and Maths (particularly worrying, given that grade G is supposed to be the level of attainment of an 11 year old).

But, aside from the small detail of 222 school days (as opposed to 192 in England), is my opening paragraph purely about another country? Is not what is described there rather typical of the inde-pendent sector of education in England in 2000? And, more to the point, is it not rather characteristic of much of English practice in all schools in 1956 when, internationally, we were doing far better in maths comparatively speaking? All of which raises in acute form the question as to why we are where we are to-day, and why our schools did not develop in the direction currently favoured by the Pacific Rim countries and by our own independent sector?

The educational world is full of *apparatchiks*, second-raters who are content to pass on the messages of others. In this it is probably little different from many other fields of endeavour. What I hope to suggest in this paper is the significance of the messages which have become the small change of educational politics in this country over the last half-century or so. What we want to consider is why it is that one professor of education can publicly refer to the apparently innocuous suggestion that the curriculum should focus in history on British history, in music on the classical traditions, and in geography on regional geography as 'the curriculum of the dead'; that another professor of education should, in her inaugural lecture, advocate a system of learning in which pupils 'actively construct their own knowledge', while dubbing the more traditional approach favoured in Europe and the Far East as 'elitist and absolutist ... perpetrated by right-wing philosophers and their colleagues in their university armchairs'; and that a third professor of education, again in an inau-gural lecture, recommends turning the educational spotlight away from teachers and teaching, and on to the pupil regarded as a social being 'the product of his or her environment, together with the creation of learning opportunities which fit'. We also know that during his or her school career 20 per cent or more of our children will be diagnosed at some time as having 'special needs'; and there are those in the 'special needs' world who take this to its logical conclusion, suggesting that we regard every child as constituting a special need.

So the question becomes to explain how it is that educational thought in our country has moved so far from the traditional vision of education as being about the imparting of such skills as are necessary to live a reasonable independent life, together with an introduction to the best that has been thought and known seen as a body of knowledge and experience, existing in its own right outside of the minds of what are the philosophical current which have flown beneath these surface changes? How is it that the proper focus of education has come to be seen not as subjects to be learned and disciplines to be acquired, but the mental structure and development of the child and his or her social environment?

Any answer to this question must begin with Rousseau, whose educational doctrines are laid out mainly in *Émile*[2] which is ostensibly an account of one child's ideal upbringing by a tutor in rural isolation away from the temptations of the city and the influence of other children. It is indeed a paradox that many of Rousseau's individualistically child-centred doctrines are now dear to the heart of an educational bureaucracy which sees social integration as a prime educational aim and will go to almost any lengths to prevent parents educating their children at home.

In *Émile*, though, there are two reasons for withdrawing the pupil from society. The first is so as to remove him from the harmful influences of society in order to allow his nature to develop in its own way. If properly developed, it will develop in a good way. According to Rousseau, vice and error, alien to man's constitution are introduced into it from outside.

But Émile's education in solitude is not purely negative and this takes us to the second reason for a cloistered education. The child has its own needs and should be allowed to develop in its own way, progressively, moving from one stage to another at its own pace and in its own time. Children are not miniature adults; in Rousseau's view, nature wants children to be children before being men. Childhood has its own way of seeing, thinking and feeling. These childish ways are largely concrete and largely sensory. So early education will avoid books and abstract thought and reasoning in favour

---

[2] J. J. Rousseau, *Émile* (1762), quoted here in the Everyman edition (London: J. M. Dent, 1911).

of direct contact with the physical world. The child should be allowed to indulge its sports, its pleasures, its delightful instincts in line with its particular stage of development. The child's needs are thus satisfied in a cocoon of self-sufficiency abandoned to play and discovery; the child is the noble savage in miniature, untroubled by the distractions and vices of society. Reasoning and socialisation, which will come, will emerge through the building on the early experiences of sensation and feeling; they will occur naturally and without the strains inherent in false society if the environment is carefully controlled by the tutor. The child will begin to realise the usefulness of reasoning in his encounters with the physical world, while he will become moral when he extends his innate feelings of pity to the other people he encounters. As he develops, he begins to move from pure instinct to a rational sociability, but this should occur not through the repressions of his passions but by allowing them to express themselves gradually and harmoniously.

In order to do this, what must be avoided at all costs in education are those occasions which would promote vanity and what Rousseau calls *amour propre* in the child. Education should not corrupt a child's spirit by exciting vicious and unrealisable desires. According to Rousseau the standard education of his time taught everything except self-knowledge and self-control, the arts of life and happiness. The self-sufficient savoyard peasant for whom Rousseau professed unbounded admiration does not need the useless facts and dead knowledge of the arts and sciences. Indeed, in Rousseau's view, only vanity and élitism could motivate a man to spend his life studying in libraries or laboratories. Rousseau is quite prepared to accept the implication of all this, that the education he is advocating is an intellectually restricted one: 'The world of reality has its bounds, the world of imagination is boundless; as we cannot enlarge the one, let us restrict the other'.[3] We should 'desire mediocrity in all things, even in beauty'.[4] Individual excellence, must be sacrificed for a life and an education which brings us closer to a natural goodness and harmony.

Émile, then, is a heady brew, combining nature worship, child-centredness, an emphasis on doing and discovery at the expense of reading and being taught, together with a pervasive hatred of the existing order of things, particularly its competitiveness and élitism from which the child must at all costs be protected. Émile is to be tutored, but much of the tutoring is negative – protecting against the civilised meddling in our nature which makes us evil – and what

[3] Ibid., p. 45.
[4] Ibid., p. 372.

is not negative is (in today's jargon) largely a matter of 'facilitating' what ought to be natural growth of the child into adulthood.

It cannot be said that anyone – even Rousseau himself – accepted every pedagogical recommendation in *Émile*, which as a prescription for education could hardly be applied to more than a very few children. Nevertheless, the spirit of Rousseau's thought has come to infuse practice in education, particularly in early stages. The key themes are those of progressive sequential development in childhood of the child as a natural growth, potentially good if allowed to develop without social interference of the wrong sort, of the vital role of play and discovery, and finally of a roosted hostility to competition and comparison.

All these themes are taken up in one way or another by the influential theorists of early education in the nineteenth century. Johann Heinrich Pestalozzi (1746–1827), unlike Rousseau actually ran schools in his native Switzerland, schools which became a magnet for educational reformers in the years after his death, culminating in a reorganisation of American elementary schools in the 1860s. He emphasised the importance of individual differences between children and also of the role of child-initiated activity, as opposed to the rote learning. Education should develop to its fullest individuality the talent nearly each person possesses by nature: each person had his or her own 'truth'. And to pass to each stage in development the experiences and tasks of the previous stage must be fully mastered. Modern civilisation and formal education do not allow the time needed for this process of organic development replacing deep learning with shallow, unassimilated knowledge which is largely verbal in nature and turning the soul from its deeper self to false and unsatisfiable ambitions.

Similar themes are also found in the work of Friederich Froebel (1782–1852). Education should be seen as part of the work of cosmic evolution, with a stress on the inner development of the individual towards full self-consciousness. It should harmonise with the stage the individual had reached starting with the youngest children with play as their first initiation into purposeful activity. He founded a kindergarten in his native Thuringia in 1837, which became a model for many similar institutions. For a time, in the 1850s his kindergartens were closed on the order of the Prussian authorities (who rightly suspected Froebel of heterodox religious views and liberal political leanings). But the ban lasted only ten years, after which the kindergarten movement and its associated psychological and educational philosophy became unstoppable in the affluent countries of the west.

Maria Montessori (1870–1952), along with Froebel, is perhaps the best known exponent of the view that in their early years children given an environment rich in manipulative materials would largely teach themselves. Although her work began with retarded children, her system or something like it is used in countless primary schools and colleges of teacher education in Western Europe and the USA. In writing as if each child contained within itself some special spark to be ignited into a bright glow, she certainly threw her own spark into the educational tinder box.

Pestalozzi, Froebel and Montessori represent what might be seen as the romantic, though practical wing of child-centrism, romantic because of the high-faluting and largely idealistic philosophy guiding their thought, practical because of their interests in actually organising classrooms. In both these ways, they are precursors of much primary and early years thought and practice today, an amalgam of sentimental romanticism about the child and a practice or set of practices which is said to be justified as practice, and insulated from any whiff of criticism from other theoretical or empirical standpoints.

It is, though, with Piaget (and in moral education with his disciple Laurence Kohlberg) that the idea of education following the sequential development of the child receives its fullest and most systematic exposition in quasi-scientific form. Piaget is mainly famous for devising a number of experiments in the 1930s which were designed to show that children developed abstract categories of thought from concrete operations according to set and pre-determined patterns. For Piaget, logical and mathematical operations manifest themselves first as overt behaviour and are only later internalised in abstract thought. Time, too, is held to be grasped as time only in a relatively late stage of child development, as is the ability to 'de-centre' oneself from one's own perspective. At earlier stages, there will be considerable difficulty for young children in realising that an object stays the same over time, and even more in recognising conservation of quantity, as a substance like water is transferred from a vessel of one shape to a vessel of a different shape. Kohlberg advances similar theses about the development of various kinds of moral reasoning in the child, again supported by observation and experiment.

From a psychological standpoint, Piaget and Kohlberg's work has been subjected to much criticism. Interesting as it undoubtedly is, it is certainly not regarded as final or even first truth. But in one unfortunate sense, it sits all-too well with child centredness in education. To put it bluntly and provocatively, the prestige of Piaget particularly, and Kohlberg to a lesser degree, have licensed generations of teachers being taught to limit their expectations of and ambitions for their pupils according to what 'psychological research' has supposedly said is possible at a given age or stage. The demands of the subject are thus regarded as secondary to contested psychological theory, theory which educational practice will obviously tend to 'confirm' in so far as it is predicated on that theory.

If Rousseau is the one great source of child-centred theory, Dewey is the other. To Rousseau's romanticism and naturalism, and its concentration on individual psychology, Dewey brings the sociological element so notably absent from the thinking of Rousseau's successors, as well as a far more directly political emphasis. For Dewey, education is above all a social and political project, and he was highly critical of what he saw as the misplaced romantic individualism of Mme Montessori and her followers. As he put it as early as 1899, in *The School and Society*, the full meaning of any subject matter

is secured only when the studies (are) presented ... from the standpoint of the relation they bear to the life of society.[5]

Not only that, in *Experience and Education* (of 1938), Dewey conceived the school itself as a 'social enterprise in which all individuals have an opportunity to contribute'. In this social enterprise, the teacher is not an 'external boss or dictator', imposing on children curricular standards alien to their current lives. He or she is rather the leader of group activities, in which his or her

suggestion is not a mould for a cast-iron result, but is a starting point to be developed into a plan through contributions from the experience of all engaged in the learning process.[6]

So, for Dewey, it is not simply that education must shadow the natural growth of the child. There is at the same time a systematic erosion of the authority, teacher and subject, in an effort to recreate both school and curriculum as miniature democracies within, responding to social needs and influences without. These themes and their educational implications are developed at great length in *Democracy and Education*, Dewey's major educational treatise, which was published in 1916.

According to *Democracy and Education*, traditional schools substitute a bookish, pseudo-intellectual spirit for a social spirit. They may secure specialised technical abilities in algebra, Latin or botany, but 'not the kind of intelligence which directs ability to useful

[5] J. Dewey, *The School and Society* (1899), quoted here in the Phoenix Books edition, 1963, p. 100.

[6] J. Dewey, *Experience and Education* (1938), quoted here in the Collier Books edition, 1963, p. 72.

141

ends'.[7] True learning, by contrast, produces skills which are trans-
ferable (in the modern jargon), socially useful and eminently
sharable. The value of an activity or of a form of social life is judged
by how far it is shared by all members of the group in which it takes
place, and by how far the group which generates it interacts with
other groups.

Dewey is, in fact, fundamentally hostile to social divisions of all
sorts, seeing them as barriers to that demotic sharing of interests
and mutual transparency of communication which for him is characteristic of true democracy, true culture and true education. Any
division between the learned and the unlearned, he sees as due to a
selfish hemming-off of one class from another. Any production of
works or thoughts which cannot be fully and freely communicated
to all men, he sees as symptomatic of a rotten, selfish and spiritual
society, 'spiritual' being for him a term of abuse. Any insistence on
the singularity of a national or local culture against cosmopoli-
tanism (multi-culturalism), he sees as offending humanity, a crime
of which all systems of education up to now are guilty.[8]

Education, then, is for Dewey either a means by which boundaries
can be set up and reinforced, or a means of breaking them down.
Education can erect boundaries of various sorts, between classes of
men, between distinct subjects of study, between élites and non-
élites, between nations. But if we fully appreciate our common needs
as human beings and the importance of solving our problems together and of democracy as a mode of living in which experiences are
shared as widely as possible, we will look to education to break down
stratifications and distinctions of all sorts. While Dewey defines culture as the capacity for constantly expanding the range and accuracy
of one's perceptions of meanings, it is clear that he is really more
interested in the former – range in terms of the numbers of people
with whom one shares perceptions, rather than accuracy.

Arguing against the identification of culture with the possession
of something inner, he writes:

> the idea of perfecting an 'inner' personality is a sure sign of social
> divisions. What is called inner is simply that which does not connect
> with others – which is not capable of free and full communication.
> What is termed spiritual culture has usually been futile, with some-
> thing rotten about it, just because it has been conceived as a thing
> which a man might have internally – and therefore exclusively.[9]

[7] J. Dewey, *Democracy and Education* (1916), quoted here in the Free
Press edition, 1966, p 39.

[8] Ibid., pp. 98ff.

[9] Ibid., p. 122.

It is hard to say whether Dewey fully realised the consequences of his view: that it would make much of the culture of the middle ages futile and rotten, to say nothing of the writings of, say, Pascal, Kierkegaard and T. S. Eliot.

He also wrote that for some (of whom he disapproves)

> feelings and ideas are turned upon themselves, instead of being methods in acts which modify conditions. Their mental life is sentimental: an enjoyment of an inner landscape. Even the pursuit of science may become an asylum of refuge from the hard conditions of life – not a temporary retreat for the sake of recuperation and clarification in future dealings with the world. The very word art may become associated not with specific transformations of things ... but with stimulations of eccentric fancy and with emotional indulgences.[10]

The conclusion to which one is inescapably drawn here is that, like Rousseau, Dewey would not have shrunk from the mediocrity which must follow upon any general acceptance of his views of democracy and education.

Dewey's reductionism regarding content is manifested in his assertion that 'in the last analysis, all that the educator can do is to modify stimuli'[11] so as to produce desirable intellectual and emotional dispositions in the pupil. We need not deny that the production of desirable dispositions is an aim of education; what is at issue here is whether they can be produced without the child being introduced to specific bodies of knowledge and experience. Can, for example, a child learn to do physics without studying the content of modern physical theory? From where else will he derive a sense of what a problem is in physics, or indeed, of its solution? Equally, can a child learn to draw or paint without being introduced either at first or second hand to the discoveries made by the great artists of the past in their masterpieces? Of the rules of perspective, say? The gaining of an intellectual disposition can be likened to the learning of a language in that both expression and discovery of new meanings depend on mastery of a pre-existing structure. And, as we learn from Aristotle, much the same is true of moral and emotional dispositions; it is only when we learned to love the good and honouring the noble requires that we are taught which things are good and which actions noble – a knowledge of the content of morality, in other words.

Dewey, by contrast, is insistent that the teacher or, even worse, a book, is not to 'supply solutions ready-made' to pupils.[12] His oppo-

[10] Ibid., pp. 135–6.
[11] Ibid., p. 180.
[12] Ibid., p. 157.

nents would agree that there is little to be said for filling the child's mind with information just for its own sake. But Dewey would reject any knowledge which cannot be busily and quickly put to use, doing something, improving social conditions, solving problems. For him unapplied knowledge is 'static' 'cold-storage', 'miscellaneous junk' cluttering the mind and likely to impede truly educative processes.

It is hardly surprising that Dewey disparages the 'acquisition of information for purposes of reproduction in recitation and examination'[13] given his stress on what would today be called active learning, which leads him to speak of 'the child of three who discovers what can be done with blocks, or of six who finds out what he can make by five cents and five cents together' as 'really a discoverer'.[14] All thinking, he insists, is research, and all research is original with him who carries it on, even if everyone else in the world already knows what the researcher is looking for. Dewey's critics can fairly point out that much of what on this view counts as research would be a most inefficient use of the researcher's time, forcing him to re-discover for himself myriads of things which are already known. More profoundly, they may question the possibility of conducting any research which does not emerge from a background of largely inactive knowledge against which the researcher makes his initial guesses as to the nature of a problem, the point of solving it, the likely solutions, the most economical methods for testing them.

The idea of each learner and each child as an original thinker, as a kind of miniature scientist researching into his own problems largely for himself, will increasingly tend to upgrade the intellectual value of early learning, and therefore downgrade the very real difference between that and the true originality which can exist only at high levels of human endeavour. Dewey, in common with the romantics, underplays the role of formal instruction in the transmission of human knowledge, or at least this is how he was and is read.[15]

There is indeed a connection between Dewey's view of the child as an original thinker and his attempt to use education and the cur-

---

[13] Ibid., p. 158.

[14] Ibid., p. 159.

[15] Perhaps at this point it is worth remarking that as a writer Dewey was nothing if not inclusive. If in many places he insisted on the child discovering things for himself, at others he also stresses the need for adult guidance and even if not over enthusiastically for bodies of existing knowledge. Nevertheless the fact remains that he did say all the things that I attribute to him, and that many of those who have read him have been influenced by that aspect of his thought.

riculum as a means of establishing a radically egalitarian version of democracy. Democracy for Dewey is not as it is for Karl Popper, say, primarily a means of removing governments regularly and peacefully; it was primarily a matter of living together, sharing experience and fraternal problem-solving. As with Rousseau and his notion of the general will, Dewey was splendidly unaware of the potential for collectivist bossiness, not to say tyranny inherent in such notions, and thus less interested than he should have been in that control of governments which is implied in the ability of the people to remove them.

Education, however, was certainly a political project for Dewey. Thereby we are all to learn about participation and communal problem-solving: hence the attacks on the inner life and on educational authorities. In the content of education, we are to concentrate on essentials, 'the things which are socially most fundamental, which have to do with the experiences in which the widest groups share';[16] hence the attacks on educational élites and assessments. In its crudest terms, what is not part of everyone's experience and problems, including those of children, is at best inessential in a democratic education, mere dead lumber from the past, and at worst a throw-back to a divided, class-ridden form of existence. But an education animated by a social spirit will be a prime means of building up a common experience in which all share, and which will break down distinctions between classes of men, between subjects of study and between school and the world outside.

For Dewey the main aim of schooling is to build up a community life:

> In place of a school set apart from life as a place for learning lessons, we have a miniature social group in which study and growth are incidents of present shared experience.[17]

It is crucial to this project that the interests of the school connect with those of the community outside. Dewey does not seek a monastic or college atmosphere, and is wary of any adherence in the school to the culture of the past. The modern world, its problems and the concerns of the future world are where the emphasis should be. This attachment to the experience of the present and to present problems leads him to denigrate the study of history and literature, except in so far as those subjects can throw light on the present. Such stress on present relevance actually takes Dewey as close as can be to a relativistic notion of truth:

[16] Dewey, *Democracy and Education*, p. 191.
[17] Ibid., p. 358.

No matter how true what is learned was to those who found it out and in whose experience it functioned, there is nothing which makes it knowledge to the pupils. It might as well be something about Mars or about some fanciful country unless it fructifies in the individual's own life.[18]

What fructifies in the life of present individuals is not that which is true in some absolute or timeless sense, but that which enables them to modify their present experiences and social conditions in response to present unsettlement. As long as a topic makes an immediate appeal to pupils, we need not ask what it is good for. It is good enough that it responds to some present interest of the pupil.

To satisfy our current biological and social needs, past authorities in education must be jettisoned. They are likely to make pupils unhappy with the modern world and to distract them from it. History and literature must be displaced from the centre of the curriculum in favour of social studies: the stress on classics and master-pieces in traditional education must be replaced by a scientific and experimental attitude, in which beliefs and values formed at first hand have far more validity than anything handed down by tradition.

With Dewey, this dismissive attitude went hand in hand with a belief in the power of unfettered and contemporary human reason to solve the problems we are confronted with, and also with a belief in the need to submit our activities – economic, educational, social – to collective central planning. It is impossible to over-emphasise the degree to which Dewey's educational views imply a specific view of man and of society; in criticising Dewey and the educational philosophy he has influenced, we will also be taking issue with the underlying anthropology and politics.

What is true of Dewey is true *mutatis mutandis* of Rousseau and the educational romantics. Their educational prescriptions are not and cannot be isolated from a general view of man and society, one which encourages free and natural individuals and which will be critical of any tendency in society which appears repressive or authoritarian. As we have suggested in considering Dewey such an approach overlooks the extent to which knowledge, learning and culture depend on external authority and are far removed from immediate political and social concerns. As far as society as a whole is concerned, a very real question must remain over the extent to which any society can be as egalitarian as Rousseau wanted or as democratic and multicultural as Dewey advocated without lapsing into anarchy and incoherence if not at least into the mediocrity of TV and the mass media.

[18] Ibid., pp. 341–2.

Some of these doubts become even more pronounced when we consider the way these approaches to education have been translated into the approach to psychology by Abraham Maslow, Carl Rogers and their followers. These approaches are not only clearly influenced by the thought of Rousseau and Dewey, but they have in their turn been highly influential in the world of education in Britain as well as the United States. Late in his life (significantly, in 1969) Maslow came to regret what he saw in America of the lack of a sense of evil, and among his students of any sense of a distinction between who should teach and who should learn. Maslow actually wrote in his diary for 14 April 1969, that the problem with the college faculties of the day was that they lack a theory of evil

> and so don't know what to do in the face of viciousness. This non-theory of evil, it occurred to me, is one peculiar version of the 'value-free' disease (which is the same as ethical relativism, of Rousseauistic optimism, of amorality, i.e., nothing is wrong or bad enough to fight against) ... What kind of educational philosophy is it that is unprepared for ill will?

The only problem with this heart-felt plea from a disillusioned educator was that for most of his career he himself had in his psychological theory and practice attempted to be a 'facilitator of learning' rather than an authority, sought to promote autonomy and self-actualisation above all else, had in Rousseauesque fashion sought to liberate feelings repressed into the unconscious, and had clung to the theory of universal benevolence – all points with obvious philosophical antecedents, and in Britain from the 1920s onwards all increasingly firmly embedded in what came to be seen as the best educational practice, in both moral and academic education.

By the late 1960s Maslow was having doubts: but doubts were only later to assail the mind of his psychological colleague Carl Rogers, the founder of what has come to be known as client-centred psychology. Central to Roger's psychology was the notion of personal growth, a notion also central to Dewey philosophy generally and his ideas on education in particular. Dewey had written in *Democracy and Education* that the process of education has no end beyond itself, that growth is the characteristic of life, and also that education is all one with growing. In sum, there is nothing to which education is subordinate save more education – a clear antecedent of the notion of 'life-long learning' and of the concept, dear to present-day educational gurus that what is significant in education is not content, but process, problem-solving and yet more education.

Rogers translated all this into psychological and educational practice. As he himself put it, in his system the teacher or professor will largely have disappeared. His place will be taken by a facilitator of learning, chosen for his facilitative attitudes as much for his knowledge ... We shall ... see the facilitator focusing his major attention on the prime period for learning – from infancy to the age of six or eight. Every child will develop confidence in his own ability to learn, since he will be rewarded for learning at his own pace.

We will be confronted again and again with the thought that what matters in education is learning not teaching, process not content. The Rogerian student

will learn to be an individual not a faceless conformist. ... He will find that learning, even difficult learning, is fun, both as an individual activity and in co-operation with others ... His learning ... will be, in itself, an experience in living. Feelings of inadequacy, hatred, a desire for power, feelings of love and awe and respect, feelings of fear and dread, unhappiness with parents and with other children – all these will be an open part of his curriculum, as worthy of exploration as history or mathematics ... the student will never be graduated. He will always be part of a 'commencement'.[19]

This is Rousseau out of Dewey, an unhappy amalgam of Dewey's growth theory and a Rousseauesque stress on the individual and his or her inner state as a subject of awe and fascination. In Rogers' own psychological practice, counselling was 'non-directive', self-directive growth from within. The psychiatrist facilitated, but made no judgement. If this non-directiveness has not yet become standard practice in education, it certainly has its toe-hold there. This is so particularly in theorising in moral education, and in the highly influential values-clarification movement, where the aim is not to tell pupils what to do, but rather to enable them to recover and expound the sources and implications of the values they turn out to have on examination of their inner attitudes to various situations, real or imagined. This parody of moral education was foreshadowed as early as 1926 by Dewey's influential disciple W. H. Kilpatrick, when he wrote that

Our young people face too clearly an unknown future. We dare not pretend that the old solutions will suffice for them ... Our youth no longer accept authoritarian morals. We must develop then a point of view and devise a correlative educational system which shall take adequate account of this fact of ever increasing change. Otherwise civilisation itself seems threatened.[20]

[19] C. R. Rogers, 'Interpersonal Relationships,': USA 2000, *Journal of Applied Behavioural Science*, 4 (3), 1968, pp. 274–5

[20] W. H. Kilpatrick, *Education for a Changing Civilisation* (New York: Macmillan, 1929) pp. 41, 49–50.

Even in 1926 relativism must have seemed a curious remedy for an impending collapse of civilisation; but one cannot fail but be struck by how old and cliché-ridden are political and educational appeals to the pace of change. As far as moral education goes however, value clarification proves to be the ultimate abrogation of teacherly authority:

> An increasing number of students are no longer willing to tolerate a curriculum that does not acknowledge their needs, interests and concerns... Are we to tell them what to value and how to live ... in the hope that they will listen? No. None of us can be certain that our values are right for other people.[21]

There are, of course, significant differences between the various figures we have looked at in this brief survey of progressive educational thought since the time of Rousseau, not least in the differing emphases given to the social context of the school. When contrasted with a traditional approach to education – as being the teaching from without of the best that has been thought and known, regardless of the child's immediate interests, social needs in general or immediate applications of what is learned – what the progressives have in common is far more striking and has been far more influential than what separates them. Standard educational thought in Britain over the last thirty years looks very much like an amalgam of the progressive themes together with doctrines of self-esteem; a stress on learning rather than on teaching; a disparagement of subjects without immediate interest and relevance; a hostility to hard and fast externally imposed standards (regarded as antithetical to the natural development of the child) and, conversely, an obsessive harping on the cultivation of individual difference; egalitarianism within school and without; a hostility to didactic and authoritarian approaches to education and morality; in the early stages particularly an emphasis on play, discovery and practical activities, at the expense of structured and particularly bookish approaches to learning; the notion of the child as a 'researcher', actively constructing his or her own 'knowledge'; and finally the idea of education itself as, in the large sense, a political project, having to do with the reconstruction of society and the self-discovery and self-creation of the learner.

To the amalgam of Rousseauan and Deweyesque ideas should be added two further themes which are currently highly influential in

---

[21] M. Harmin, H. Kirschenbaum and S. Simons, *Clarifying Values Through Subject Matter. Applications for the Classroom* (Minneapolis: Hart, 1973), p. 31.

education: while not explicitly present in either thinker they certainly sit well with their ideas. The first of these is the notion of self-esteem and the hostility to sharp or externally imposed discipline. That self-esteem is an *idée fixe* in Britain of 2000, and not merely among educators, hardly needs underlining. While Dewey would doubtless have been critical of the notion as currently deployed (if it was unhealthily 'inner' and not linked to actual problem-solving) and while Rousseau was, of course, the self-critical, self-analytical author of *Confessions* (though that itself could be seen as the ultimate tribute to his own self-esteem), self-esteem can be seen as a logical extension of some of their ideas, as we have suggested in considering Maslow and Rogers.

Thus, from Rousseau we certainly derive the notion that human beings are naturally good: 'the first impulses of nature are always right'; 'God made all things good, man meddles with them and they become evil.' The child, if not exactly a noble savage, should learn that all his passions are good, provided they are not perverted or unnaturally repressed. And what is *amour propre* but an obsessive absence of self-esteem, seeking compensation and reinforcement from the ever fickle and unreliable opinions of others?

As far as Dewey is concerned, hostility to class-divisions and a stress on the contributions each individual has it in his power to make, however backward on conventional criteria, certainly forms the basis for the cultivation of individual self-esteem. For, without the confidence which comes from self-esteem, individuals will not play the part in group work and discussion which Dewey is hoping for, nor will they give their own growth the significance Dewey accords it.

Relativism, like self-esteem is not explicitly part of the programmes of either Rousseau or Dewey. On the other hand, both espouse forms of egalitarianism which are conducive to relativism. Rousseau is highly critical of the pretensions of cultural, academic and social élites; in *Émile* it is the humble Savoyard vicar whose wisdom is esteemed. Dewey regards all social groups as having a valid contribution to make to the educational project, however unqualified they may be on existing criteria. He inveighed against national sovereignty and was always in favour of the 'new and broader environment' which would result from the intermingling in schools of young people from different races, customs and religions.

None of this is precisely relativism, but it certainly suggests that educators should not seek to impose of pupils the cultural standards of existing élites. It would provide a very good basis for the theories of thinkers such as Althusser or Foucault, for whom much of the existing school curriculum and educational organisation (including literary canons and traditional styles of assessment) are little more than the means by which those currently in power simply reinforce their position, parts of the ideological apparatus of state hegemony in Althusser's terms. It would also provide a ready foundation for feminist and neo-Marxist pleas that the voices of the white middle-class males be silenced in order that we (or, more accurately, our children) attend to those of the dispossessed and the previously unheard (women, ethnic minorities, homosexuals, the traditional working class). Both Rousseau and Dewey explicitly saw many judgements of cultural evaluation as little more than the positioning of those who have much to gain from refusing to admit other voices into the pantheon. Of course, as things stand now in Britain, precisely the reverse is true. One has to move heaven and earth to get compulsory Shakespeare papers or grammar into public examinations, and over 500 academics from university English departments (including Oxbridge professors) condemn governmental attempts to draw up a list of recommended authors from before the twentieth century as 'philistine'. We cannot know if Rousseau or Dewey would have approved, but such reactions are certainly in the spirit of their thought.

So, one suspects, is the hostility one finds in British education to objective testing, and most especially to the testing of intelligence. Such measures are decried variously as being 'unreliable', simply a measure of how far the norms of existing élites have been internalised and, above all, are divisive. While Rousseau nor Dewey would not have gone along with the extreme environmentalism of some current thought – according to which there is no such thing as native intelligence, or if there is, it cannot be measured – there are certainly aspects of their thinking which would support attacks on any current types of test. From Rousseau, they would appear simply to reinforce existing and suspect modes of thought (analytical, life-denying, 'logocentric', in to-day's jargon); from Dewey they would reinforce undesirable divisions in society, as well as privileging the modes of thought of those already dominant. While neither Rousseau nor Dewey believed nurture was all in upbringing, they would both obviously be unsympathetic to anything (such as intelligence tests) which appeared to cast doubts on (in Rousseau's case) the spark within each child or (in Dewey's case) the validity of every perspective on a question. The way they each conceive democracy and equality would undoubtedly have made them and those influenced by them hostile to the notion that people should be graded for intellectual ability on a metric scale, particularly if there was any suggestion that there was something final and definitive about the results of such grading. The suggestion that there might be offends

Anthony O'Hear

anyone with either sentimental or egalitarian leanings, which goes some way to explain the unprecedented disdain in which Sir Cyril Burt is currently held in educational circles. Burt claimed to have produced good evidence for innate intelligence, and evidence that it could be measured. His detractors, after his death, accused him of fraud, an accusation widely and uncritically accepted, and anyone casting doubt on it is likely to receive short shrift in most departments of education today. But the accusation is itself suspect. It has itself been trenchantly criticised, and its lazy repetition in academic circles is itself a scandal.[22]

Before closing this essay on the philosophy underlying current educational orthodoxy, it is worth remarking once more that – on his own admission – Rousseau's educational proposals are hardly suited to mass education. But, perhaps more surprisingly, no more are Dewey's.

John Brubacher in his *A History of the Problems of Education*[23] describes the laboratory school Dewey founded in Chicago in 1894 as follows:

> Dewey thought it was an archaic practice for elementary schools to spend 75 to 80 per cent of their time on verbal studies. While such a proportion might have been proper before the invention of printing, in the twentieth century it amounted to forcing a middle- and upper-class education on the mass of the population. In place of such an education Dewey substituted one centering in ... the current social occupations of the home and community with which the child was becoming increasingly familiar. Thus, Dewey's school started with household occupations. From here foods and textiles were later traced to the source of their production. Still later, occupations were seen in their historical setting. Number work was done incidentally to occupations like carpentry and cooking. Reading and writing began in the children's keeping of their own records. These and other activities were all conceived in a social context, for it was Dewey's idea that education was the regulation of a process whereby the child came increasingly to share in the social consciousness.[24]

Much of this could have been predicted on the basis of Dewey's writings; indeed, part of the practice is actually laid out by Dewey in *The School and Society* in 1899. Equally, the extent to which Dewey's practice seems unremarkable to us today shows how far

[22] See Robert Joynson, *The Burt Affair* (London: Routledge, 1989).
[23] John Brubacher, *A History of the Problems of Education* (New York: McGraw-Hill, 1966).
[24] Ibid., p. 389.

152

ideas of the sort which he expounded so insistently have captured the less than commanding heights of educational theory during the course of our century. It is thought worth observing here that Dewey's own school started with three teachers for thirty-two pupils, rose to sixteen teachers for sixty children and ended with twenty-three teachers plus ten assistants for 140 children. Whether or not a child-centred education such as Dewey advocated is a good thing, we cannot but agree with Dewey and his followers that to be successful an education based on the child, his interests and ever-changing personality is bound to be extremely labour intensive. We should remember this point when we hear – yet again – that education is 'under-resourced'; conversely we might observe that there must be something very peculiar about a teaching system which fails to produce some impressive results when operating with the pupil-teacher ratios Dewey allowed himself. We might also re-call the findings of Robin Alexander in Leeds as to the extremely high amounts of time wasted in primary schools when pupils are broken into groups to carry out their own tasks (up to 40 per cent). We should never overlook the sheer inefficiency of teaching methods other than interactive whole-class teaching, in terms of pupil–teacher contact and pupil distraction.

The myths, though, continue to be promulgated. In his *John Dewey and the High Tide of American Liberalism*, Alan Ryan had this to say about Deweyesque pedagogy:

> His (Dewey's) stress on task-oriented and co-operative learning remains the basis of good elementary school teaching today – indeed, not only there but all the way up to graduate school. To the extent that countries such as Britain practice it more effectively at primary level than does the United States, and Japan and China all the way through the educational system, the loss is not Dewey's but the present generation of schoolchildren.[25]

For those who have read *Worlds Apart*, it is surprising to see British educational practice held up as a model. Any loss is *our* children's precisely because *they* have Dewey inflicted on them.

I will close this essay with three specific, but not uncharacteristic examples of how educational theory translates into contemporary practice in Britain. The first of these concerns the very practical matter of classroom organisation; but underlying the practice is the rather more profound question of what classrooms are for.

Dewey reports in *The School and Society* that he found it very dif-

---

[25] Alan Ryan, *John Dewey and the High Tide of American Liberalism* (New York: Norton, 1996) p. 187.

ficult to find the desks and chairs he needed for his University Elementary School in the Chicago of the 1890s. Finally, overlooking the fact that reading and writing are certainly types of work, one dealer said to him: 'I am afraid we have not what you want. You want something at which the children may work; these are all for listening.'[26] Even if the dealer could not supply Dewey with furniture, he gave him what he wanted philosophically in the admission that old-fashioned school furniture was not designed to enable pupils to move around the classroom at will. Nearly one hundred years later Her Majesty's Inspectors of Schools lambasted Shakespeare's school, King Edward VI School at Stratford-on-Avon for its reliance on 'traditional' methods; they seemed particularly concerned because at Stratford many lessons were, in the old sense, didactic: but, even worse, in many of these lessons pupils were listening 'attentively' and even 'with evident enjoyment'. Instead of treating this observation and the excellent academic record of the school as an answer to Dewey's story, the Inspectors insisted that this attentive and enjoyable listening must stop: 'the needs of the pupils in the late twentieth century require the introduction of new procedures, new methods and new courses'.

If the Inspectors repeated revolutionary ideas of the eighteenth and nineteenth century as though they were established wisdom in 1989, these ideas also find more than an echo in current teacher education. In a report in *The Guardian* (4 December 1990), Edward Pilkington wrote about the School of Education at Roehampton Institute, one of the principal institutions of teacher training in the country:

> Only five weeks into the course [students] have begun to absorb the message that will be hammered home with monotonous regularity throughout their four years at Roehampton: children should not be told what to do, but encouraged to learn for themselves. Their tutor, Graham Welch, assistant dean of education, tells the class that the key to learning is play: 'You have to realise that everybody including big kids like us, learns through play.' This approach rapidly becoming the norm in teacher training establishments and primary schools, stems from the idea that children learn at their own pace and according to their unique level of understanding. The traditional model of teacher standing in front of the whole class cannot work because the lesson will be too simple for some pupils, while leaving others behind. A more democratic and appropriate approach, says Roehampton, is to start with each child's understanding and develop from there.

[26] J. Dewey, *The School and Society*, p. 31.

Thus the institute advocates that children should be given some control over how they spend their time in school, or in Roehampton – they should have the right to negotiate their own curriculum. 'Negotiated curriculum is an idea rooted in a concept of democracy', says Graham Welch. There is a lot of evidence to suggest that children as young as three are better motivated if they have a say in the way their day is organised.

It is not too hard to recognise the roots of this talk of learning through activity and of pupils learning for themselves. In common, though, with many places where there is much talk of democracy, negotiation and participation, at Roehampton in 1990, according to *The Guardian*, openness did not extend to the admission of pedagogical viewpoints other than those espoused by Rousseau, Dewey and their followers.

A third vignette from the contemporary educational landscape may be drawn from the interim report of the National Curriculum Working Group on Music of 1990 which offered the following prescription for music teaching:

> Knowledge about music should be taught in the context of practical musical activities: that is, the needs of a particular task in listening, composing and performing should determine the facts to be taught. (Section 3.8)

That this statement should be offered without defence or comment – and similar statements may be found in discussions of all the other subjects in the National Curriculum – shows how far ideas on learning through practice and discovery, rather than through laid-down programmes of knowledge to be mastered, have come to dominate educational thinking. So there is no need to be surprised that the authors of the music document place stress on pop and rock music of various sorts (after all, do we not know that we need to modify traditional ideas of culture to respond to the demands of youth, and that as long as any topic makes an immediate appeal, we are not to ask what it is good for?) or that they make the apparently bizarre suggestion that children of seven or eight years old devise their own ways of notating sounds (for haven't we learned that childish spontaneity and experiment is of far greater experiential and educational worth than the absorption of information and solutions provided by others, teachers and the like?).

These three examples illustrate fairly comprehensively a whole philosophy in practice. We have said enough of its educational implications and presuppositions. What these examples bring out is something of its political implications and presuppositions, anti-elitist, anti-meritocratic, anti-dogmatic, collectivist, self-consciously progressive, egalitarian, adumbrating a form of radical democracy in which notions of authority and of quality and, in the final resort, of truth itself have become suspect. Teachers may not think of themselves as political radicals or as philosophers; but the ideas which have come to dominate their profession in this country since the war are closely linked to the politics of radical egalitarianism, and, more remotely, to the philosophical sources of that radicalism.

What did John Dewey Want?

ALAN RYAN

Introduction

Although this essay focuses on the ideas of one individual—the American philosopher of education, John Dewey—its purpose is to raise questions about those ideas rather than their author. Dewey is famous for inventing (or spreading) some familiar ideas: that educational reform is at the heart of creating a democratic society, that the classroom is as important to democracy as the polling booth, that the central aim of education is to foster the individuality of the child and that teachers must teach children how to think for themselves rather than pass on cut and dried knowledge. These ideas have been resisted by philosophers who have thought that the aim of education is to teach children some defined and circumscribed skills, or to transmit to them as much factual information as they can usefully be given during their school years. They have also been resisted by thinkers who have wanted to limit the scope of education, to say that schools exist to serve limited, non-political purposes, and that 'schooling' properly ends at sixteen, eighteen, or twenty-one when it sends adequately educated students out into the world to earn a living, raise a family, and do their wider social and political duty.

Of course, the opposition is not as stark as that; writing a century ago, Dewey expected most children to leave school at fourteen, he expected them to learn a great many facts and to acquire a great many skills, and he had no difficulty in distinguishing schoolteachers from politicians. Still, he had a distinctive view of the purpose of education; he defined the animating principle of modern liberal societies as 'intelligent action', explained the point of democracy as 'full and unfettered communication on the basis of freedom and equality', and looked to education to bring everyone within the scope of liberal democracy so defined.

There has recently been, both in Britain and in the United States, a 'back to basics' movement. Since the call for 'back to basics' amounts to a rejection of the ambitions of 'progressive education' it is not entirely astonishing, although it certainly is astonishing, that some advocates of back to basics have thought that the influence of John Dewey is at the root of many of the problems of contemporary education. Richard Pring, Professor of Education at Oxford, tells the story of encountering the late Sir Keith Joseph, then Secretary of State for Education at a public meeting, and being berated by him for corrupting British teachers by introducing them to Dewey. Dewey's ability to enrage his critics almost fifty years after his death is impressive. After all, he was born in 1859 in Vermont, grew up in a devout Congregationalist household, went to the local university, did graduate work at the newly founded Johns Hopkins University, and spent the whole of his life as a professor of philosophy, most importantly at Chicago for ten years from 1894 and at Columbia University in New York from 1904 until not long before his death in 1952 at the age of 92. He was far from being a rabble-rouser. He was a very dull lecturer; and he was a baffling writer—not exactly boring, but certainly very often inscrutable. But in his lifetime and ever since, he has been a lightning conductor for critics, mostly from the conservative end of the spectrum, but also from the far left. He has been accused of promoting 'child-centred education'; of having a naively Rousseauist faith in the intrinsic goodness of children; of having wanted to teach children how to think, but undermining in the process the task of giving them something to think about. The Marxian left always complained that he believed in the possibility of democracy in the teeth of the inequalities and oppression of capitalist society, while the right accused him of encouraging otherwise satisfied workers to aspire to a level of education and a degree of self-government that are sheerly impossible. The devout accused him of having undermined traditional religion as an indispensable classroom aid, and the aggressively atheistic thought he made far too many concessions to the godly.

I am not about to defend Dewey; he is distinguished enough to look after himself, and so quirky that it would be an impertinence to get in his way. I shall claim that a world in which an education of the sort he advocated was a reality would be a better world than ours—for most, but not for all, of us; but I shan't suggest that the mass production of such an education is even possible, let alone that it is easy. As to Dewey's influence, I believe the truth is disappointingly simple: it was vastly less than his detractors believe, and vastly less than his disciples hoped. To the extent that he had a direct impact on classroom practice it was because he caught a tide that Froebel, Herbart, Mme Montessori and Margaret Macmillan set in motion. So far as Britain is concerned, where Dewey's views about educational practice could not be assimilated to theirs, his views made little headway. Even in the United States, they made less than one might suppose. The decentralisation of American education, the domination of discussion by conservative and Christian forces, and the utilitarian emphasis that most school boards placed on the education they were offering, meant that Dewey, who was an urban, secular, socialist and utopian philosopher was unlikely to have much practical impact. Left-wing English enthusiasts for progressive education, whether at secondary schools such as Dartington Hall and Bedales, or at Bertrand Russell's Beacon Hill and A. S. Neil's Summerhill, had their own reasons for taking little interest in Dewey, some of them to do with their greater political intransigence, and some to do with their interest in sexual emancipation—a subject on which Dewey was utterly silent.

Why does Dewey have the reputation he does? What follows will explain that in passing. But here are some elements of the answer. First, Dewey appeals to teachers because he was a teacher-centred theorist, and teachers have always been at odds with the school boards that employ them. The usual division between child-centred theorists and syllabus-centred theorists left Dewey cold, and did no justice at all to the views he in fact held. In 1895, he published a short piece called 'My Pedagogic Creed', from which I shall shortly quote at some length; its content explains why teachers thought he was wonderful—even if they never 'applied' his work in the classroom. The second is that he thought that the object of education was—*inter alia*—to encourage in children the capacity to think critically. This is associated in the minds of Dewey's detractors with a hostility to the idea that education should involve learning substantial quantities of facts, so Dewey is blamed for what critics think are the failures in factual teaching and learning characteristic of British and American schools in the past forty years or so. The third is that Dewey's educational philosophy was unabashedly political. Its politics are not easy to describe, but they are certainly democratic, liberal-to-socialist, and reformist. Dewey imagined education as the process whereby young people are socialised into an adult world; but the world into which he wished them to be socialised was not the world as it is but the world as it might be made. Most critics complained that Dewey was a utopian radical. But one astute early critic, his former teacher the psychologist G. Stanley Hall, observed that Dewey could easily play into the hands of the conservatives; the emphasis on the need to socialise children into loyalty to their community might be meant to encourage loyalty to a future and better society, but it could be distorted so as to promote the socialisation of children into the community as it now exists. Forty years later, Hofstadter's *Anti-Intellectualism in America* blamed the 'Life Adjustment' classes inflicted on 1950s high school children in the United States on Dewey. Needless to say, it was not Dewey's intention to stimulate a movement embodied in such multiple-choice questions as 'do we need to use shampoo?' and in classes on how to become popular.

Both from left and right, however, the defenders of high intellectual standards dislike any idea that education is essentially political. Many writers on education believe we can have an educational system that is somehow *politikfrei*. Dewey himself insisted on preserving the elementary distinction between the classroom and the political platform. But *Democracy and Education*—the most famous of his books, published in 1916—treats Plato and Rousseau as the two most interesting educational theorists a writer on education can engage with, and neither exactly kept politics out of education. What was most interesting about them from Dewey's point of view was that they stood to either side of him on almost every important issue. However, there was one methodological issue where they were on the same side and at odds with him. Since Dewey was frequently denounced for his 'Rousseauist' tendencies—particularly for believing in the intrinsic goodness of the child's nature, it is an issue worth getting out of the way. Both Plato and Rousseau thought that nature set a standard for education; education was a matter of bringing the child's mind and character into line with what nature endowed him or her with. Dewey disliked appeals to 'nature.' He refused to say that nature sets moral or political standards, and thought that identifying the 'natural' with what is good was a crass philosophical error.

In *Democracy and Education*, however, it was the contrast between Plato and Rousseau that most concerned him. Just like Dewey, Plato saw that education required the socialisation of the child into the community he or she was destined to join; and the community Plato imagined in the *Republic* was even less like the community they could encounter in everyday Athenian life than the community of Dewey's imagining was like urban America. But the divergence imagined by Plato was, of course, in exactly the opposite direction to the one imagined by Dewey. The community Plato had in mind was hierarchical and despotic; it was not only undemocratic, but anti-democratic; its conception of individual happiness was for each of us to find an appropriate slot in the social (and therefore the natural) order, and to realise our potential by doing what that slot required of us.

This Platonic vision has much in common with the vision of education that seems to be held by the present Labour government; this is not surprising, since stripped of Plato's metaphysics, the emphasis on employability that dominates contemporary government policy is the standard non-liberal, narrowly vocational vision of education. Rousseau, in contrast, minded very much that the individual whose education he lovingly described in *Emile* should grow up free and uncorrupted, and fit to be a citizen of the democratic republic delineated in the *Social Contract*. The trouble was that he could be a citizen of nowhere else. Rousseau supposed that young *Emile* had no chance of growing up free and uncorrupted in eighteenth century France, and one of Dewey's objections to the whole Rousseauian enterprise was that it is essentially defensive. *Emile* was to be educated untainted by the social influences that would corrupt him. To Dewey, this seemed a slightly insane exercise, even in imagination; we only become the persons we are by learning how to live with others in a community. Nor did Dewey suppose that preserving anything was what education was about. He certainly shared Rousseau's antipathy to the concept of Original Sin, for its denunciation of which *Emile* was condemned and burned by the public hangman; but he did not follow Rousseau in saying that everything was good as it came from the hand of God and depraved only through the influence of society. The canard that Dewey was Rousseauist in this sense is oft-repeated, but becomes no less silly by repetition. To say there is no Original Sin was only to say that human beings could build a happier and freer society without their efforts being undermined by a sense that it was hopeless because human beings were irredeemably flawed.

A fourth reason for the dislike with which Dewey was regarded by both the Christian right and the hard left emerges when we see why Dewey denied the existence of Original Sin. The reason Dewey wished to deny Original Sin was, oddly enough, because he wanted to preserve a religious attitude to the world while disabusing his readers of any hankering after 'supernaturalism'. As his essay *A Common Faith* written in 1934 insisted, his intention was to remove the taste for religion—that is, for the organised, separate, theologically-encumbered practices of particular and contradictory faiths—while encouraging a taste for the religious, that is, for the frame of mind which sees nature and the world at large as a proper home for the human species. The trouble with religion is, or was, more properly a problem with the kind of high-minded New England Congregationalist protestantism practised by his mother.

Mrs Dewey's God was emphatically the God of the last judgment, and of standards we could never hope to meet. The consequence for Dewey was what he termed 'an inward laceration', and as a form of moral training he dismissed it as 'constantly lifting the plant out of the ground to see if its roots were growing'. For anyone who believes that education must be much more than vocational training, and also believes that taken literally all faiths are simply false, Dewey's desire for a naturalistic but essentially religious attitude towards the tasks of the teacher has a certain attraction—though it also threatens a certain embarrassment. Naturally enough, his atheist friends wished he would not mention religion at all, and his devout critics complained that he was an atheist who hadn't the courage of his lack of conviction. At all events, Dewey's attitude towards Original Sin was interestingly complex. It was quite unlike Russell's bracing but simple observation that nobody ought to teach who did not have a profound sense of Original Sin—a view that he claimed to have been forced to when he found one of the children at Beacon Hill putting an open safety pin in another child's soup.

What a difference a hundred years makes. It is an important fact about Dewey's views that they were formed a century ago. This is not a polite way of saying that they are out of date; but they certainly need to be understood in context. That context is both like and unlike that of our own day. In one respect, it is oddly like our own time. Dewey wrote when American cities—especially the Chicago in which his ideas were developed between 1894 and 1904—were growing in a quick, brutal, and chaotic fashion. In terms of town planning, Chicago did better than many cities because the aftermath of the great fire that all but destroyed it in the 1870s was the pulling back of the city from the shoreline of Lake Michigan, with results for which we can be grateful today. In other respects, it was as bad as anywhere, and a proper place for Jane Addams to build her settlement at Hull House. In Dewey's day, unemployment often reached twenty-five percent, and almost a quarter of the population was thought to have been temporarily homeless in the depression years of the early 1890s. Only a quarter of the population could boast four American born grandparents, and local politics were hardly cleaner than the stockyards—another reason why the settlement house movement set up a voluntary alternative to the non-existent official welfare state. In addition to migration from overseas, there was migration from the country into the town. In the population as a whole only one child in seven went to high school, and it seems unlikely that more than a third got all the way through elementary school.

As to the education they got, it was essentially rote learning of more or less useless information. Dewey fought against this on several fronts at once. One object of his antipathy was the sheer awfulness of education by drilling. When critics worry about Dewey's opposition to an education that consists in a Gradgrind-like instance on 'the facts', it is worth pointing out that it was a very extreme version of such an education that he disliked. Lawrence Cremin's short history of American public education offers some vignettes of the sort of classroom Dewey wished to avoid—among them the English classes for immigrant steelworkers, where burly Polish workmen sat in a classroom chanting 'I have a yellow flower, Jane has a blue flower'. We are used to primary classrooms where children work in groups around small tables, assisted by their teachers; Dewey was used to the kind of bleak classroom where one teacher memorably responded to an inquiry about the complete absence of interesting materials on the walls by pointing out that the children were supposed to face rigidly to the front and there was not supposed to be anything to distract them from teacher and the blackboard. How much room, if any at all, there might be for educational drills was something on which Dewey did not commit himself. This was not evasiveness, but something implied by Dewey's view of himself as a philosopher and not an 'educationalist'. He was content to leave the discussion of educational techniques to those who had inquired into the efficacy of different methods. Indeed, he would have thought the philosopher no more entitled to dogmatise on technique narrowly defined than to dogmatise on the way to change a car tyre. What Dewey set out to do was explain why we needed to educate children at all—not a foolish question, since many societies have got along entirely satisfactorily without bothering to invent the school—what it was that an educated child ought to be able to do, and why teachers mattered so much.

Let me start with 'My Pedagogic Creed'; it is an astonishing piece of work, and explains what I mean by saying that Dewey was not a child-centred theorist of education but a teacher-centred theorist. It is also very distinctly a work of 1895 rather than 1995. It ends with the rousing declaration:

> I believe, finally, that the teacher is engaged, not simply in the training of individuals, but in the formation of the proper social life. I believe that every teacher should realise the dignity of his calling; that he a is a social servant set apart for the maintenance of proper social order and the securing of the right social growth. I believe that in the way the teacher always is the prophet of the true God and the usherer in of the true kingdom of God.

It is not hard to see why teachers might be drawn to Dewey, and why their employers might be less so. A strikingly Deweyan idea is that of a social servant 'set apart,' and it points to one of Dewey's passions that it is rather hard to share, or even to get clear enough to reject. Dewey believed that society socialises the next generation into adult membership in all sorts of ways and all sorts of environments, and that the teacher is only one of them and the school only one of the appropriate environments, along with home, work, museums, political rallies and many more. When Dewey years later wrote an essay for the *New York Times* on 'Schools in Utopia', he began by observing that the most surprising thing about schools in utopia was that in utopia there are no schools.

Their non-existence follows from Dewey's philosophical account of education; the abolition of schools in utopia is on a par with Dewey's desire to abolish the church in order to save religion from its formal institutionalisation. The same thought recurs in his desire to blur the difference between democracy as a set of formal institutional arrangements for the conduct of politics and democracy as the habits of everyday life. It is not obvious what to do with the antipathy to institutions that have been 'set apart'. On the face of it, when we distinguish one set of social arrangements from others, we do it in virtue of their purposes, their patterns of institutionalised authority, their recruitment for membership, and so on. An army, for instance, is a social institution that exists to provide defence; it recruits people to bear arms, to transport, feed, and supply those who bear arms, and to manage those who perform all these tasks. Its 'set apart' quality is to that extent absolute: it exists to provide military defence, and not something else. This is not a matter of personnel. Fifteen people could during the afternoon be a rugby team, and the same evening become a military formation. The functional difference between the team and the squad would be complete, though their membership was identical.

A way in to what Dewey might have wanted is to reflect that there are different ways of meeting these various social functions. So, we might provide for our defence by a standing army with a permanent established membership or by a militia that came together only periodically. Their function would be the same, but a standing army might be said to be 'set apart' in a way a militia is not. This difference was the subject of heated political debate from ancient times until the nineteenth century; and the debate still continues as a debate over the merits of a 'volunteer'—or mercenary—army as contrasted with those of a conscript force. Dewey may have had in mind what the advocates of militias had in mind. Just as they thought it was the task of any able-bodied man to go and fight for his country when needed, and a task that should not be handed over to professionals, he may have thought it was the task of all adults to transmit to the next generation what they needed to know in order to become fully participating members of the community in their turn, and that handing it over to professionals was a sad necessity from which utopia might be exempted. Even that thought is vulnerable to the same objection as the defence of a militia. Once warfare becomes more complicated than can be handled by a citizen

militia, a specialised army is essential. Once a society needs to transmit an elaborate body of knowledge rather than generalised cultural know-how, schools, colleges, and universities are essential. No
doubt, many more things could be passed on in the course of work,
entertainment, family life, and so on than we presently imagine.
Still, it seems hard to believe that in utopia we shall recapture the
simplicity of a tribal society and dispense with educational institutions 'set apart.' None the less, just as the eighteenth century dislike
of standing armies informs twentieth century discussions of the
best way to recruit a modern army, so Dewey's dislike of splitting
off education as a specialised activity can inform our discussion of
the role of the family in education, or the proper relations of family
and school, or the place of the teacher in the community.

Liberal and vocational education

One element in Dewey's thinking that is especially relevant today is
his disquiet about what passed for vocational education in his own
day, as well as his disquiet about most proposals for improving
vocational education. British anxieties about the employability of
the least qualified forty per cent of teenagers and American anxieties about the 'functional illiteracy' (and for the matter of that the
functional innumeracy) of the same proportion of American
teenagers have led, reasonably and unsurprisingly to a concern for
the vocational implications of secondary education. As so often,
confusion is caused by running together two very different ideas of
vocationally relevant education. One focuses on the need to give
school pupils skills that will later allow them to be trained 'on the
job', but not on teaching them those 'on the job' skills at school.

This emphasises literacy and numeracy, as well as habits of attention and orderly behaviour, but not, so to speak, machine drawing,
metal-working, carpentry and the care and maintenance of
computers and computer networks. The other takes for granted the
need for high levels of literacy and numeracy, but concentrates on
the skills required in employment—anything from metalwork
through information technology to bookkeeping. It is the latter that
is usually meant by discussions of vocational education in an
American context. It is the former that is usually meant when
British policy-makers worry about employability.

Dewey was a pragmatist, in the technical, philosophical sense of
that term. Put briefly, that means that he explained the truth of
statements about the world in terms of their usefulness in helping
us to understand and control the world more effectively. This made

experiment central to understanding the world, and in Dewey's hands at least downplayed the 'merely spectatorial' approach to the world. It is not too much to say that this conception of philosophy saw even perception as a form of working on the world rather than passively receiving data from the world. With work thus placed at the centre of our understanding of the world—I shall say a very little about his view of art a little later—it is easy to imagine that Dewey wanted to turn liberal education into vocational education. Anyone who has read *The School and Society* with its descriptions of the children of the Lab School growing wheat in the schoolyard, harvesting it, grinding it, baking bread, and playing at selling the results to one another, may well have begun by wondering whether Dewey wanted schools to produce little workers for American farming, commerce, and industry. The truth, as readers of *School and Society* soon discovered is that Dewey was more interested in turning work into a sort of philosophical instruction. Work was, or rather work should be, one of the main ways in which grown-up men and women participated in the life of their society. Work was a form of social service as well as a necessity forced upon us by the world and our needs, and one of the many things wrong with industrial society is that work too rarely feels like this. For children to encounter work in the preliminary way they did it in the Lab School was part of a training in a full engagement with the outside world, with their society and with themselves, and part of a liberal rather than a vocational education. Education was not a preliminary to work in the everyday sense, but a training in how to extract from every activity its full meaning. That applied to growing wheat, to harvesting and cooking, as much as to mathematics. In a letter he wrote a little before the school opened, Dewey produced a wonderful spiralling diagram of the ways in which cookery would teach the lesson that rusting and cooking were related processes of oxidisation, manifested in very different ways—which, whatever else it might be, would hardly be an unchallenging programme for eight year old children nor the most obvious way of turning them into wage slaves.

Dewey took a fierce line against most of the schemes to set up special 'vocational' schools that were produced before the First World War. His objection was not to the detail of the curriculum, but to their divisive effect in segregating a class of school students who were destined—or doomed—to go into humble occupations and to stay in them all their lives. In this way, he anticipated the social objections to selective secondary schools that have often been voiced in Britain, and to both the elementary schools of before World War II and the secondary modern schools of the post-1944 settlement. Dewey was all in favour of education designed to help young people to obtain work and better work. Both Hull House in Chicago and the Henry Street Settlement in New York had programmes to help fourteen and fifteen year old students better themselves at work that he very much approved of, and for which he occasionally gave lectures. But once again, very much in line with the complaints of critics of British elementary education before 1944, Dewey deplored the way in which children left school at thirteen or fourteen years of age with no resources to help them to acquire new skills and make their way to something better than simple manual labour. To establish schools with no higher ambition than the production of competent wage slaves was not what he thought might improve matters; and he thought it was particularly intolerable to deprive students of a liberal education under the pretence of providing them with vocational training. A hundred years ago, he pointed out that it was likely to be self-defeating in any case; such was the speed of change in modern industry that the most useful skills that children could acquire were those that allowed them to re-educate themselves for the rest of their lives.

For all the strength of his feelings about the wickedness of narrowly vocational education, Dewey was not in fact very interested in secondary education. Like many other philosophers of education, he thought that much of the damage we do to children we do by the time they are ten years old. (On the whole, the evidence suggests he was right). It is therefore the beginnings of what we usually think of as education that he most cared about. What he thought good secondary and university education might be like is interestingly difficult to tell. He sometimes observed rather cynically that if our primary educational practices were hopeless, it was no wonder that what happened thereafter was pretty awful. Yet, he can hardly have held that view consistently: not only did he himself do something out of the ordinary by insisting on pursuing graduate studies at the brand new Johns Hopkins University, he went on to work in universities from 1883 to 1930, and when he formally retired from Columbia in 1930 at the age of seventy, he kept his office and went on supervising graduates until 1939. A man who studies and works in university departments of philosophy from the age of eighteen to the age of eighty can hardly think the whole time that what he is doing is irreparably damaged by the weaknesses of primary education. Neither did he; the scepticism was part of an attitude that he described by calling himself a 'tremendous optimist about things in general and a terrible pessimist about everything in particular'.

At all events, the usual understanding of the nature and purpose of vocational education was not Dewey's. His notion of integrating education for work with education more broadly was not meant to supply the workforce that the existing capitalist order required, but to supply the self-managing workforce that would be needed when we remembered that the point of work was not only to fabricate motor cars and washing machines, but to build a world that human beings would wish to live in.

He kept even reformers like William Wirth, the great Superintendent of Schools at Gary, Indiana, in the years around World War I, at something of an arm's length. Wirth's experimental schools in Gary were organisationally interesting because Wirth had designed them to be operated on the 'platoon' system, whereby the physical plant of a single school (considered as an architectural entity) was used continuously by what were two separate 'schools' (considered as organisational entities). By tinkering with the school day a little, things were managed so that one school used the assembly hall, gymnasium and workshops while the other used the regular classrooms, and vice versa. Not only this, but the children were taught the arts of building and maintenance so effectively that Wirth used to boast that his eighth-graders could dismantle their school and reassemble it as efficiently as any adult builders. Dewey thought this was perilously close to teaching technique and providing a marketable skill. Given his antipathy to the way in which employers everywhere and always attempted to avoid paying the taxes necessary to sustain a civilised society, Dewey was also unwilling to endorse an educational project that might amount to paying the training costs that employers ought to be willing to pay for themselves.

Imagination, socialisation, and reform

But it might be thought to be pretty obscure what is left of Dewey's pragmatism if it does not amount to an enthusiasm for an education that teaches children how to be practical. (It might be observed in passing that Dewey himself was tolerably practical; he had for some years a small farm on the eastern end of Long Island where he kept hens—so that when he appeared as the guest of honour at some distinguished event, his hostess exclaimed in shock, 'my goodness, it's the egg man.') The answer is that Dewey's idea of education was built, as his critics have often complained, around the idea of teaching children problem-solving skills. He explained all this at length in a terrific book called *How we Think*, published in 1911, and used for years in teacher-training colleges in the USA. It had an odd fate inasmuch as it was based on Dewey's antipathy to the method of recitation, and was none the less widely taught in recitations, with trainee teachers learning great chunks of it by heart and reciting them back to their instructors.

The basic thought is one that any enthusiast for the philosophy of Sir Karl Popper will find attractive, save for an emphasis on verification that would no doubt have had Dewey thrown out of Popper's seminars if he had ventured into them. In the last few years of the nineteenth century, and the beginning of this, teachers were much attached to Johann Herbart's five part schema for teaching something to a class. Herbart had argued that all instruction could be broken down into five formal steps, regardless of subject-matter. Although Herbart was eager to arouse the interest of children in what they were taught—and was indeed criticised for pandering to the infantile need for excitement as a result—his all-purpose account of instruction gave children rather little to do in the process of learning whatever they were supposed to be taught. His five part schema was 'preparation; presentation; comparison; generalisation; application'. Preparation was a matter of getting the children to contemplate the subject ahead of them. If the subject was rivers, for instance, the teacher might ask them about streams and brooks they had seen, or about other forms of running water; Herbart thought that this stirred 'apperceptive masses' into action, but setting aside the psychology, one might think that this is at any rate one way of getting children to focus on what they are about to study. During this stage, the class would be told what the point of the lesson was. 'Presentation' is the stage of presenting the facts that one hopes they will absorb. How this is to be done will differ from one subject to another and at different ages; but the aim is essentially that particular facts are brought vividly before the children. The really educative part lies in the next two stages. For it is by comparison and generalisation that children are got to understand—in this instance— 'what makes a river a river', that is, some conceptualisation of the subject before them is established. Finally, their grasp of that is extended by their seeing that the essentials of rivers are common to all of them and some other features are accidental and common only to a few.

Unsurprisingly, Dewey thought this was too rigid, and got things the wrong way round. Its picture of how one might prepare a class was well enough for the teacher, but the impression left was that thinking was incidental to the acquisition of new information, whereas, for Dewey, it was the other way about. Dewey had his own five-stage story, not in competition with Herbart's but as a schema for how we really get to understand things. For Dewey, thinking about a topic involves 'i) a felt difficulty; ii) its location and definition; iii) suggestion of possible solution; iv) development by reasoning of the bearings of the suggestion; v) further observation and experiment leading to the acceptance or rejection; that is the conclusion of belief or disbelief'. Without a felt difficulty to focus the mind, nothing that Dewey is willing to acknowledge as thinking at all takes place; we simply drift on mindlessly taking things for granted.

If this problem-identifying and problem-solving process is to be made the basis of education, it takes an extremely intelligent teacher to do it in an articulate and disciplined fashion—though many teachers teach in the way this suggests both intuitively and very well. But Dewey supposed that the purpose of teaching in the light of these ideas was to develop intellectual discipline, to help children focus their minds upon problems, to get them to learn how to avoid wasting time by fruitless speculation without cutting short useful speculation. No simple rules can be given for how much time should be allowed for speculation, nor for how the mind is to be got to be flexible, imaginative, sceptical and yet hopeful of achieving a solution. Dewey did not wish to provide a formal lesson-plan; his view was rather that unless we understood education as helping children to learn how to think, we shall not be educating children at all.

'Problem-solving' education has a bad press at present for all sorts of reasons. One is the widespread suspicion that it fosters a taste for the project method and results in a general collapse of standards. Dewey certainly thought that projects were, done well, a good way of learning. If they were not, it would be hard to see why scholars are supposed to acquire a Ph.D. as the culmination of their education. But Dewey was cautious about projects: their purpose was mental training and discipline, not free expression. Because the Deweyan classroom has a teacher at its centre, it has present at least one person who knows exactly where the class should be going and why; Dewey was deeply opposed to what he dismissed as 'messing about', and was in fact wary of calling himself a believer in progressive education. To the extent that a 'project' is simply a controlled experiment, Dewey was in favour of the project method; otherwise, not. Dewey's admirer, William Kirkpatrick, was perhaps over-enthusiastic in his defence of the project method; but Dewey was averse to selling panaceas, and never went so far.

The emphasis on problem-solving makes it all the harder to set out the communitarian side of Dewey's educational theory as clearly as it needs to be set out. Dewey's picture of education by problem-solving looks at first blush like a very individualistic model of education. It may seem that each of us gets hold of his or her problem, speculates about solutions, engages in the usual back-and-forth to get the problem clearer and the solution more exact, and ends up with an answer that provides yet further problems to resolve. This is to mistake the accidental for the essential. There is nothing in Dewey to suggest that the entire class will not pile in to the discussion, and everything to suggest that he imagined that a well-organised collective discussion was just what would happen.

Dewey was insistent that we are products of the situations in which we find ourselves, and that both our problems and the resources we bring to the solution of those problems are collective. 'How we think' is an aptly chosen title. However clever, original, and imaginative any individual may be, it remains true that what he or she thinks is their share of what we think.

Dewey acknowledged some difficulties in his picture of thinking as a matter of constantly solving problems and in the process throwing up more problems for solution. Some subject-matters seem resistant to analysis as problem-solving. The one he most minded about was art. The purpose of art, said Dewey in *Art as Experience*, is to enhance our experience of the world, not to tell us anything in particular or to resolve a problem. Dewey cared very much for modern art—he was a close friend of the irascible Albert Barnes, and thus one of the very few educated persons allowed inside the Barnes Foundation, and he was a good friend of Henri Matisse, who painted his portrait. But Dewey also insisted that *Art as Experience* did not put forward a pragmatist theory of art: pragmatism was a theory of truth, and art was not about truth. This suggests that if art features in education—and it surely does so in Dewey's view—some parts of education are not about puzzle-resolution in quite the way *How We Think* suggests. Even then, Dewey might have gone some way towards assimilating artistic creation and the scientific exploration of the world. An education in art-appreciation is frequently cast in a problem-solving mode; once we know what an artist or a composer was trying to accomplish, what counted as success and failure within his or her context, and what conceptual and technical resources he or she possessed, we begin to see their problems and the resolution of them. This, after all, is the backbone of Gombrich's *The Story of Art*, and its plausibility is suggested by the way in which a difficulty about the spectator's relation to post-1945 painting is precisely that we have more trouble than we formerly did in figuring out what the artist wanted to do and whether he or she did it successfully.

Alan Ryan

Culture, mono- and multi-

Among the things that Dewey shares with us is the fact of living in a multi-cultural society which felt uncomfortable about being one. On the subject that most exercises us, namely the educational difficulties that result from tensions between white and black citizens, he wrote nothing. On cultural and moral pluralism, he wrote a good deal. Dewey was one of those who took the American motto *e pluribus unum* very seriously. That is, he took both parts of the equation seriously. Writing at time when ultra-patriots denounced so-called 'hyphenated Americans,' he defended what he called 'good hyphens'. Good hyphens unite, bad hyphens separate; the genius of American nationality was its ability to take the infinite variety that incoming cultures offered, and turn it to a common purpose. This is something that the United States has done since its foundation. Britain has been a more pluralistic society than many of its inhabitants have appreciated, but it is only in the past fifty years that an articulate response to multiculturalism has been needed. So far as education in the narrower sense was concerned, the implication of Dewey's enthusiasm for pluralism was that a classroom was a place where students could study, say, American history with a view to seeing their own ethnicity's contribution to the growth of the society they now inherited. This was not the defence of the melting pot, which was a concept he disliked; it was the view that we might offer an image of a future culture which could sustain a common sense of national identity without excluding particular and more local identities.

This, on the whole, seems the right approach. It may well be harder to achieve than Dewey hoped, but it is not itself an ignoble ambition. It is not, as it is sometimes said to be, a post-modernist view, but a staunchly modernist one. Dewey had few of the doubts about cultural hegemony that recent multicultural theorists have expressed, and that was no bad thing. It would be a lot easier to build a tolerant and intelligent society if more people understood their own particularities and their own local allegiances as something they could bring to a common project rather than something that required them to defend themselves against everyone else. Dewey thought of the United States as building a common culture out of a fairly fragmented and localised set of cultures; in modern Britain, we are moving hesitantly towards a greater acceptance of diversity and variety after two centuries of operating a highly centralised state. The slogan *e pluribus unum* is the right one in both contexts.

Conclusion

I do not propose that Dewey holds the answers to the problems of British education. Nothing and nobody holds all the answers, if only because it is absolutely proper that a great diversity of different goals should animate the educational system of a large and complex country. My object has mostly been to show that whatever else might have been going on in the past twenty years it isn't the subversion of a once great educational system by the ideas of a long-dead American philosopher of notoriously unreadable writing habits. Historically, of course, the idea is silly, since most of the things that we associate with very modern teaching methods date from some years after Dewey's death, while the more general movement towards individual teaching in classrooms designed around small children, and with the use of imaginative apparatus to bring children from the world of play to the world of schoolwork owes more to Montessori, Macmillan, Froebel, and behind them Pestalozzi and other European writers of the last century. Dewey's focus was on something other than the details of what happened in the classroom, though he agreed that it was in those details that success and failure lay. If there were really a Deweyan education system in this country, it would be strikingly different from what it is. It would be more experimental, less assessment driven, more—but very differently—demanding of teachers; it would also be more demanding of pupils, since they would have to take more responsibility for their own development.

Educating for Citizenship

DAVID ALTON

Two short paragraphs, 42 and 43, in the White Paper, *Excellence in Schools*, published in July 1997, announced the UK government's intention to educate for citizenship:

> Schools can help to ensure that young people feel that they have a stake in our society and the community in which they live by teaching them the nature of democracy and the duties, responsibilities and rights of citizens.

How they will deliver this remains unclear – not least to the Government itself – which is perhaps why they then followed the time honoured course of setting up an advisory group 'to discuss citizenship and the teaching of democracy in our schools'. (When in doubt – set up a committee.) The membership of that Committee will wield enormous influence in shaping an agenda which cuts to the heart of how a person perceives their relationship with the wider community. It is foolish to underestimate the high stakes involved as politicians seek to define citizenship.

The debate about 'educating for citizenship' has become a cipher for a more fundamental debate about philosophy and theology, relativism and absolutism, values and virtues, the individual and the community. Some are using it as a smokescreen to see off religious education and the daily act of worship in schools – which in the light of the extraordinary outpouring of spontaneous, but frequently unstructured, religious feeling over the tragic death of Diana, Princess of Wales, is a lamentable response to a nation trying to find spiritual meaning to questions of mortality and immortality.

If all that emerges is a view of citizenship which encourages another series of miserable little charters, linked to consumerism, choice, entitlements and rights, it will be another wasted opportunity. Nor should we contemplate a return to the mainly abandoned teaching of civics – a dreary litany of constitutional questions. If citizenship is merely taught as civics it will be an empty cask drained of all its richness. Here, then, I would like to consider two things:

1 The circumstances which led to the 1997 Government White Paper;
2 The political and educational response.

175

David Alton

The White Paper had its genesis in 1990, when Lord Weatherill, the former Speaker of the House of Commons, issued his report 'Encouraging Citizenship' (the report of the Commission on Citizenship). The Commission spawned the excellent *Institute for Citizenship Studies* which works alongside other charitable bodies such as the *Foundation for Citizenship*.

The Secretary of State for Education, David Blunkett, was a member of the Weatherill Commission which declared that 'citizenship should be a part of every young person's education from the earliest years of schooling and continuing into the post-school years within further and higher education'. There is no reason to believe that anything which has happened since 1990 has changed David Blunkett's views. Quite the reverse.

The role of education in the formation of citizens became the central concern of Mrs Frances Lawrence following the tragic death of her husband, Philip, outside his London school. After the killing of James Bulger and the massacre at Dunblane there was similar national introspection. However, the publication of Frances Lawrence's personal manifesto; David Selbourne's *The Principle of Duty*,[1] Amitai Etzioni's *The Spirit of Community*,[2] and Jonathan Sacks' *The Politics of Hope*,[3] and his 1990 Reith lectures, all played a significant part in challenging the previous orthodoxies of individualism and rights. In the latter Dr Sacks says 'it is as if in the 1950s and 1960s we set a timebomb ticking which would eventually explode the moral framework into fragments. The human cost has been colossal'.[4]

In higher education, at the *Centre for Philosophy and Public Affairs* at St Andrews, at Leicester University and at the Liverpool John Moores University, significant work has been undertaken into values education and the development of citizenship. Professor Peter Toyne, the Vice Chancellor of Liverpool John Moores, has said that 'citizenship stems from the process of education'.[5] It has become the first University in the United Kingdom to commit itself to develop a strong sense of citizenship among all of its 20,000 students.

That formal education should play its part in promoting the

[1] D. Selbourne, *The Principle of Duty* (London: Sinclair Stevenson 1994).
[2] A. Etzioni, *The Spirit of the Community* (London: Fontana Press: 1995).
[3] J. Sacks, *The Politics of Hope* (London: Jonathan Cape, 1997).
[4] J. Sacks, *Faith in the Future* (London: Darton, Longman & Todd, 1995).
[5] P. Toyne, The Hockerill Lecture, 1995.

virtues of honesty, compassion, respect, responsibility and justice has also been recognised by Parliament and within the school inspection framework of the Office for Standards in Education (OFSTED), who are already required to give attention to spiritual, moral, social and cultural development. This has been further reflected in the establishment of the Values Education Council (VEC), and through the School Curriculum and Assessment Authority (SCAA) initiative in creating the National Forum for Values in Education and the Community. SCAA's much-awaited statement on the promotion of values was published in 1998.

Nicholas Tate, its director, rightly asked what should be the 'ends' of education and whether the teaching of 'facts' could be separated from 'values'. Children spend 20 per cent of their time in schools so the importance of a school's role is obvious. Historically, universities and schools recognised their role in preparing men and women for their private and public lives. However, one of the casualties of the pell mell rush towards a more individualistic approach has been civic responsibility. 'Looking out for number one' has a poisonous effect as individualism encourages people to opt out and to privatise their lives – becoming limited by the narrow confines of their job or their home. Only in Britain would we turn 'community service' into a punishment dispensed by magistrates. Citizenship has also been a casualty of the sheer complexity and overpowering nature of modern life. So often this has incapacitated citizens. We have come a long way from Athens and on the road we have been robbed of our inheritance. Ill-prepared for the ethical and moral dilemmas, robbed of the concepts of duty and service, utility and functionalism have turned us into slaves of everything from a genetically manipulated reproductive system to the servility of consumerism. We are less like citizens and more like slaves

The educators have become what C. S. Lewis in *The Abolition of Man* memorably called 'the conditioners'.[6] These 'conditioners' have made 'men without chests' from whom we expect 'virtue and enterprise'. Lewis concluded that through modern formation 'we castrate and then bid the geldings to be fruitful.[7] Aristotle urged that one educate for virtue, for duty, and for the common life. The conditioners say its all a matter of individual opinion; that individuals are not responsible for their actions. And what have been the consequences? What is the dowry the conditioners can hand to their daughters? What is the legacy for the men without chests?

In the nineteenth century Carlyle called it 'the condition of

[6] C. S. Lewis, *The Abolition of Man* (Oxford: OUP, 1944).
[7] Ibid.

England' question. In what condition do we find our country today? How a nation treats its children is a pretty good test of its claims to be civilised. It also sets in a proper context the scale of the challenge in forming tomorrow's citizens.

Eight-hundred thousand British children now have no contact with their fathers; since 1961 marriage breakdown has increased by 600 per cent with the number of divorces doubling since 1971. Many children have no experience of family life and no model on which to build loving and caring relationships.

Children are daily robbed of their innocence. Computer pornography, much involving children, paedophile rings – many operating with the connivance of people in authority at children's homes and in social services or special hospitals – compete with the daily fare of advertising targeted at children. Never ending computer games, films, and TV programmes saturated with violence, complement the pimps and drug pushers who operate like urban cadres on our streets, recruiting children and young people at every opportunity.

Broadcasters have colossal power in forming citizens – who spend an average twenty-seven hours a week in front of their TV sets. In a lecture to the television industry Bruce Gyngell, Managing Director of Tyne Tees Television, asked 'What are we doing to our sensibilities and moral values and, more important, those of our children, when, day after day, we broadcast an unremitting diet of violence ... television is in danger of becoming a mire of salaciousness and violence.' By contrast, in an interview in the UK press, Oliver Stone, who made *Natural Born Killers*, is quoted as saying: 'We poke fun at the idea of justice, at the idea of righteousness, at the concept that there is a right and a wrong way.' These sentiments should be a central concern for all who care about the formation of citizens.

In his book *Britain on the Couch*, the psychologist Oliver James asks the question 'Why are we unhappier than we were in the 1950s despite being richer?'[8] Clinical depression, he says, is ten times higher among people born after 1945 than among those born before 1914. Women under the age of thirty-five are the most vulnerable. The paradox is that we are told that we have never been more materially affluent and yet, says James, modern life seems less and less able to meet our expectations. We feel like losers, even if we are winners.

According to Gallup, in a survey of comparative attitudes in 1997 and 1968: in 1968 62 per cent thought behaviour was getting worse; today it is 92 per cent; in 1968 28 per cent thought they were

---

[8] O. James, *Britain on the Couch* (London: Century, 1997).

happier; today the figure is 7 per cent with 53 per cent believing that life is becoming unhappier. Only 1 per cent believed that standards of honesty in contemporary Britain were improving.

Consumerism, material gain, the high-tec, high-powered information laden lives of the 1990s are mirrored by collapsed family life, broken communities, the instability and insecurity in employment which accompanies market forces, and a widespread sense of isolation, from which flows loneliness. Like the disappointed ancient Greeks who finally climbed Olympus to search out their gods, modern men and women have scaled the peaks of prosperity and found nothing. They realise that instead of truth, they have been peddled a gigantic lie. When they ask for bread, we fill them with broken glass.

So many of our modern contemporaries find a void on the mountain top and resort to the escapism of the drugs scene, the couches of shrinks, the embrace of astrologers, and the clutches of the black arts. This modern loneliness, which breeds despair, is fed by a diet of nihilism and materialism initiated from outside the home or the community. One German study states that between the age of three and thirteen a child watches an average of 107 minutes of TV each day. The German child psychologist, Mrs Christa Meves, found that 44 per cent of pre-school children preferred watching their television than to being with their father. Forty-nine per cent of videos bought or rented in Germany contain violent material.[9]

The poison is often in the dosage and this will intensify with digital TV – the ultimate amalgamation of the internet and TV as they become one, the proliferation of video material and games, the ethical and conceptual dilemmas posed by the use of virtual reality and subliminal techniques; these are the new environment for Britons, and everybody else, on the couch.

Virtue must be promoted; vice can make it on its own. Instead of virtuous citizens, we have been forming couch potatoes rather than discerning men and women with civilised and civilising attitudes. We have learnt everything except the ability to become fully human. We are no longer Romans but we are nothing else either. And who is to blame?

Parents blame teachers and vice versa; both blame the state. The politicians blame the broadcasters. Fear induces panic and while latter-day Luddites would happily smash the internet and the TV sets – or string up newspaper editors – liberals are frightened to concede that anything at all is wrong, fearful that an honest admission would bring down their whole edifice.

[9] C. Meves speaking to conference in Vienna in September 1997.

David Alton

Rosalind Miles, in *The Children We Deserve* eloquently sums up the problem:

> Part of the experience of growing up is learning to negotiate and to have social skills that come from relating to other people. If a child comes home from school, raids the fridge, and disappears to their room to the TV or computer console, that child is alienated. He or she will become cut off from real life and will come to expect instant gratification attuned to their needs. This is the foundation of yobbishness and violence.[10]

Academics, as ever, agonise over the empirical evidence. The evidence of our own eyes should be quite enough. However, there are studies which reveal that TV can trigger suppressed fears of children, or neurosis; that the lowest school achievers watch most TV, while the highest achievers watch the least. Some studies suggest that not only can obsessive TV watching lead to retardation in language and mental performance but it is blatantly obvious that programmes promote anti-parent feelings or ridicule institutions, as well as triggering solitude and inability to integrate. In day-to-day conversation people talk endlessly about TV figures and characters – not about reality.

The internet may permit me to kiss my wife goodnight from New York or Paris, but it is not and never can be real. The danger is that we simply escape from reality. In the *Pensees*, Pascal says we are always trying to flee reality to near-real worlds, for example a love of the past can become an attempt to escape the harsh challengers of today. Modern media has encompassed a new ideology of virtual reality to emerge.

Truth is a casualty as simple slogans, repeated ad nauseam in the media, become true. Why should we care about reality when the virtual will suffice? In addition to nihilism, reflected in political negative campaigning, spin-doctors ensure that the image and virtual-reality politics counts more than substance or truth.

In our homes, the ideology of virtual reality allows us, through computer software, to kill, maim, brutalise or abuse another, without any apparent consequences. We start to feel like gods, as creators of the world with all of life's chances at our fingertips. God and creation become nothing but human invention. For some this is confirmation of Nietzsche's philosophy that man creates the universe and it is a new extension of the serpent's promise in the Garden. In the Middle Ages, Thomas a Kempis well understood this impulse when he wrote in the *Imitation of Christ* that 'because men wanted

[10] R. Miles, *The Children We Deserve* (London: Harper Collins, 1994)

to become God, God wanted to become man'[11] – to sanctify and redeem us from this conceit.

In response to all this, families are patronisingly told to get a grip and use the off-button. Yet vast numbers of households no longer house families where there are parents to perform this task; others, house tired, pressurised stressed parents who use the TV to replace the hearth or the baby-sitter and simply fail to discern between different categories of programmes. One sixteen-year-old girl told me, 'I live as a stranger in my own family'.

The destruction of family life leads inexorably to a dysfunctional society. Melanie Phillips in *All Must Have Prizes* perceptively analyses the consequences of this collapse.[12] In the American context, Allan Bloom in *The Closing of the American Mind* spells out the implications for citizenship when personal commitments and bonds can be broken or sloughed off, when the concept of fault is abolished, and when children's interests are reduced to the deceit that they would be somehow better off:

> Of course many families are unhappy. But that is irrelevant. The important lesson that the family teaches is the existence of the only unbreakable bond, for better or for worse, between human beings.[13]

It is within the family – the basic building block of society – that a love of civic life must first be cultivated. Young women, like the sixteen-year-old girl I mentioned, must not be strangers to their parents, or in their own homes. Ironically, those TV-resistant families who do shield their children may breed emotionally more stable and more mature children, but we will see another elite emerge: children unscathed by the ravages of uninhibited exposure to the electronic media.

There is plenty we can do in the three areas of technology, the law, and education, to support the family, but political will would be required. These should be central questions for the politicians and media. They are certainly central questions about the formation of citizens. The Archbishop of Canterbury, George Carey, perceived this when he said in a House of Lords debate in 1996, that the nation was being threatened by a tendency 'to view what is good and right as a matter of private taste and individual opinion only'.

[11] Thomas a Kempis, *The Imitation of Christ* – a new reading of the 1441 Latin autograph manuscript by William C. Creasy (Macon, Ga: Mercer University Press, 1989).

[12] M. Phillips, *All Must Have Prizes* (London: Little Brown & Co., 1996).

[13] A. Bloom, *The Closing of the American Mind* (New York: Simon & Schuster, 1987).

What sort of values have the conditioners, the men without chests left us with? They have replaced the Beatitudes with the Me-attitudes, and with individualism, relativism, syncretism, libertarianism and false liberalism. In fashioning a 'who-can-I-blame?', 'who-can-I-sue?', 'what-does-it-matter?', 'why-should-I-care?', society, they have left us poor beyond belief.

The human ecology is in tatters. Consider again our children: In 1996, 46,000 children were on child protection registers; 64,000 children are in Local Authority care; while a recent ICM poll found that 28 per cent of British parents thought their children were running wild. Crime is largely committed by young people – with 50 per cent of all crimes committed by those under twenty-one. Ten times as many crimes are committed as in 1955 and the crime rate is forty times that of 1901. In the United States, a baby born in 1990 and raised in a big city has a statistically greater chance of being murdered than an American soldier had of dying in battle in World War Two. What goes into the formation of these young people is far more important than the debate about curfews and custodial sentences.

In Britain hardly a family or community is untouched by crime, violence or drugs. More than 160 babies were born addicted to purified cocaine during one twelve month period alone; and a recent study by the University of Manchester found that in the North West, 71 per cent of the region's adolescents had been offered drugs over a twelve month period.

Before we are born we are more likely than ever to be violently done away with. Only four out of every five pregnancies now goes full term. Six hundred babies are aborted daily. Since 1990, if you have a disability you may be aborted up to and even during your birth. One hundred thousand human embryos are now destroyed annually in British laboratories. Euthanasia and eugenics are regularly practised – not just in Holland and Scandinavia – and the old mistakes – which have led to episodes of genocide, racial theories, corrupt medical ethics – are dressed up in the new guise of genetics.

Everything is reduced to a matter of personal choice. The word itself originates from the same Greek word as the word heresy. My right to choose – and never mind the consequences – is the modern heresy. Human life is reduced to a commodity: bought or bartered, experimented upon, tampered with, destroyed or disposed of at will. 'If it's right for me, it's right per se.'

In *The City of History* Lewis Mumford perceptively and prophetically saw how the balance of civil society was threatened:

Before modern man can gain control over the forces that now threaten his very existence, he must resume possession of himself. This sets the chief mission for the city of the future: that of creating a visible regional and civic structure, designed to make man at home with his deeper self and his larger world, attached to images of human nature and love.[14]

Mumford foresaw the need to address the question of human development and personal expression. He appreciated the scale of de-industrialisation which would occur, the social problems which would flow from this and the need to invest heavily in education: 'Not industry, but education will be the centre of their (cities') activities.'

In practice, over the thirty-five years which have elapsed since Mumford argued for the centrality of the personal formation of citizens, economic and industrial regeneration have taken priority. Failure to appreciate the role of education in fostering a civilised society, where personal civic responsibility is cultivated in each person, has threatened the delicate balance which enables society to function.

Among the consequences have been:

- the increasing isolation of the individual within the context of the modern urban environment;
- the fracturing of community bonds and their corresponding effects on the relationship of individuals to the state;
- the low levels of participation in the institutions and processes of local and national government;
- the lack of understanding about civic responsibilities and duties in the democratic state;
- the lack of a co-ordinated approach towards corporate responsibility and involvement in the community; and
- the failure of citizens to understand what responsible citizenship in modern society really means.

Civil society has become uncivil as modern citizenship has become perceived in terms of rights alone. This in turn breeds unrealisable demands and a cult of selfishness which is bound to flourish in a climate of materialism and consumerism. It is further entrenched in the isolation of individualism and the marginalisation of ethics. Is it any wonder that society becomes chronically disordered?

Rights and choice are the new civic dogma. Rights have replaced duties as propagandists demand the right to a job, the right to an education, the right to a child, the right to drugs, the right to

[14] L. Mumford, *The City of History* (Harmondsworth: Pelican, 1961).

pornography, the right to kill, the right to die. Displaced are the ancient duties to work, to acquire knowledge, to care for the family, to cherish and to respect life. Choices are no longer conditioned by consequences. The delicate balance of civil society is thus broken. In his justly famous book *After Virtue*, Alasdair MacIntyre poses the central question of whether new communal and civic relationships can be snatched from the poisonous clutches of individualism.[15]

This is the second area which I want to explore: the political and educational response. Failure to address at any level of the curriculum the role of citizens and the question of citizenship in modern society, the absence of a coherent approach in industry in cultivating corporate responsibility or civic engagement; and the general lack of understanding about what are a citizen's duties and responsibilities in a democratic state, are the key questions for the twenty-first century. Failure to address them properly will lead to further civic disengagement and dysfunction.

If we were to educate for citizenship and to take seriously the civic deficit we would enshrine the duties of each person: to live peaceably; to participate in civic government; to contribute to the resourcing of commonly beneficial institutions; to acquire knowledge and to encourage the pursuit of knowledge in children; to learn respect for the needs of others; to behave ethically; and to appreciate how legitimate rights have been acquired and to cherish them. We need a greater concern with how civil society is made, how it decays and how it might be preserved. Civic education is a *sine qua non*.

If a civil society is to withstand the ambitions of those who wish to usurp it, fundamental shared principles must be widely held and understood in the political community and beyond. A nation or community will not survive for long if its civil structures are corrupted or decaying or if its rulers and citizens do not pursue civic virtues; A respect for the sanctity of human life, respect for law, a sense of personal responsibility, public spirit and munificence, firmness of purpose, discernment and foresight, perseverance, and a sense of duty might be chief among these civic qualities. Aristotle celebrated justice, wisdom, temperance and courage as the cardinal virtues and associated with these were magnanimity, liberality, munificence, prudence and gentleness. Christ offered the virtues of faith, hope and charity – (the love of God in its original meaning). If such indispensable virtues are not passed from generation to generation, civic fabric is bound to crumble.

These are not new concerns. In the *Politics* Aristotle's *koinonia*,

[15] A. MacIntyre, *After Virtue* (London: Duckworth, 1981).

184

communal existence, was not about civic structures or forms of government but about the qualities in man which made civic co-existence a possibility. Civic virtue was exemplified by a concern for the rights of others, in the civilising of the polis and through sense of justice. Aristotle said we are not like 'solitary pieces in chequers' but need to cultivate a common life.[16] Cicero, in his work, 'On Duty' also saw the need for active participation: 'the whole glory of virtue is in activity'.[17] Aristotle believed that civic virtue could and should be taught.

Aristotle also held that there was something innate about a citizen's desire to participate in the public life. *Zoon politikon*, political animal, is a phrase which he coined in his *Politics* and which remains in regular contemporary usage. Today it has perjorative connotations: for Aristotle it was an honourable phrase denoting a citizen who strove for others. For Aristotle, communal existence – koinonia – was not about civic structures or forms of government but primarily about the qualities in man which made civic co-existence a possibility. Man alone, he argued, had the logos – the ability to speak, but more than that: the ability to use reason and to act as a moral agent. 'Man alone has the special distinction from the other animals that he also has perception of good and bad and of the just and the unjust.'

Aristotle described the *polis* as 'an association of free men' which governed itself; where the citizen 'takes turn to govern and be governed', familiar territory for the modern democrat always expectant of losing or winning public office. The *polis* became the school of life. The *polis*, through its laws, religion, tradition, festivals, culture and participation in its common institutions, shaped each citizen. Its architecture, its theatre (the nearest equivalent in Athenian society to our concept of a free press: particularly plays which dared to satirise and to explore controversial questions), its orators, its laws: all were manifestations of the common life and all required the commitment of the citizens. It was a duty to engage in the polis, sharing in the glories as well as the burdens. A man who withdrew from the life of the polis was not perceived as simply minding his own business, living a private life, but being a worthless good-for-nothing. The city's business was everyone's business and participation in the life of the city was crucial to a person's development. Taking part was not an optional extra.

Rewards and punishments help to mould a man's attributes and Aristotle held that a man would endure danger because of a combi-

[16] Aristotle, *Politics*, Books 1–2 translated with a commentary by Trevor J. Saunders (Oxford: Clarendon, 1995).
[17] Cicero, 'On Duty' in *Speeches* (London: Heinemann, 1931).

David Alton

nation of civic commitment to the common good and a fear of the shame and legal penalties, the punishments, which would attach to cowardice or civic indolence. *Aidos* – fear of shame, of how you would appear to other citizens – is for Aristotle the balancing scale in the civic question. It balances the cherished ideal that the citizen would want to act nobly and altruistically.

Closer to our own times, Gertrude Himmelfarb in her book, *The De-moralisation of Society, from Victorian Virtues to Modern Values*,[18] reminds us that the Victorians also focused on good character and personal responsibility. They spoke not so much about values but of virtues – a more demanding test. No doubt there was an element of romanticism implicit in the Victorian emphasis, calling up medieval codes of courtly chivalry: the virtues of mercy, religion, compassion and courtesy. But the caricature of Victorian virtue as largely hypocritical and enforced by Dickensian schoolmasters is just that: a caricature. The Victorian pursuit of virtue was as much about encouragement as it was about imposition. It was primarily aimed at creating a civic community of citizens who respected one another and were determined to advance and improve themselves. Perhaps it is best revealed in the civic municipalism of Chamberlain's Birmingham.

It is a pity that the word 'values' has become interchangeable with the word 'virtues'. Leo Strauss was right to muse on the mystery of: 'how a word which used to mean the manliness of man has come to mean the chastity of women'[19]. Friedrich Nietzsche was, in the 1880s, the first to stop talking about virtue and to use values in the modern sense of describing collective attitudes and beliefs. 'Transvaluation of values,' as he put it, disposed of virtue and vice, classical virtues, Judaeo-Christian virtues, good and evil and conveniently accompanied 'the death of God'.[20]

Alongside virtue, value is a weak word. It can mean anything people want it to mean, which is why it works so well against a backdrop of syncretism and relativism. Everything becomes neutral and non-judgemental, nothing is absolutely right or absolutely wrong. A return to the concept of civic virtue would prove to be the best defence against civic disaggregation and provide the basis for a new civic settlement: a settlement about more than a devolved Scottish Parliament or reformed House of Lords.

[18] G. Himmelfarb, *The De-moralisation of Society: From Victorian Virtues to Modern Values* (Institute of Economic Affairs, Health & Welfare Unit 1995).

[19] Quoted by Himmelfarb, ibid.

[20] See F. Nietzsche, *The Genealogy of Morals* (Harmondsworth: Penguin, 1997).

Virtue, is a word which is not simply about personal preference or personal views. It is about character and the formation of the citizen at the deepest level. Civic life and politics are conditioned by the culture in which they grow. If the character of the citizen has not been fully formed – and is deficient in virtue – is it any wonder that social anarchy results? Can we avoid this? Can civic virtue be taught? Can we educate for citizenship?

Since the virtual disappearance of civics courses, even that narrow preparation for citizenship has not been a priority in schools. The many other pressures of the National Curriculum mean that provision is patchy at best and non-existent at worst. One survey suggests that nearly a third of primary schools are not addressing the themes of citizenship, while Leicester University's Centre for Citizenship Studies has published valuable data – including a plea by almost half the primary schools for more staff training, and access to resource material and visiting speakers.

The last thing which teachers or pupils need is another subject for examination. That is not what the White Paper and any subsequent legislation or curriculum requirements should seek to achieve. We need a sustained, rigorous and properly resourced approach to a subject which cuts to the heart of how a society functions. This should replace the 'mission statements' of many educational institutions which simply contain lip-service reference to citizenship. The reality is that most pupils, students, administrators, teachers, and faculty members could not tell you how that objective relates to either the curriculum or to the day-to-day policy of the institution.

When we recognise academic achievements and sporting prowess, we should recognise instances of good citizenship. In many American universities credits are given for community work. We need to practice and experience citizenship – as well as analyse it. Service learning, where those with advantages teach literacy to the disadvantaged, especially commends itself to me.

At school prizegiving and at degree day ceremonies, citizenship awards should be presented and form a recorded part of individual records of achievement.

For most young people civic education is generally acquired as an incidental, through contacts with voluntary projects and contacts with individual teachers or because of an event or political policy which directly impinges upon them. We must be far more systematic, and in courses at every level ask the tough questions about the purpose of education, about what is expected of democratic citizens, and about the skills we each require to live peaceably. It is part of the mission of a school or university to educate for democracy, to develop citizenship skills and to form men and women for others.

David Alton

This should particularly appeal in the context of a Britain which commentators are claiming has been fundamentally changed and which, in an unfocused and often inarticulate way, has learnt compassion and a care for the disadvantaged from its dead princess.

How a citizen acts as a moral agent affects everything from how they treat their environment and their neighbours to the pursuit of ethical standards in commerce or the embrace of civic duties. It is not a spectator sport or the preserve of a few well-meaning specialists.

Before the collapse of the Soviet Union many of us saw first hand the consequences of the destruction of civil society. Loss of freedom is all too obvious when you have been run over by a tank. The corrosive effect of materialism and individualism is less obvious. Here the devil arrives in carpet slippers.

Early twentieth-century Marxist obsession with production, the division of labour and class structures has been matched by individualistic indifferentism in our own times. The disfigurement of civic culture and the suppression of civil order have been the principal casualties. At its worst atrocious power has come to be exercised by a rump over the rest of the human race.

If we are to avoid such disaster each of us must understand our duty to our country and to the community The complete citizen will be a virtuous citizen: one who has been formed to consider and care for others. We will each still have our individual frailties, weaknesses and vices, but even from the worst of us some good can be extracted. In his *Fable of the Bees* – or 'Private Vices, Publick Benefits' – Bernard Mandeville recognised how this might happen:

> Thus every part was full of Vice
> Yet the whole mass a Paradise....
> And Vertue, who from Politicks
> Had learn'd a Thousand cunning Tricks;
> Was, by their happy influence,
> Made Friends with Vice: And ever since
> The worst of all the Multitude
> Did something for the Common Good.[21]

---

[21] B. Mandeville, *Fable of the Bees,* edited with an introduction by Phillip Harth (Harmondsworth: Penguin, 1970).

Being Human: Science, Knowledge and Virtue

JOHN HALDANE

I

In February 1997, following the announcement that the Roslin Institute in Scotland had successfully cloned a sheep ('Dolly') by means of cell-nuclear transfer, US President Clinton requested the National Bioethics Advisory Commission to review legal and ethical issues of cloning and to recommend federal actions to prevent abuse. In the meantime he directed the heads of executive departments and agencies not to allocate federal funds for 'cloning human beings'. The Commission consulted with members of relevant academic disciplines and other professions, representatives of interest groups and members of the general public, and received written submissions. Unsurprisingly, given the prospect of human cloning and the sensational announcement in January 1998 by the American physicist-cum-embryologist Richard Seed that he would aim to clone himself (subsequently he has decided that his wife would be a better subject), public debate in the US has been fairly voluble.

In Britain a similar consultation exercise has been engaged in by a joint working party of the Human Fertilisation and Embryology Authority and the Human Genetics Advisory Commission, established (in the same month as the US President's request to the NBAC) to advise government on human cloning issues. This reported in December 1998 and like the National Bioethics Advisory Commission has cautioned against the non-therapeutic (reproductive) cloning of human beings. Howard Shapiro, Chairman of the NBAC recommended to President Clinton a three to five year period of study and reflection before the preparation of a code of ethics on human cloning. The HFEA/HGAC group has proposed permitting therapeutic cloning but banning cloning for reproduction.

These recommendations are not likely to resolve the issues or even to be particularly effective in controlling practice. Determined individuals are able to pursue the project of human cloning in secret and in parts of the world in which there is no relevant legal regulation and in which ethical considerations play little role in public policy. In addition, the issue of therapeutic cloning in which human embryos are created—in this case in order that stem cells can be harvested for genetic transfer—is also open to familiar anti-abortion objections. In British laboratories alone about 100,000 embryos are experimented upon or destroyed per annum.

There has been much written from ethical, political and scientific perspectives on the details of these matters, and here I wish instead to consider the broad philosophical context within which the issues are discussed. Along the way, however, I shall present a case against reproductive human cloning.

II

In the course of its review the US National Bioethics Advisory Commission made a point of stating its awareness that, and I quote:

> ... the formation of appropriate public policy with respect to cloning human beings in this manner depends on more than the potential benefits and harms of reproductive cloning itself. It also depends on the traditions, customs and principles of constitutional law that guide public policy making in the United States.[1]

This is a very interesting observation and one to be applauded for its sensitivity to the wider normative context within which public policy must be formulated. Benefits and harms are hard enough to assess and calculate; taking account of traditions, customs and legal principles is a more difficult task given the number, range and generally uncodifiable character of these. Yet for reasons that will soon emerge I think this broadening of the ethical and philosophical setting does not itself go far enough. It is a very good beginning, but there is an even broader context to be comprehended, that created by the question what is it to live a good human life?

Of course, in the United States the relevant traditions and customs include ones in which individual liberty is given prominence and often priority, and this fact is liable to be seized upon by those such as Richard Seed who advance a free-market, libertarian agenda. European culture is less individualistic and more communitarian in orientation, and more accepting of social regulation; and these facts should be taken account of in the fashioning of policy. It is also worth noting, however, that in the US (as in the UK) there is more than one such tradition or custom. This plurality is reflected in the sorts of discussions that go on nowadays and it is not something that we can expect to pass away. At the same time, it would

[1] *Cloning Human Beings* (Washington: National Bioethics Advisory Commission, 1997).

be premature to identify it with relativism or even to suppose that it provides a good case for this, for apart from the fact that some traditions bear little rational scrutiny there is the fact that the plurality has arisen out of the common condition of human animals.

III

So much has already been said and written about cloning, reproductive technologies and genetic engineering that one might wonder what could now be added, in particular, what a *philosopher* could hope to add. Clearly it is not the business of philosophy to determine what scientific enquiry may achieve; nor is it the task of philosophy to predict social trends. So far as these matters are concerned anything a philosopher might say would just be amateur speculation. It does not follow, however, that philosophy has nothing practically useful to offer. Not every fact is a scientific one, and not every question about public policy concerns what people would do. There are facts about human life that are not reducible to any physical (or social) science; and there are issues about what we should do, not just about what we could do or would do in certain circumstances.

The study of human life and the regulation of action and emotion by norms and values is very much the business of philosophy—as indeed is the preliminary task of conceptual clarification. The phrase 'clarity is not enough' has been used in criticism of an exclusively analytical style of working fashionable among Oxford-trained philosophers for a short period in the 1960s. The criticism is apt, but of course it presumes that clarity is a necessary condition for progress in philosophy. And clarification is usually called for. In the present case, as soon as mention was made of gene-based cloning commentators and others began to discuss the implications of replicating adult humans and contemplated the prospect of several 'identical individuals'. This reveals scientific ignorance and intellectual confusion. As a matter of logic individuals must be numerically distinct and hence cannot be one and the same person. As a matter of fact a clone would be a biological twin rather less similar to its partner than has hitherto been the case—for the clone of an adult would begin as a baby and lag behind its 'parent' thereafter. In addition, genetically identical twins often differ physically and psychologically and only the crudest determinism would support an expectation of extensive qualitative similarity in these respects.

On the other hand it is a confusion to suppose that whereas reproductive cloning involves the creation of a human embryo, therapeutic cloning does not. The difference lies not in what is created but in what is done to or with it. Reproductive cloning plans to preserve the embryo, therapeutic cloning plans to dismember and then destroy it. Of themselves, without supplementary premises, these observations do not constitute an argument in favour of or against any policy but they are made necessary by the obscurities surrounding the very idea of human cloning.

Moving to the policy questions, my general concern, which applies equally well to other reprogenetic matters and to almost all morally charged issues—is that discussions (and I include ethical discussions) are conducted in at most two and more often just one dimension(s). One dimension produces a line, two constitute a plane; essential as these elements are in the constitution of something solid they are not themselves sufficient for it. For that we need to achieve depth.

The one dimensional discussion is conducted in terms of welfare, more precisely in terms of harm and benefit. The second dimension added to this, often by professional ethicists, concerns rights (and corresponding social duties). Sometimes these two dimensions are collapsed back into one, as when it is argued that rights and responsibilities ultimately concern what is of benefit to an individual or perhaps to society. Even when they are kept distinct, however, there is a tendency to suppose first, that these features exhaust the range of relevant 'ethical' and 'philosophical' considerations; and second, that they can be weighed against one another in some more or less precise way—by some kind of moral mathematics—bringing together utility summing, and rights vectors.

So far as the second supposition is concerned while no-one really believes in the possibility of precise calculation there is a sense that there are broad bands and thresholds within and between which credit and deficit transfers can be made. So, for example, it will be said, in noble opposition to utilitarianism, that it would not be permissible to violate the *right* of one for the *welfare* of some small number. However, things change as the scale of potential benefit rises. This way of thinking is intelligible but it suggests a fundamental commitment to consequentialism. Whereas the idea of the right of the innocent, for example, was originally conceived of as something inviolable, i.e. as something that could not be infringed or transgressed *whatever the consequences*.

Those who still try to uphold the idea of inviolability are sometimes seen as indifferent to human welfare, for it is clear enough that if one denies oneself the very possibility of certain courses of action, then it will happen that there are circumstances in which one will refuse to countenance an option even though performing it might produce great benefits. In an effort to show that they are not indifferent to welfare, advocates of inviolability appeal to the idea that one may sometimes act (or refrain from acting) for the sake of some good (or the avoidance of some evil) even though in doing so one may cause harm. They then point out that in determining the permissibility of this the relative impact on human welfare is a factor to be taken into consideration.

This appeal to 'the principle of double effect' is sometimes said to be casuistical (by which, contrary to the original meaning of the term, is meant devious or deceptive). More subtly it is sometimes held to show that advocates of inviolability are themselves ultimately consequentialists. Neither charge is warranted so far as the logic of double effect is concerned. In essence the principle concerns the scope of morally permissible action. It maintains that while it is always wrong intentionally to bring about a bad effect or an evil end—the death of an innocent, for example—it is sometimes permissible to act in a way that one foresees will have bad side effects. In brief, one may not directly intend harm but one may countenance it as an unintended effect of doing good.

It would indeed be devious (and thus in the pejorative sense 'casuistical') to redescribe an intended and primary effect as a secondary and unintended one; and unscrupulous persons have certainly sought to pervert double-effect thinking along these lines. For example, if it is wrong intentionally to kill the innocent, then it will not do for a terrorist who plants a bomb beneath the car of an innocent driver to redescribe matters by saying that his intention is to advance his political cause by causing an explosion, and that any injury to the occupant of the car is a merely foreseen and unintended effect. This will not do because it is false. The terrorist does not hope to achieve his political goal by destroying cars but rather by injuring and killing people. This latter is therefore an *intended* means to a further end. Admittedly, unlike the intention of a homicidal psychopath, the harm caused to innocent occupants may not be the terrorist's only intended aim, but deployed as a means it is certainly intended and not merely foreseen. Accordingly, it is wholly excluded by the principle of double effect.

The charge of concealed consequentialism is no more convincing. Consider what is precluded: one may not aim at a bad effect as a goal, nor use one as a means to a good end. What one may do in pursuing a good end is to deploy means which though not in themselves bad are foreseen to have additional and bad effects. This does not at all say that the end justifies the means, since it insists that some means are never justifiable (killing the innocent, for example).

Moreover, elaboration of the principle involves the requirement that where unintended bad effects are foreseen they must be proportionate to the goods achieved. In other words in eschewing both evil ends and evil means one does not yet have a morally free hand. One will still have done wrong if in pursuing a small good one causes— be it unintentionally—a great harm. This element of weighing outcomes does not constitute consequentialism; indeed it only enters in *after* non-consequential values have been taken account of; which is to say once they have been respected.

The relevance of this style of reasoning to the argument of those opposed to therapeutic cloning on anti-abortion grounds is worth pointing out since it is not always understood. Suppose, what is admittedly controversial, that it is wrong intentionally to kill or to injure an embryo. If that is so then it is plausible to suppose that it is worse still intentionally to create an embryo in the knowledge that one will then intentionally kill or injure it. This is what therapeutic cloning involves. An embryo is created by nuclear replacement in order that cells may be taken from it. Thereby it suffers injury. Indeed, further development would be impossible or at best abnormal. Accordingly, it is destroyed in, or subsequent to the process of cell removal.

I assume that even advocates of this procedure would allow that to create embryos *just* for the sake of dismembering them would be wrong. Their claim, of course, is that the creation of embryos for experimentation and therapy is justified by the end it serves. Perhaps that is so, but we should now be able to see that if it is wrong it cannot be saved by appeal to double effect. For just as the terrorist intends and not merely foresees the harm to the car occupant, so the medical scientist intends and does not merely foresee injury to the embryo. In each case this has been chosen as a necessary means to an end; and to the extent that these ends are taken to justify causing harm the moralities in question are consequentialist.

IV

The opposing position that certain policies remain excluded, especially those that would challenge inviolable values, is an absolutist one. There is now a general avoidance of such ideas. This is probably because it is supposed that absolutes are only intelligible within a religious framework. There is some irony in this given the marked tendency in the latter half of the twentieth century for moral theologians to abandon absolutist ethics in favour of forms of consequentialism, viz. 'situation ethics' and 'proportionalism'.[2] In any case the supposition that absolutism only makes sense on religious grounds has to contend with the fact that arguably the three greatest moral philosophers, viz. Plato, Aristotle and Kant, *all* maintained that rational reflection unaided by any kind of religious revelation establishes that there are unconditional norms and absolute values, and that these set inviolable boundaries to prudential calculation.

Whatever the abstract theories of these particular philosophers it is a recurrent conclusion of serious reflection that beyond the realm of individual and collective advantage lie considerations about what is permissible, impermissible, or required, and that these set limits to consequential calculation. The sense of this, if not the philosophical language and argumentation, is in fact quite common. People will spontaneously exclaim that something would not be right, or that it would be unjust, or cruel or cowardly, and so on. These verdicts are quite independent of any thought of whether the proposed policy would be advantageous or disadvantageous, and they are not always liable to be withdrawn when it is claimed that, whatever may be said about the action itself, great benefits would flow from it.

It may be said that this sense of moral limit is what is captured by the ethics of rights and duties, and therefore that these ethical concepts are enough to guide the pursuit of welfare and the causing of harm. So, for example, welfare is to be maximised up to the point where no rights are violated. As I remarked, however, most of those who talk of rights do not think that they are absolute, and they generally allow that things may be done to an individual if the benefit to others is very great (or the others are very many) which it would be wrong to do if the benefits were less (or the beneficiaries fewer).

Notice, the difference lies not in the condition or circumstance of the victim but in the condition and circumstance of others. Not only is the status of the innocent not absolute, it is not, at least on most versions of this approach, something possessed independently of the interests of others. In this connection some readers may recall the counsel attributed to the chief priest Caiphas in one of the accounts of the trial of Jesus 'it is expedient that one man should die for the sake of the people' *John* 18: 14.

Moreover, and this is the point I want to emphasise, the ethics of

---

[2] The principal advocate of the first is the Protestant moral theologian Joseph Fletcher who sets out his position in *Situation Ethics: The New Morality* (London: SCM Press, 1966). Perhaps the best known proponent of proportionalism are the Catholic writers Charles Curran and Richard McCormick; see, for example, R. McCormick and C. Curran (eds) *Moral Norms and the Catholic Tradition* (New York: Paulist Press, 1979).

John Haldane

rights fails to explain the sense we have that to act in a certain way would not just injure others materially or morally, but would undermine the person who acted in that way. The best way to develop this thought is by reflecting on two different perspectives represented in the history of moral philosophy and to be found deep in most reflective people's moral thinking. First, there is a conception of morality which sees it as consisting in a system of principles and rules (mostly negative or proscriptive ones). The Judaic 'Decalogue' in its non-theological commands is an important and enduring example of this: 'Thou shalt not kill. Thou shalt not commit adultery. Thou shalt not steal. Thou shalt not bear false witness against thy neighbour. Thou shalt not covet thy neighbour's house ... nor anything that is thy neighbour's' (*Exodus* 20).

As in the biblical example of Moses and the 'children of Israel', the natural context for this conception is that of a community or society in which co-operation and the avoidance of conflict are very important for the achievement and maintenance of certain goods. Unsurprisingly, therefore, two ideas are associated with it. First, that of a social contract involving mutually binding obligations agreed to explicitly or implicitly—and most likely tacitly. Second, that of agent/patient reciprocity. By this latter I mean the assumption that anyone who can and should be a beneficiary of moral consideration must themselves be capable of according it to other beneficiaries. In other words every moral patient must be a moral agent and vice versa.

This social (or, better, societal) focus is intelligible and in terms of the conceived function of morality important and defensible; but today we are perhaps better placed than in the past to see that it omits certain classes of beings who there are reasons to suppose deserve of moral consideration and respect. First, there are those who as a matter of circumstance lie outside the contract, for example members of other and distant societies, and isolated individuals outwith the bounds of our or any other society. Second, there are those incapable of moral deliberation and thus who cannot satisfy the condition of patient/agent reciprocity. Among these might be included human beings who for one reason or another lack competence. This would cover both those who have lost the relevant abilities such as the senile, and those who have not developed them, such as retarded adults, children, and foetuses. As well as incompetent humans there are non-competent animals to be considered. Focus on the latter has been a common feature of recent writings by Peter Singer who has described the enlargement of the domain of beings worthy of consideration, beyond the field of those capable of according it, in terms of an 'expanding circle' of moral concern.

Other writers have insisted that animals and even plants and primitive organisms possess moral rights and to that extent enjoy moral standing analogous to that of persons.

Besides straining a moral vocabulary developed to describe the position of participating members of human societies this way of thinking is not necessary in order to accord respect to non-humans and to nature. Interestingly, Roger Scruton—an atheist philosopher working within the broadly Kantian tradition that defines moral worth in terms of the potential for reciprocity, and one not known for progressive moral sentiment—has recently found it appropriate to invoke the idea of a 'natural piety' felt in the presence of something other than oneself, and to cite this response as a ground for acting respectfully towards its objects.[3]

Given the limitations of the conception of morality as a system of principles and rules governing human interaction, and the possibility of grounding conduct in a sense of what is felt reflectively to be appropriate, one may turn to the other main perspective on value and action, that which locates morality *within* a broad structure of rational sentiments, motives and behaviour—as that part of the whole of a person's normative outlook that is sometimes termed 'the moral psychology of virtue'. Unlike the rules-based approach this ('aretic') philosophy of virtue is concerned not just with setting requirements and limits to action (responsibilities and duties) but with introducing values that might inform the general direction of one's life—not just drawing an outline but filling in the shape. It also has a wider concern and serves to link questions of conduct with a view of the world and of the human way of being; in short, with metaphysics and with philosophical anthropology.

In fairness it should be noted that in recent years advocates of utilitarianism and of the ethics of rights have acknowledged the need to address the role of virtue in morality, but they have thought of it as something secondary to the value of good outcomes or the requirements of principle, viewing it as a disposition to promote the former or to discharge the latter. This is both question-begging in its assumption that virtue is secondary, and restrictive in confining its operation to the sphere of morality as those other theories conceive of it. In contrast, proponents of virtue argue either that *it* is what has priority over welfare or rights, or that if not prior to these other factors it is equally fundamental; and to this they add that the perspective of virtue is broader than that of ethics. Virtue consists in the possession of values that shape and animate one's entire range of sentiments, reactions and conduct. Put broadly, to be virtuous is

---

[3] See Roger Scruton, *Animal Rights and Wrongs* (London: Demos, 1996).

to be disposed towards human goods and to be inclined away from human evils.

The ancients and the medievals saw clearly that virtue is called upon quite generally in the effort to live a good life. While bearing on one's relations with other competent, adult members of society it also touches upon a far wider constituency of concern and is also necessary for the management of affairs in which others have no place. The obstacles to human fulfilment are many and various. Some are local and avoidable such as social inconveniences, but others are global and inescapable such as illness and death. These various factors, the coming to terms with which is a part of living well, set the conditions for the project of being human.

V

Thoreau observed that 'the mass of men lead lives of quiet desperation'.[4] It is clear enough what he meant by this, and the popularity of self-help literature suggests that anxiety, disappointment and frustration remain features of modern life. Indeed, notwithstanding material affluence the sense of insecurity would appear to be more widespread. One analysis sees this concern in terms of the feared loss of preferred goods. For example, having worked to secure a good job, or having acquired or inherited the means to sustain a leisured lifestyle, or nature having bestowed a good physique, a man or woman might then come to see that these goods are vulnerable to fortune, and might become increasingly desperate as they contemplate the prospect of their loss.

Significant as this is, however, it does not reach the desperation felt by those whose reflections go deeper. Their concern would not be assuaged by the assurance that what they have valued will be protected, *per impossible*, against the tides of misfortune and the ravages of time. For part of what they (and here I must say 'we') doubt is whether the preferences one has, and for the sake of which one has struggled, *ought* to be satisfied. And a reason for doubting that they ought to be is that commonly their satisfaction does not bring contentment. Not infrequently, the educated, liberal, middle-class think that this is an anxiety that others less cultured than themselves ought to feel. I agree that those who have pursued material goods at the expense of the cultivation of the aesthetic or the cultural have chosen the lesser part, but I also note that among those whose feel this superiority many have abandoned spouses and partners (not

[4] Henry David Thoreau, *Walden* (London: Dent, 1974) p. 5. He went on to add that 'what is called resignation is but confirmed resignation'.

being 'obsessively faithful'), encouraged abortions for reasons of convenience (not being 'fanatically pro-life'), and cultivated appetites far removed from human needs (not being 'obsessively puritanical'); and further note that not everyone feels at ease with the pursuit of these preferences. In particular, women are more likely to be used and abused in these 'non-material' respects and to feel that fact as the years advance.

There is more to a good life than observance of moral responsibility, and more to moral value than welfare and rights. There is the question of virtue: the cultivation of habits of action and reaction directed towards human well-being, which is to say—conceiving of this good as something dynamic and maintained by activity—towards being-human well. Hitherto I have been speaking of the life of individuals, but the same holds good at the level of society. Hard enough as it may be to shape policy in accord with welfare assessed impartially, and with rights accorded universally, there is also the need to consider social virtue. It takes a good deal of dialectical ingenuity—though somewhat less rhetoric—to establish the conviction that questions about collective virtue are incoherent.

The attitudes developed in the course of cultivating virtue constitute a form of *demeanour*. This is a way of being, formed and held constant in the face of such facts as that we grow old, that we are more or less talented, that we have varying personalities, that we are vulnerable to abandonment, betrayal, loss, sickness and death. Virtue, and the happiness it brings, lie in proper concern and appropriate indifference to these realities; attitudes that should be informed by a wise assessment of the conditions of life and an ennobling sense of the possibility of living well under conditions given and not chosen. We will not develop this outlook if we see nature always as something to be overcome, or if we always give priority to the satisfaction of antecedent preferences—preferences held prior to the discovery of natural obstacles or, assuming those to have been identified at an early stage, counterfactual ones. Additionally, recalling that a great part of what it is to be human is to teach others what this should involve, we cannot help cultivate a demeanour of reasonable acceptance if we do not have and show it in our own dealings with given circumstances.

The good life is necessarily one achieved under limits—that is what makes it good and makes the living of it something that merits praise. Put another way the virtues are capacities forged in the face of adversity: courage in the face of danger, justice in the circumstance of shortage or in that of wrong-doing; fortitude in the face of difficulty; perseverance in the context of enduring opposition and so on.

John Haldane

The relevance of these reflections to aspects of the issue of reproductive cloning should be clear. According to non-consequentialist moralities the creation of human beings exclusively for the client's benefit is a violation of the ethical requirement not to use others only as a means. That is true even where the embryo is cultivated to term. So much the worse where embryos are created, for client's benefit, in the expectation of being destroyed as is the case in both therapeutic and non-therapeutic cloning. According to the wider perspective of virtue, reproductive cloning is also a breach of the philosophical responsibility to live within human limits according to norms of openness to the being of others. I recognise that of itself this latter consideration may be held to be inconclusive, but I hope nevertheless that its significance may yet be felt and taken account of.

Some of the ethical objections to cloning concern contingent matters of safety, such as the risk of transferring mutations in the somatic cells of donors. In the course of time, due to ultraviolet radiation and chemical contamination, body cells are liable to be damaged. In itself this may not matter if the process of replacement proceeds normally. However, cloning from adult body cells carries the risk of creating an embryo out of mutant genetic material. The resulting clone would then have a greater chance of developing cancer and could also be expected to have below average life-expectancy. Additionally, as the efforts involved in the production of Dolly the sheep showed, embryos created by cloning are likely to suffer developmental abnormalities. The reason for this is not yet established but it seems likely that the 'reprogramming' of transferred body cells is often incomplete.

The risks of malformation and early death provide a good reason not to clone. However, they are contingent and consequential factors which one can easily imagine being overcome through further scientific research; though that research will itself involve creating embryos for experimentation and destruction. Turning from physical dangers there are other harms to be contemplated. The process leading to the production of Dolly required the surgical removal of more than 400 unfertilised eggs from donor ewes. Current practice concerning human in vitro fertilisation (IVF) involves on average the recovery of 10 eggs per woman donor. Sheep are more highly reproductive than humans: a fertile ewe has over ninety percent chance of becoming pregnant through a single mating; a fertile woman has about a 33% chance of pregnancy through intercourse, and rates drop to 10–20%. under IVF. These figures suggest that any clinic seeking to clone a human being will require well over a 1000 eggs gathered from over 100 women (or fewer women and more harvestings). The potential for exploitation of donors and of clients is evident and need not be elaborated.

I return, however, to the broader issues of virtue and demeanour. Bringing another human being into existence is one of the fundamentals of life and should be regarded as such. It involves opening oneself to physical, emotional and moral challenges so various and considerable that some decline the option, preferring instead to develop their own projects. Yet for most people the challenges are felt to be worthwhile and are accepted as the corollary of creating another human being. The sense of otherness which is felt at the sight of a new born child registers a combination of continuity and difference that contributes in part to the value of conceiving and having children, and also underlies many of the common difficulties in parent-child relationships. By contrast, the deployment of genetic science in the service of reproductive cloning suggests a wish to assert one's own being, extending it into space hitherto occupied by uncertain otherness. In this respect the wish to clone also marks a failure to have cultivated the sort of respect towards human existence that is now widely encouraged as a proper response towards the lesser being of non-human nature.

In reply it may be said that the development of selective cloning offers the prospect of bringing children into being whose initial condition and subsequent development are likely to be better than those of natural offspring; and who, because they are possessed of characteristics chosen by their 'parents' are more likely to be loved and cherished. But that very reply illustrates the perspective I have been concerned to oppose. A good human life is not one that tries to overcome human contingencies, but is one that is developed within the context of them. In having children we carry forward the human enterprise not as a form of self-advancement but as a way of enabling others to realise the value of shaping a life in circumstances which are given rather than chosen. Reproductive cloning aims to overcome that limitation but thereby threatens the very possibility of a meaningful life.

If this style of thinking seems less clear and determinate than that represented in the appeal to rights and welfare, then I suggest readers consider the possibility that the latter fails to represent the complexity of human values, and that in this of all matters it is dangerous to sacrifice accuracy for simplicity. Discussions of the ethics of human cloning and of other contemporary moral problems generally lack a dimension that I believe to be essential, namely, a phenomenology of human value, that is to say, a descriptive account of

John Haldane

the meaning and value of living a human life. Progress in this regard would be an important contribution to moral philosophy and, given the policy implications of cloning and related bioethical issues, to the conduct of public affairs.

Index of Names

Index of Names

Index of Names